My Best Friend is a

Liar

The Real Life Story of a World Class Con Artist

MELISSA SPROUSE BROWNE

An Expose to Help You Learn to be
Smarter than the Con!

CONTENTS

ACKNOWLEDGMENTS

This book wouldn't have been possible without the support of my family and the friendship and assistance of Linda Wilson. One of the best things to come from a terrible situation is the realization that I have a true friend in her, one who is not a liar.

I also would like to thank each person embroiled in this web of deceit for sharing his or her story. It's not easy admitting you've been conned and I admire every single one of these victims for taking the initiative to fight back.

INTRODUCTION

And I quote…

"He jumped up and wrenched my arm sideways as he pulled me up the stairs. The burn of his hand twisting my arm was searing and my legs dragged uselessly along the stair treads. "No, no, no!" I cried as I tried to jerk away. Where is Mrs. Ray, I desperately thought. Please let her come and save me! I realized he was overpowering me and I was forced all the way up the stairs. No help was in sight. Spinning me around, he violently pushed me into his bedroom and threw me onto the bed.

Crushed by his weight, I sank deeper into the mattress as he fell on top of me. His sweaty hands rubbed across my breasts and up and down between my legs and thighs. Already exhausted from the struggle, I didn't even fight any more. Submission and disgust was all I could manage. I just laid there and let him have his brutal way.

My eyes shut tight to block him out, I felt him slide my pants and underwear down my legs and drop them off onto the floor. He yanked open my legs and kept trying to force himself to go inside of me. I was nervous and my body shook from the force and the pain. Screaming as loud as I could, I cried for him to stop. He penetrated me and I kept screaming. Nothing would stop him from disrespecting me and my body.

The savage finished his business, saying, "Don't you tell no one."

I cut him off, "I already KNOW don't tell no one our secret." I was too familiar with that old line. The only thing Jake did different from the other rapists was he gave me a wash cloth and helped me into the bathroom. I stood at the sink, gingerly washing myself and holding a hot towel to my bottom, trying to find some comfort and relief. I decided right then that if this was love, I would rather hate."

Wow, that was terrible. But not for the reason you might imagine. The above passage is from *The Fight for My Love: Final Chapters* manuscript written by Sharon Johnson, who claimed to be my friend for a year and a half. However, this passage wasn't actually written by Sharon Johnson, it was written by me. Sharon provided the framework for that part of the story, but relied on me to rewrite it. I was horrified at the story she told, her own story of being raped as a child.

What horrifies me now is her true story, and the childhood rape she lied about to gain sympathy as a part of an elaborate long-term scam. The web of deception she created over a period of several years touched people from all walks of life, from street-wise men and women to educated professionals, everyday folks and even those on the edge of celebrity. She said over and over how she was going to be famous. As it turns out, she will be, just not for the reasons she imagined.

As a small business owner, I've opened several different ventures in my life. Graphic design, editing, real estate, senior care – I've done a little bit of everything. I am adamant that customers and clients be treated fairly and honestly at all times. To have been taken advantage of in such a sick and horrible way by Sharon was beyond infuriating. As a citizen and as a Christian, I don't abide by criminals hurting dozens and dozens of people without consequence. Finding out she used my name and reputation to further her dark designs shocked me into action.

An unlikely alliance formed from a core group of victims, converging on the local sheriff's department on a chilly winter afternoon. Had Sharon happened upon this group of people she sought to keep permanently separated, she would've fainted dead away.

Sharon spent her life getting things through any means necessary. Services, clothing, furniture, valuable time from busy professionals – her appetite for fame and wealth was never sated. Her ego was untouchable; the sense of entitlement she exuded when running a con was practiced and believable, making her very dangerous.

The majority of her victims were roped into her dark world through one of two lures she commonly used. The first lure she used was the Tyler Perry story. A famous name, Tyler Perry is a respected actor, director, writer and producer whose successes are numerous and well-known. His studio is based in Atlanta, Georgia, which is conveniently only a four hour drive from Columbia, South Carolina. Sharon concocted the tale that Tyler Perry bought the rights to her book *The Fight for My Love: Final Chapters*, and was making a movie about her life. For the rights to her manuscript, Tyler paid her six million.

A whole host of lies originate from the Tyler Perry lure. The reality show about her family, the offers to appear on actual reality shows, working with Tyler Perry on the movie production and casting calls, meeting with Fantasia Barrino from American Idol fame, hooking up with Domonique Scott from TLC's former reality show The Sisterhood, the need for a business manager and a publicist, and even her association with gospel artist Wess Morgan and singer Fantasia Barrino's mother can be tied back to the Tyler Perry lure.

Secondly, you might be told about her daughter, Barrio, who died at the age of ten. Sharon frames this child's death as a case of malpractice by the local hospital, wherein she sued for damages and was awarded $81 million. There are several offshoots of the Barrio lure, to include the You, Too Foundation, Barrio Bath and Beauty, the Back to School Bash, and the Empowering Women to Excel conference. All of those activities, the foundation and the product line are based on the premise of Sharon's large settlement and her desire to act as a philanthropist and entrepreneur.

By running a real life, in-person variant of the infamous Nigerian email scam, Sharon's complicated, years in the making confidence game would make the Nigerian Prince proud.

The Secret Service refers to a variation of one of Sharon's brand of scams as Advance Fee Fraud or 4-1-9 Fraud. The 4-1-9 section of Nigerian penal code deals with these schemes, where a person or persons are made to believe they've been singled out to participate in their "share" of a large sum of money. Creative in nature, victims give up their own money in expectation of a large windfall in the very near future. These cons are created to look like a short and smart return on your initial investment. In Sharon's hands, a 4-1-9 fraud concept is a piece of cake.

Her tendency to make herself appear to be more than she was, coupled with her total lack of empathy and propensity for lying repeatedly, makes her a textbook psychopath. Her icy cold stare, with the feeling you're looking into a blackness totally devoid of emotion, can be intimidating. Her goal each morning is to win whatever game she's chosen to play that day, from convincing a facility to hold her event without paying the upfront deposit, to humiliating a close confidant by lying about her character, all while feeling no remorse.

The people Sharon chose to include in her lies were all people from whom she wanted something. As she never worked at a legitimate job for very long, and her live-in boyfriend seemed to also be forever unemployed, her needs were many. First, she needed a place to live. By her own admission, she has moved over ninety-five times in the last ten years. These multiple moves resulted from the pattern of renting a place, not paying and ultimately moving out in the dead of night.

Sharon also needed money to operate. She'd run one scam to get funds, then run another using the money she just received from the previous scam. Her maneuvering was endless, moving from one practiced lie to another with incredible ease. Anyone confronting her stories was met with indignant rage, sometimes coupled with crocodile tears and a sad story.

The trail of money leads many places, but most of all, it will lead to her final comeuppance. Dozens of bank accounts, opened at an assortment of well-known financial institutions including Bank of America, Wells Fargo/Wachovia, TD Bank, SunTrust, Woodforest Bank, First Citizens and others, were used in a shell game to move funds from one account to another. In several instances, basic checking accounts were opened and used to facilitate the writing of plain old bad checks.

Sometimes, Sharon would open a free checking account at a bank simply to have a reason to go into that branch. By conducting a very low level transaction or just talking to someone at the branch about the possibility of opening an account, Sharon could take up enough time inside while one of her victims waited outside on her to finish "transferring the money" or "checking on the wire," then she'd return to give a fresh excuse as to why there wasn't any money that day.

Sharon spends every waking moment scheming and studying ways to make her lies look good. Thirsty for fame and desperate for legitimacy, she latches onto celebrity any way she can to convince the unsuspecting she's telling the truth.

The cast of con game players is enormous. Sadly, many have yet to realize that not only are they in the game, but they are being expertly played by Sharon for her own benefit.

There are many sayings we all hear, from "if it's too good to be true, it probably is," to "Caveat Emptor" – commonly known as buyer beware. They are certainly appropriate here. If you're involved with Sharon Johnson, you've already been scammed. She's going to constantly tell you, "It's all good," while taking your hard earned money and living like the queen she believes herself to be. But don't feel bad, you are not alone. The many victims identified in this exposé could cry a river of tears to the bankruptcy and foreclosure offices where they've ended up while Sharon lived the good life.

Learn the lesson so many of us learned too late to make a difference and avoid being the target of the next great con artist to follow in Sharon's footsteps. Protect yourself and thoroughly investigate any situation where you're asked for money. All may not be as it seems. When someone asks for your pity, be sure she deserves it. The person closest to you may not be your best friend at all, she may be the devil.

THE LURE, PART I: TYLER PERRY

CHAPTER TWO
The Famous Tyler Perry
◇◇◇◇◇◇◇◇◇◇◇◇◇◇◇◇◇◇◇◇◇◇◇◇◇◇◇◇◇◇◇◇◇◇◇◇◇

"I have a secret to share with you," Sharon whispered to me with glee in her voice and a gleam in her eye.

"Tyler Perry has bought the rights to my book and is making a movie based on my life!" The lynchpin in one of her main go-to cons, Tyler Perry's name has been uttered thousands of times by Sharon and her flock of followers.

"I'm fixin to get on this plane to meet Tyler Perry in Atlanta for a few hours," Sharon claimed in late May 2013. Other goodies include, "I'm at Tyler Perry's studio, working on a casting call for my movie." Or, "Tyler Perry's gonna hook me up with Oprah and we're going to her show in Chicago." Better yet, how about, "Tyler Perry's people gonna do all the work on my magazine for it to come out at the conference I'm havin.'" Linda Wilson, Sharon's assistant, was present when Sharon told me Tyler Perry was going to make a movie about her life and base it on her book. Linda had just been told the same story. There are two very different stories Sharon rolls out at game time, but she gets a lot of play out of Tyler Perry. It's an easy story to explain and a real hit with her usual type of victim.

Sharon had already confided in Linda that her funds didn't come from Tyler Perry, which is the reason Linda was so amazed by the Tyler Perry offer. What a blessing to have millions of dollars already in the bank and then have another six million thrown your way. Success breeds success, right?

The Tyler Perry story goes back a few years. Back in her crack dealing days, when Sharon first tried to put her book together, she met a professor from a community college who taught writing and English. The professor wanted to help her change her life, so he agreed to meet with her on a regular basis to coach her writing skills. She told him about the book she was writing, which was the beginning of *The Fight for My Love* manuscript.

The further he became involved in her world, the professor believed her back story and mildly suggested she seek representation from a publicist. He talked about others who've overcome a rough start, only to find success later. A shining example of victory in perseverance he mentioned was Tyler Perry. With a childhood of abuse, Tyler found inspiration from the Oprah show to write what would become his first musical. After sticking with it for years, he finally found success. Sharon's interest in his fame was instant.

Their shared experience of abuse made Tyler's

interest in Sharon and her life story plausible. As a prominent celebrity, he has access not only to personal funds but to many sources of studio funding for pet projects, such as *The Fight for My Love*.

The confusing parts of the Tyler Perry story are time and money. First, while a genuine movie production does take time, sometimes a year or more, Sharon's movie has taken multiple years. Second, the money's always different. One figure bandied about is six million dollars. Depending on the target, Sharon sometimes confuses the amount paid by Mr. Perry with the amount she is supposed to have won in the wrongful death lawsuit over her daughter, Barrio. Eighty-one million is the bigger number you'll hear her mention. In fact, the fraudulent documents she's created support that piece of fiction.

All of these stories about Tyler Perry need to have an anchor in reality, so Sharon cooks up ways to bring her fantasies to life. Meetings, out of town trips, conference calls and dinners fit the bill perfectly. Except for the hard fact that not only is Sharon uninvolved with Tyler Perry, he's never even heard of her.

Sharon went with Andi James and Patricia Sullivan to meet Tyler Perry in Atlanta. This four hour trip (or was it a "three hour tour?" Apologies to Gilligan's Island fans.) happened in 2012. Sharon's crew didn't meet with him, but Sharon told them to say they did. This fake meeting was disclosed by Andi to Tom Blackstone, another famous name sucked into Sharon's circle of despair. She questioned the setup, wondering why it would be so important for them to say they had a meeting that didn't actually happen. Tom could've used this information much sooner than it came to him. Another clue to the truth, it came as too little, too late.

Once the word was out about her Tyler Perry deal, Sharon mentioned it early and often in most conversations. For something she framed as a secret, it didn't take much for her to spill plenty of details.

"I'm going to a casting call in Atlanta in October. I want you and Becca to go with me," Sharon mentions at a meeting we had about the book editing. "It's gonna be two nights in Atlanta at Tyler Perry's studio."

Becca Kelley (a graphic designer that works with me) and I were all about going, and looked at the calendar to see what we'd need to rearrange to make the drive to Atlanta. Sharon's description of the studio matched anything we found online, so it smelled credible.

"Say hi to Tyler Perry workers," Sharon said on a phone call to me one weekday afternoon. Instead of being in Columbia at my office, she'd gone to Atlanta on short notice to handle a request from Tyler's studio.

"Hi, Tyler Perry workers," I responded, feeling foolish as I matched her speaking style.

"Imma try and get this work done here so I can get home and meet with you," Sharon said, promising a meeting to give the details for the movie production. This phone call could've been made from anywhere. Anywhere but Tyler Perry's studio, that is. Sharon's M.O. is to walk away from everyone when she's on the phone. That way, she can say whatever she needs to convince the person on the other end of the line.

Keeping a piece of reality in her back pocket, she comes up with an actual person affiliated with

Tyler's operation. Sharon's contact at the Tyler Perry studio was a man called Lee Daniels. Mr. Daniels is a producer Sharon claimed was chasing her to do the book as a movie.

Sharon kept saying she didn't want to deal with Tyler Perry, she's not a Tyler Perry fan. But the money won and she told a select few she was working with him because of the name recognition and money.

Sharon claimed there was a contract in the mail, sent certified by Lee Daniels to get the movie done. Linda was with her virtually day and night, yet Sharon claimed to never have time to get the package from the post office. Now, if someone sent me a contract worth millions of dollars, I'd be waiting at the post office the moment it opened.

Here's another time issue with this story: If she's working with Tyler on casting calls and visiting the studio frequently, shouldn't the contract have been signed months ago?

"Isn't that ironic that I told that lie on Tyler Perry and now he's actually interested in me," Sharon confided to Linda. She admitted it was a lie.

As far as we know, Lee Daniels has never actually made contact with Sharon. Early on, Ms. Sullivan supposedly sent a copy of *The Fight for My Love* to Tyler Perry and didn't receive a response. That likely fueled her dislike for Tyler, since he had no real interest in her project.

Now that you know what the first lure is, keep reading to see how Sharon Johnson used it for years to get her way, swindling and cheating untold numbers of victims along the way.

The *Be Smarter than a Con* Takeaway: The old adage, "When something sounds too good to be true, it probably is," offers a good rule to live by. Don't check your brain or skepticism at the door.**

CHAPTER THREE
The Fight for My Love

Sharon's main claim to fame is her book, *The Fight for My Love*. It is this book that provides the basis of her Tyler Perry scam. She works an endless string of lies, incorporating this book into a variety of situations where either Tyler Perry or Marlon Campbell (Tyler's cousin) is working on a movie based on her book.

Depending upon when you run into her, you may get a copy of the original version, or perhaps one of the later incarnations. It's been written, ghost written, edited, re-edited and repackaged multiple times. You may see the one with the black cover and the faded red heart graphic, which is the original. Or, you may see one with a better cover that incorporates Sharon's photo on the front. There's also a version with a different title, called "Let Truth be Found." Or, you'll see the latest known iteration with a grey background and a broken heart graphic on the front.

The last cover is the most appropriate. In the name of this book, Sharon has broken many hearts with promises she never intended to keep. After I edited her book in Spring 2012, Sharon once again reinvents this piece of literary trash by slapping a new cover on it and posting it on amazon.com under Dream Development Publishing. The involvement of Patricia Sullivan, Sharon's publisher and favorite co-conspirator, in this rebranding is clear. The book's description sounds like the same copy Ms. Sullivan has written previously and the most telling part of the new cover is the question on the back asking, "Is this real?"

The manuscript I first saw was rough, to say the least. Riddled with grammar errors, it was either an attempt to be true to the words and speaking cadences of the poor South or it was simply just bad, uneducated writing. A critical clue in debunking her story of coming fame and fortune should have been the condition of the manuscript.

"I want my picture on the front, I got some professional ones done for it," Sharon said as we discussed how the book should look at one of our early meetings. The photos were professional quality, so I didn't object to using the image. Her dress was semi-formal and tasteful, making its incorporation into the graphic design fairly easy. She offered very little input beyond that remark on the cover design, save for a few comments on the back cover wording.

Using my graphic design skills, I clipped her image from the background in the original photo, added her to the area near the main title and felt satisfied with the result. Sharon seemed thrilled.

"I got a surprise for you," she teased once the cover was complete.

"Ok, I give. What?"

"The book people, Destiny Image, are so impressed with your design that they're gonna give you an award."

"You're kidding. Why?"

"Mm hmm, they said they like it, it's real good and will give you an award when we walk the red carpet together at the movie premiere in L.A. I want you to go with me for it."

Flattery, especially when used by a sociopath, is often a way to get someone to think she is sincere by giving personal praise. Wielded by Sharon, flattery is compelling.

"Wow, that would be amazing. I've never been to California. I'd love to go!"

That exchange set off a world of worry for me personally, as I kept thinking about the cover design and how little time I really spent on it. I began to agonize about the minute details of the background pattern, displeased that it didn't exactly line up. Seeing things that no one else would probably even notice, I made minor tweaks to the design. Sharon didn't know I did a thing, and frankly nobody would notice a difference. I just wanted it to be right.

The only significant change Sharon wanted to the cover was the addition of the wording, "Published by Dream Development, LLC." This inclusion was confusing, since I had been told numerous times the publisher was Destiny Image.

Beyond making the cover, the work at hand was

editing. Knowing from the first look at the manuscript the time to edit would be significant, I asked Sharon how in-depth she wanted me to go. She settled on a light edit to save time and money.

Thinking the story was something of value to Tyler Perry, I looked forward to the project. The odd thing to me was her not wanting to spend a lot of money for editing services. Moreover, I thought it peculiar Tyler Perry's people wouldn't want to edit the work themselves.

As a small business person in a tough economy, you take work when you can get it. Hence, I became Sharon's editor of the moment.

The plot of *The Fight for My Love* Sharon frames as an inspirational love story, with a target demographic of women readers. For the technical production, she insists on crème interior paper, "because professionals use crème and amateurs use white paper." She gleaned this little tidbit from Linda Wilson or Patricia Sullivan, or perhaps both, since those ladies have previous publishing experience and Sharon has none. Now, Linda served as Sharon's personal assistant for a number of months and gave up countless hours trying to assist her with all her daily tasks.

The emailed Word document of the manuscript was a combination of a previous shorter version of her story and additions she's dictated to someone else to type. Stand alone pages were sent as well. The ones directly typed by Sharon were difficult to interpret. For example, "she weared a scrabbles dress," was meant to read as, "she wore a strapless dress." Spelling, grammar and sentence structure are foreign to her.

The chapters to be edited were sent with the caveat, "chapters one through thirteen have NOT been edited at all." Any previously edited content was not obvious, but those chapters were especially challenging. Later, I found out the emails from Sharon about the book were actually written and sent by Linda Wilson, but the content was uniquely Sharon.

Here, feel my pain: "What I do remember is at the age of 6 going to Benson school in kindergarten I was living with my grandmother who lived in a one bedroom shotgon house."

So, maybe that wasn't so terrible. The truly horrible passages were the ones dealing with the childhood rape and subsequent abuse of both Sharon and her children by the male character, Timmy. These paragraphs were flat descriptions, very much telling and not showing the action. To make it work, they were rewritten to convey the action. A word of advice: don't ever offer to rewrite the rape of a child, it will haunt you for a very long time.

Throughout the editing process, Sharon wanted a lot. From requesting inclusion in the Library of Congress to purchasing ISBN numbers, formatting text and writing disclaimers to protect the names of the people behind the characters, she knew how to make her goal seem real.

Linda assisted by obtaining the Library of Congress Pre-Assigned Control Number, which was added to the front of the manuscript. Linda also sent over a series of minor edits for groups of pages I'd completed at a time, but they were signed as if sent by Sharon herself. At the time, I didn't realize the major point: these edits were well conceived, spelled properly and used correct grammar. Sharon never could have sent them.

The chapter organization was an ongoing struggle, with rearranging and renaming occurring in several phases. Linda had started going through the book with her and discovered the timeline didn't work. "The story she was telling didn't make sense. I didn't realize it at the time, but it all had to be a fabrication," said Linda. "She'd ask me where in the story I thought something should go, and I'd go back to something I previously read and ask her why things didn't line up correctly."

Toward the end of the re-org, she wants to add a chapter of redemption, showing who she is today and what she'd do differently if given the chance. Her life today is billed as a study in Christian kindness, a victory over the old ways she clung to for so long. The redemption chapter summed it up this way, "I lost a lot of so-called friends, but sometimes you must leave good people to avoid bad situations. The past must stay where it belongs. My life of pain is over. With prayers and the help of people who love me, every day is better and today, I'm a new woman getting geared up in a new life that is healed."

Going a step beyond, Sharon claims to submit her manuscript to the Writers Guild of America East in New York for a ten-year registration period. Worried another author would lay claim to her very special work, Sharon wanted proof to show the world it was all hers.

Multiple proof copies were ordered through CreateSpace for Sharon to "review and edit." The actual purpose? Propaganda. She needed actual copies of the book to sway others into doing her bidding.

Another plank in the legitimacy platform, holding a physical copy of the book helped her get her way.

"I want a website just for my book," Sharon demanded at a meeting in March, 2012. "I need my bio, a Paypal order link, description of the book, some reviews and links to other sites."

Sharon had a few different domains of her own to point to this site and was planning ahead for people to order this book through both her directly and Paypal plus through the dedicated book website available as an option tied to CreateSpace, amazon.com's publishing arm. She wanted to sell as many books on her own as possible, since Destiny Image was taking thirty percent of her sales as their cut.

Trying to corner the market on Fight for my Love names, she had me purchase a couple more domains. These were utilized right away to bring the newly created website to life on the internet. Why these domains weren't purchased and utilized directly by Tyler Perry's people remained a mystery. A hot property and the subject of an upcoming movie, The Fight for My Love deserved a website. Sharon convinced me to make it happen.

**The *Be Smarter than a Con* Takeaway: Someone who holds himself out as a successful author and business executive will have evidence of this success. Best selling books on amazon.com are easily found; in fact, any book for sale on amazon.com shows a sales ranking under the title's product details. **

CHAPTER FOUR
Reality Show About Sharon's
Life and Family

"What are you doing today?" I'd innocently ask.

"Filming," she'd reply.

Someone was producing a television show about her life and struggles, that is, if you believe Sharon.

"TLC is picking up my show. It's gonna be called *From the Streets to the Suites*. It'll air next year," Sharon boasted. To go along with this charade, the network supposedly bought her a home in Charlotte. Yet, she's always in Columbia. The Charlotte house must sit empty all the time.

Sharon and her children work out all of the titles for their projects themselves. They create a list of suggestions and then give one another feedback on how viable each one sounds.

"I need you to fix this treatment for the reality show," she said while handing me a black and white printout of a Powerpoint presentation. It had pictures of

Sharon and her family in a series of circles, with names below each photo. Clearly not a power user of Powerpoint, or any program that allows the insertion of images or graphics, this piece of work was just bad. The photos were stretched out of proportion, the copy didn't flow properly and there was no way anyone would take that document seriously in any industry, ever.

A treatment for a television show is a brief synopsis of the idea and how it's suited for television. It's not a full script. This particular treatment was generated by people associated with the business manager, as a first attempt to get a reality show on the line for her. At least that's what Sharon said about it.

High resolution photos were needed to fix and rebuild this so-called treatment. Sharon promised to provide them within the week. Almost a year later, they've yet to arrive.

Working on a treatment for a possible show shouldn't have been necessary if this concept had already been bought by the network. Her request was very out of place.

Sharon always said Toron Woods worked for Flipup Entertainment and was involved with TruTV network. If you Google "Flipup Entertainment," the top resulting company provides DJs and bands for events such as weddings, parties and corporate functions. They are not involved in the world of reality television at all. Toron was one of those names Sharon threw around casually, meaning to impress those around her with her connections in media and television.

Linda confirms Toron's company name as Flipup Entertainment. "His company used to come up on

Google, so I know it was real," she shared. Twitter has a user called @flipupagency, with references to Toron, so Sharon's version of their name is almost correct. Classic Sharon – her information is close, but not quite right.

Sharon started off with Toron Woods, whom she met through Wess Morgan. Toron came to Columbia, along with Jay, her business manager from Charlotte, and they came to Sharon's house at Woodman Farms. Toron flew in the night before with his assistant and had a breakfast meeting with Linda and Sharon about what he was going to be doing for her. The idea was to polish her, get her into different events and on the red carpet at key functions. He was going to charge her on the order of ten thousand dollars a month and help her get her reality show. He was highly recommended by Wess.

Jay was just taking notes at this first meeting. He talked to all of her family members and they even went to Calvin's grandparents' house and the hair salon where Kandi Buttons worked. All of those folks were interviewed and then the crew went to California Dreaming, a nice regional chain restaurant, for lunch. They also had a camera guy with them to create a bit of documentation for later review.

The two producers are supposed to both return to Columbia a few weeks later. True to form, Sharon created friction between Toron and Jay, tainting their relationship.

In May 2012, Sharon planned a meeting with Toron during a trip to Virginia Beach. Linda worked on the arrangements and knew that Sharon was responsible for Toron's airfare, hotel and all travel expenses. This meeting was to discuss her possible reality show and interview her daughter Myesha. Toron was only there with her in Virginia for a day and a half, so Sharon paid for all of that.

Not really – I actually paid for all of that. The same day, May 29, 2012, Sharon came to visit me. She told me she needed fifteen hundred dollars to send to Smith Publicity for the promotion of her book. Her money was tied up and the lawyer was working on it, so to take care of her book publicity, she wanted half of the money from me and the lawyer was going to supply the other half. Instead, she used the money to pay for Toron's travel and kept the balance. However, it took until September, 2013 to discover what actually happened.

"I gotta take this call," she'd say and walk away from you and everyone else within ear shot of her conversation. Sometimes, the secret call was from her business manager. Sometimes, it was from her attorney. Sometimes, it was the network. These mysterious calls were offers for her to guest on other reality shows, separate from the one being produced about her family and life. If you believe she's a hot commodity in the reality show circuit, you need to re-evaluate yourself. Claims from how she's been offered to be on other reality shows, primarily the *Iyanla, Fix My Life* production on Oprah's OWN network, figure prominently in her discussions with targets.

She really ramps up this story during the summer and fall of 2012. She hones in on a scenario where Iyanla will be attempting to reunite her with a brother she hasn't seen or spoken with in years. The cause of their estrangement: his incarceration.

Along this same time, one of Sharon's daughters was pregnant. With the due date in September, Sharon wanted to have a big baby shower for her in July.

Her cajoling about having the baby shower at my house was never ending, so I relented and agreed to host the shower. I am blessed to have a nice home overlooking the Saluda River and having a party there wasn't a big deal. However, a week's worth of preparation went into making the yard, pool and tiki hut not just presentable, but perfect. Right before the baby shower, I lifted something wrong and my neck suffered the consequences.

The day of the shower was stifling, with temperatures hovering in the mid-nineties. With my neck in agony, I got ready anyway and played the role of hostess. The camera crew was due to arrive early, so everything was double checked to make sure the house and grounds looked their best.

Instead of the reality show crew arriving first, Sharon and Calvin came ahead of everyone with a truck full of food. Aluminum food service trays, almost a dozen of them, filled with home cooking, were set up on the river side of the wraparound porch. Becca, Melissa's friend and a favorite of Sharon's from The Marketing Division, gave the buffet the once over.

"If I can't identify it, I can't eat it," Becca declared.

That's good logic. No argument from me on that point.

Becca was over to help with the preparations and stayed to lend a hand for the baby shower. The guests piled onto the porch, almost three dozen strong. The party started, with guests helping themselves to food and drink. The party progressed, but without the reality show crew.

It couldn't be more obvious something was amiss when a friend of the family, Sharon's cousin's husband Louis Benjamin, showed up with a personal Sony Handycam to video the event. We played along, letting him conduct terribly unprofessional interviews with myself and Becca and then Sharon herself, who sat over by the pool, under the umbrella to save herself from the heat of the brutal July afternoon.

Watching Louis film Sharon was enlightening. Totally at ease and confident in her surroundings, Sharon gave the air of someone not only used to attention, but who craves it. The explanation for cousin Louis as the camera man was thin. "They were too busy to get down here from Charlotte today," Sharon said.

If she's the focus of an entire reality series, how could the crew assigned to her project be suddenly too busy to attend a major family function?

This ruse of shooting the reality show went on for months. In October, 2012, she claims to film for several days and includes Wess Morgan, the gospel artist, in this version. He was in the Columbia area and Sharon convinced him to come over to her home in Woodman Farms. "The team wanted to get some footage of me and Wess," Sharon said on a late afternoon call.

"I'd love to meet him and see how your show is going. May I come over," I asked, genuinely hoping for an invitation.

"It's going to be pretty late when we're done for the day, but I'll call you when the producer says we're clear."

She called back around ten that night, with the news that everyone is too tired and has gone back to the hotel to sleep. Including Wess.

Everyone is asleep at ten o'clock at night, according to Sharon. How odd. The entire film crew went to bed with the chickens, just like they're eighty years old. Whatever you say, Sharon.

This routine of just missing the film crew or a celebrity Sharon's working with became a pattern.

At year's end, Sharon's other daughter gave birth at the local hospital. She said the film crew was driving the staff crazy in the birthing center. I went to see Sharon and her new grandchild, but even my unannounced visit still didn't match up with the crew's presence.

How easy it would've been to simply ask one of the nurses or hospital staff working the maternity ward if a full camera crew had been filming in their midst. There was even time away from Sharon during that visit when it could've happened. But the bubble of oblivion still surrounded me and the questions went unasked.

**The *Be Smarter than a Con* Takeaway: When nothing you're told by someone ever materializes, and excuses are offered frequently, your red flag antennae should be all the way up. Don't be afraid to ask questions and remind the person what you were previously told. **

CHAPTER FIVE
The Business Manager and The Agent

A link to legitimacy, as are so many people in Sharon's world, her business manager labored under the belief that Sharon was wealthy and would pay him a large fee for his services.

As late as May, 2013, Sharon used the name and company information for the business manager on her documents. Meant for use in the commission of a swindle, the always mentioned, rarely present business manager was alternately blamed for things going wrong and praised for getting her guest spots on a number of popular reality shows.

He made connections on Sharon's behalf, introducing her to people in the entertainment industry. Her closest target, Fantasia Barrino, was served up on a silver platter by the business manager, who thought he was making a smart move. Sharon was introduced and began to use more and more tales of spending time with Fantasia (or as she called her, Tisa) in her con games.

A rube for a year and a half, Sharon circled him like trash circles a drain. Pushing as hard as she could for him to break her into the business, she used every weapon in her arsenal to convince him of her wealth and worthiness. Her back story was sad enough, intriguing enough, sordid enough and relatable enough to deserve her own reality show. Overcoming abuse, drug dealing, having children at a young age and crawling out of the deeply wretched public housing complex where she spent most of her life had to mean something. The business manager agreed, and tried to make things happen for Sharon.

In her usual fashion, she made a lot of promises to her business manager. An exorbitant fee would be paid to him, just as soon as her lawyers got the funds released. But in the meantime, could you buy me a steak at Outback?

"She didn't get any money from me," Jay said in early 2014. "I never gave her anything beyond paying for dinner."

As the person responsible for her professional projects, Jay felt he had a good handle on where she was supposed to be and when. Surprised was his reaction when he was informed she was working on a casting call for a movie trailer with the female filmmakers from Columbia. No idea, in fact.

Her perfume line for Fantasia, the magazine Out in the Street, the reality show, the books, the movie, her women's fashion boutique, the bookstore, the charity work and women's conferences all combined to make Sharon look like the up and coming entrepreneur. But as an insider, Jay knew the perfume line, the magazine, the reality show appearances and a show dedicated just to her and her family had yet to materialize. He began to feel bad about putting Sharon together with Fantasia and her people. She never delivered on her promises to dump a hundred thousand dollars into a marketing campaign for this fragrance that Sharon and Fantasia were to design together. After all, Sharon's years of experience in creating fragrances for family and friends was enough to warrant an actual star to put her faith in her abilities. With her settlement from the hospital and funds from Tyler Perry in the bank, dropping a hundred thou' shouldn't be a problem. Not a problem at all.

Sharon continued to call Jay, even after he started to distance himself from her. "She called a few months ago and we didn't have much of a conversation. Anything she promised me, let's just say it didn't pan out. It didn't pan out and I think it's not going to."

**The *Be Smarter than a Con* Takeaway:
If you're a business person or simply someone who has been asked to participate in a so-called business venture, find out all you can about the other participants. If you don't know your potential partner, look into that person's character and references. Do your due diligence by researching the information that person provides for verification.**

CHAPTER SIX
The Publicist
∞∞∞∞∞∞∞∞∞∞∞∞∞∞∞∞∞∞∞∞∞∞∞∞∞∞∞∞∞∞∞∞∞

If you spend a lot of time watching television and don't have a formal education to give you a frame of reference on how the world really operates, you will come up with some unusual notions. Sharon, who never received her high school diploma, thought having a publicist would make her claims of celebrity interaction, book tours and speaking engagements more legitimate. Of course, she was right, to a point.

She hired a Columbia woman who owns a marketing and communications firm to be her liaison. This publicist has a number of reputable clients and by adding Sharon D. Johnon to her esteemed list, Sharon gained a measure of credibility. What's more is Sharon's other unsuspecting accomplice, the business manager, helped Sharon seem on the level to the publicist.

Sharon called and said, "I'm gonna be on Fix My Life with Iyanla and I need a publicist. I want to get my book out and put everything out there." Sharon met with the public relations expert by herself in early 2013 to set the terms of their working agreement.

"The only thing she told me was that she was going to be on the Fix My Life show," said Bebe. "Her producer/ business manager set up everything, as far as I knew. The conference she had last year at the Hilton downtown gave her credibility in my eyes so I agreed to work with her."

Additionally, the main reason Bebe took Sharon as a client was because she thought Linda was still working with her in some capacity. Bebe and Linda knew each other previously, outside of their mutual connection to Sharon.

At the beginning of their association, Bebe arranged for a photo shoot in Charlotte, North Carolina for Sharon to get some nice, professionals shots to use in crafting her PR campaign. Sharon's business manager hired the photographer and Sharon paid for the whole thing in cash. Patricia Sullivan attended the photo shoot to provide Sharon with moral support. So far, so good.

Next, Bebe started setting up a book tour for Sharon. Interestingly, the cover on *The Fight for My Love: Final Chapters* book Sharon intended to promote was quite different than the version created just last spring. This time, the cover was black, with plain artwork. Sharon's photo was prominently displayed on the back; she wore a purple outfit without shoes of any kind. Bebe's team rewrote the back cover copy for her. Yet, for some reason, Sharon left intact the acknowledgements section from the version immediately preceding this one.

The book tour excited Sharon, who shared it with Melissa during a late evening phone conversation. She could barely contain herself when talking about the many churches and bookstores she'd visit in the coming months.

While crafting the plan for the multi-city book tour, Sharon conceived a genius idea to host another women's conference. This scheme has worked so well in the past that Sharon can't pass up the opportunity to hold another one.

Acting on Sharon's behalf, Bebe made the arrangements for the Medallion Center, which was conveniently located in the center of Sharon's world on Garners Ferry Road. Planned for May 25th, Bebe thought she was setting up the launch of a new magazine owned by Sharon called Out in the Street. However, Sharon's plan was to have another women's conference in the Empowering Women to Excel line.

A media buying budget was needed to promote this event, whatever it was to be. Bebe and the business manager agreed to a total budget of eighty thousand for the whole conference. Both Bebe and the business manager thought nothing of proposing such a large amount, as Sharon is independently wealthy as far as they know.

Sharon's second payment for Bebe's services came due shortly thereafter in the amount of one thousand dollars. Bebe expected to be paid this amount monthly for representing Sharon's interests and event planning.

Sharon gladly wrote her a check.

It bounced.

And so began a months-long chase between Bebe and Sharon. Excuse upon excuse was used, finally resting on an old favorite. "My money is being held up at the bank.

I'm gonna get it for you, Ms. Sullivan is supposed to get it transferred, but I don't know what she's doing!" claimed Sharon.

Bebe's never been paid since and the check is still outstanding.

"She always had money for whatever we needed at the beginning. I guess I was lucky that she paid me the first month," said Bebe.

The *Be Smarter than a Con* Takeaway: When you're dealing with a client who wants to pay with cash for everything, be on the alert. More often than not, something's not right in that situation.

CHAPTER SEVEN
Making it Look Good

Trips to Hollywood, awards shows (including the Dove Awards, from which she proudly displayed the program she picked up while attending), pictures with a cast member from the TLC network's production called The Sisterhood – Sharon has been all over the country in her quest to become a reality star.

She posts a photo of herself standing in front a building literally labeled Hollywood Producers. For some of her low level victims, seeing her in such a place could be enough to convince them she is there for a meeting about her upcoming movie.

Early morning phone calls from Sharon claiming to be in Hollywood were always interesting. I'd ask why she's calling so early, only to hear her say she gets up really early to start working on her day. The time difference between the East and West coast is three hours. To receive a call from Sharon at 7:00am EST meant it would've been 4:00am PST. Assuming she really was where she claimed to be, that meant she was getting very little sleep. A normal person doesn't function well without the proper amount of sleep, but Sharon rolls on, regardless.

Communicating her daily routine through Facebook posts, Sharon enjoyed telling the world about her television and radio interviews, her meetings with so-called Hollywood producers, her book signings and encounters with celebrities.

"Leaving AIB TV station, in ATL, it's been a good day," she wrote in mid-May, 2013. "Leaving V103 radio station in ATL," she writes later the same day. A photo of Sharon with an internet talk show host is posted with a caption about getting ready for her interview. The purpose of these missives is to make unsuspecting marks believe she has something big going on in her life.

One of the big trips out west was timed in conjunction with the BET Awards in late June 2012. "Imma be out there to meet with the attorneys and Al Sharpton to get my funds released," Sharon told Linda when discussing the planned excursion. Linda and Tom believed this story, since a lot of the discussion over the past months focused on the discrimination she was suffering at the hands of Big Finance, AKA Bank of America, First Citizens and the like. Tom even suggested to Sharon she seek celebrity input into this crazy process.

The common theme from Rev. Sharpton was helping those aggrieved by the system, so he seemed like a perfect person to get involved. Plus, his name recognition would bring much needed sunlight to the situation.

With the majority of her funds tied up, getting to California might be a problem. Sharon's solution was to have her attorney pay for her airfare, ground transportation and lodging, which seemed logical to Tom and Linda. If the attorney had verified the existence of these funds, then there's no reason why he wouldn't be comfortable paying her way to meet with him in Los Angeles. Right?

Ms. Sullivan paid for the trip to Hollywood. Sharon went out there for the BET Awards. This trip was all about Sharon wanting to attend the BET Awards and nothing else. Her dream was to walk the red carpet with the stars and, together with Patricia Sullivan, Sharon got to live that dream.

Kandi Buttons traveled to Los Angeles with Sharon as part of her mini entourage. Kandi has helped put Sharon together with hair, clothing and makeup. Surely working on a shoestring budget, she's expected to make Sharon look like a million bucks. Sharon brought her along as her personal stylist. Kandi attended the BET Awards with Sharon, Calvin, Ms. Sullivan and Sharon's daughters, but not as celebrity guests. Tickets are available for purchase as a part of the BET L.A. Live Experience. The VIP Experience does include red carpet access. Just like most things in life, if you are willing to pay the right price, anything is possible. Even without the VIP tickets, there is a free Fan Fest component available to the general public for each day of the event leading up to the final evening's award telecast.

It's easy to insert yourself into the celebrity circle,

just by showing up. Sharon's goal was easily attained this time.

The trip wasn't quite as happy for everyone, though. Someone stole five hundred dollars from Keisha's purse. Sharon told Linda that Kandi lost her purse at the airport in Charlotte and when she found it, the money was missing. Several of Kandi's friends questioned whether Sharon had anything to do with the missing funds.

Sharon went on a series of trips out of town over the course of 2011 – 2012. Linda believes Ms. Sullivan, Taci Davis or Talitha Long paid for the majority of Sharon's vacations. None of the trips was work related, as Sharon has no actual work to do on anything, ever. From Los Angeles, where Sharon said she always stays at the hotel where Whitney Houston was found dead, to Atlanta, to Charlotte, to Virginia Beach – Sharon kept the road hot.

A compliment to her many trips and schemes, she works a set of paperwork as her mainline propaganda. She has a great deal of almost somethings, such as a magazine cover but no magazine contents; a planned book launch for her constantly repackaged book; a casting call for the non-existent movie; and of course the bank statement for the fake bank account containing her millions of dollars in lawsuit funding or rights purchases from Tyler Perry. Making it look good in Sharon's world takes time and materials. Just imagine if she would spend that time creating a legitimate business or charitable organization how much good she could do for the world.

**The *Be Smarter than a Con* Takeaway: If someone's bragging about meeting famous celebrities and is also a serious user of social media, beware when there's no evidence of these celebrity encounters. You hear a story that's exciting and amazing, yet no photos or comments about it have been posted. Be suspicious. **

CHAPTER EIGHT
Dream Development

◇◇◇◇◇◇◇◇◇◇◇◇◇◇◇◇◇◇◇◇◇◇◇◇◇◇◇◇◇◇◇◇◇◇◇◇

A corporate structure created for the smell of legitimacy, Dream Development LLC was registered in the state of South Carolina in May, 2011. The registered agent of service lists Sharon, but at one of her dozens of previous addresses.

Later, Sharon morphs this company into Dream Development Publishing. She doesn't put together anything new, but simply uses the moniker of Dream Development by adding Publishing to the end. She publishes the October 2012 version of her book under that name on amazon.com.

Dreaming of success, Sharon's mock corporation is another of her paper tigers. She seems successful, but none of it holds up to even the smallest amount of scrutiny.

When a normal person opens a business, it has a specific, stated purpose. Not Sharon – she has used Dream Development for myriad purposes, including her entrepreneurial endeavors, book publishing and now movie making and reality shows.

The purpose of Dream Development is purposely unclear. Sharon creates the name and identity on the fly, selling this company in the commission of her crime of the moment.

Choosing a company name is a task usually related to the product or service the company provides. For Dream Development, the name couldn't be more appropriate. Whatever Sharon dreams of, this company can be. Serving as an all purpose catch-all for her game of the day, Dream Development gets attached to as many unrelated activities as her other business organization, the You, Too Foundation. Using the names as virtually interchangeable, Sharon and her co-conspirators attach projects to each entity when selling themselves to a new mark. The corporate structure of the You, Too Foundation is non-profit, but Dream Development, LLC is a limited liability company.

In the strictest sense, Dream Development is a non-profit because it has no official business to conduct. In the more literal interpretation, it's a real money maker since anything gained from its use sure won't be claimed on any tax return.

By setting up this fake front, she creates the perfect hiding place for her true intentions. Renting an expensive house, she wants to "have the company pay for it," leading the landlord to believe Dream Development's corporate funds will be a guaranteed payment source for the life of the lease. What's uncertain is whether or not she gives the actual federal tax identification number for Dream Development when she's using its name for her criminal activities. She's amassed a list of other active tax IDs by promising to pay a vendor and then insisting her accountant needs your tax ID in order to cut you the check. The check never comes, but your tax ID gets repurposed by Sharon.

She believes her corporate name can go on forever. All the while, the normal corporate filings required are ignored. A corporate tax return has never been filed, nor will ever be filed. Any money gained through this business finds immediate conversion to personal funds. The cash on hand in Dream Development's balance sheet means cash in Sharon's pocket.

Running a company requires attention to detail. Reports with various entities must be filed, both initially and through a regular, ongoing basis. Election of a corporate status, establishment of a withholding number for employment taxes, new hire reports and a quarterly tax filing are just a few of the procedures a business owner must follow to keep the organization running within the boundaries of the law.

It may be that, just like famous gangster Al Capone, Sharon's downfall comes through the guise of government prosecution for tax evasion. Tax evasion is the illegal avoidance of taxes by individuals and corporations. By misrepresenting the true details of income, profit or gains, the government (and fellow taxpayers) gets cheated.

While she is expertly running a racketeering enterprise, her monetary gains are still considered taxable income. The IRS is brutal when you don't file and even more so when you don't pay.

**The *Be Smarter than a Con* Takeaway: Protect your identifying documents. Business owners and employees need to exercise caution when providing official information, such as your EIN (employer identification number, AKA Tax ID). Make sure the party requesting the information has an actual need for it. **

THE LURE, PART II: BARRIO JACKSON

CHAPTER NINE
Barrio's Story
∞∞∞∞∞∞∞∞∞∞∞∞∞∞∞∞∞∞∞∞∞∞∞∞∞∞∞∞∞∞∞∞

Barrio Sharell Jackson was born to Sharon in February, 1985. It's believed she was born with a congenital heart defect. A single mother, Sharon had borne two other children by that time, yet she was just eighteen years old. Her lack of formal education and absent parents of her own meant Sharon had no one from which to model appropriate parenting behavior.

She was interested in living the good life, meeting and dating older men and looking good. The care of her children came in a distant second to her blossoming social agenda. Even today, Sharon will tell you she's not into watching babies, even if they are her own grandchildren. The maternal instinct didn't take hold with Sharon, then or now.

A short life was in store for this child called Barrio, as her mother failed to provide adequate care. It is likely the lack of properly scheduled treatments and administration of medication throughout her life that ultimately led to her death in August, 1995 at the tender age of ten from rheumatic fever due to heart disease.

Barrio's birth was partially recounted in *The Fight for My Love* manuscript. As shocking as the death of a child usually is, even more so is how Sharon chose to process this loss.

Her obituary appeared in The State newspaper, South Carolina's largest daily. It read, "Services for Barrio Sharell Jackson, 10, of Fort Jackson Boulevard, will be held at 3:30pm Tuesday at Rehobeth United Church, with burial in New Light Baptist Church cemetery of Hopkins. Visitation will be from 7 to 8 tonight at Tompkins Funeral Home.

Barrio died Thursday, Aug. 10, 1995. Born in Richland County, she was a daughter of John H. Jr. and Sharon Johnson Stearman. She was a student at Moore Elementary School, where she was a member of the newspaper staff and the D.A.R.E. Club. She was a member of Rehobeth United Church.

Surviving are her parents of Columbia; sisters, Myesha Jackson, Aneshia Jones and Ceira Nicholas, all of Columbia; and a maternal grandmother, Bernice Jackson of Columbia."

The visitation was only an hour long, which is short by any standard. It's suggested by several sources that Sharon didn't stay for the full funeral and burial, choosing to leave before it was over. Perhaps the grief was overwhelming.

A trip to the graveyard across from the New Light Baptist Church in 2013 revealed no marked gravesite for Barrio Jackson. Every single grave marker was read, yet Barrio's name was nowhere to be found. The church doesn't have a complete record of those interred in their cemetery, so confirming her placement was impossible. If she is indeed buried there, it is in an unmarked grave.

A child. In an unmarked grave. However brief, Barrio's life had meaning in God's great plan. In death, though, while her soul surely serves the Lord, her memory only serves Sharon and her nefarious purposes.

What's more, no one tends to her final resting place. No flowers of any sort, no remembrance on holidays, or any other day. It's almost as if she's forgotten. Almost.

Barrio's untimely death has given Sharon ammunition to fire at unsuspecting marks throughout the years by playing on the sympathies of good and decent folks.

A child's death is usually accidental and fairly immediate, or the result of an identifiable illness. If Barrio's heart condition warranted ongoing medical care, the child's health would have been declining prior to her death. Curiously, Sharon married a man named John H. Stearman just two short months before Barrio's passing. With a child in poor health, Sharon decided to finally commit to an official, legally-sanctioned marriage. Possibly the marriage would provide some much needed stability to the lives of her children.

"I met her on Read Street in Columbia one day, back in 1991," explained John Stearman as he talked about how he met Sharon. Now, Read Street is straight up hood, a known drug area and familiar locale for deputies making arrests. It's an impoverished neighborhood, but ironically nowhere near her home base of Garners Ferry Road.

"Me and Sharon was ok. She had some other goals in life that we both came to understand and face. I was in my drug selling state of mind and was not trying to see or hear anything else! She's a lot younger than me by eight years. She showed me a few things about life. I'm ok with that," he said.

The marriage license filed in Richland County, South Carolina plainly states the residence of Mr. Stearman as Goodman Correctional Institute on Broad River Road. An inmate with the South Carolina Department of Corrections, Sharon married him while he was still incarcerated. As of June, 2013, no record of a divorce exists in South Carolina. If she has terminated this union, it was done so in another state.

The marriage did nothing for Sharon or her children. He dropped away, fading from her life like so many others. He is currently serving a long sentence in the federal Bureau of Prisons facility in lower South Carolina for armed robbery of a federal Bank in SC in 2001. The correspondence with him was conducted through the prison email system. She has certainly had enough years of continuous separation to qualify for a divorce, but still hasn't pursued the dissolution of her marriage.

"And no, I'm not Barrio's father," John said. "I don't have no children."

As usual, Sharon's dishonesty, this time about the parentage of her deceased daughter, serves no purpose but her own. Since she had just married John when Barrio died, maybe Sharon thought she was doing the right thing by listing him as the father. Maybe it was just another lie.

Sharon's grief found a useful outlet. A sure fire sympathy getter, Sharon discovered her loss of this child opened doors blocked beforehand.

To monetize the situation, Sharon started using Barrio's name as the basis for her "line" of bath and beauty products, aptly called Barrio Bath and Beauty. This perfume line has no formal manufacturing process. Rather, it's concocted in Sharon's kitchen with a chemistry set and instructions from the internet. She employs the professional catalog I produced, along with a few sample bottles, as part of her propaganda for those she's targeted for a con.

The general pitch used for Barrio Bath and Beauty goes like this:

"The Barrio Brand is in honor and remembrance of Barrio Sharell Jackson, the young daughter of Sharon D. Jackson. Although her years among us were cut short, she left an everlasting impression of love and joy to remind us of all that's amazing, fabulous and good. To this end, we invite you to explore Barrio Bath and Beauty products and find yourself!

Sharon D. Jackson is a successful published author, speaker, entrepreneur and philanthropist who believes through God all things are possible.

The Barrio Bath and Beauty Products line was established in 2011 by Sharon Johnson, founder and CEO of P&P Enterprises, LLC. For several years, Sharon has created fragrances and beauty products for family and friends. She now brings that experience and creativity to the Barrio brand to produce some of the most sensational and unique fragrances that will have your friends, family and even strangers giving you compliments on how clean, fresh or sexy you smell, the choice is yours! So, go ahead and explore, enjoy by finding yourself!"

The Barrio lineup proclaims to offer products for both men and women. The namesake item, Barrio, can be purchased as a lotion, perfume, soap, body wash or body spray. Ranging in price from seven to forty dollars, the fragrance combines raspberry, pomegranate, Fuji apple, vanilla orchid, purple passion fruit, sheer woods, musk and a touch of floral to create a "bright and airy fragrance for the woman who has a playful sexiness, combined with chick style and confidence." The tagline: A Mother's Gift to the World.

Next up is Heaven's Pleasure, so you can "feel like an angel." The product description calls it a fruity, aromatic floral fragrance with notes of purple passion fruit. The best part? It's for the woman who truly knows how to please her man.

If that's not appealing enough, Sharon offers the Fabulouso fragrance. She describes it as, "top notes of marshmallow and sea breeze, along with Brazilian cherry and sheer amber. For the woman who exudes class and perfection, 365 days a year." The same options are used for the majority of these products as offered for the Barrio signature perfume.

The Fight for My Love scent's advertised as a blend of fruits, including tropical mango, wild strawberries and raspberries, with an added touch of vintage floral and a background of hot skin amber and warm soulful amber. This berry blend, "brings out feelings of joy, passion and flirtation for the woman who is feeling playful and sexy," according to Sharon.

A totally new word, Sharon calls this next fragrance Sunde. Pronounced as "sun dee," this one is for the woman who wants to make the first impression last over and over again. A mixture of grapefruit, orange and fresh ozone (really, she said ozone), combined with passion fruit sorbet and a touch of jasmine, the Sunde perfume is billed as exotic and tropical.

Her line for men starts with the fragrance called Calvin, which is named after her live-in boyfriend and sometimes fiancé Calvin Jones. Two out of the three bottles of Calvin we have as samples have labels, but one octagonal shaped bottle is just dark blue with no markings or labeling whatsoever. It's supposed to have a blend of rich spices, oriental woods, musk, moss and amber, for the man who has romancing his woman on his mind. This assortment is priced from six to thirty dollars.

The second product in the men's department is called For Kai's. Sharon envisions this one for the hard-working man to be sporty and fresh.

Finally, The Fight for My Love for Men claims a luxurious blend of blackberry, Asian pear, moss, sea spray, amber and leather to create a bold, modern effect that women find hard to resist. The tagline: For the man who knows what he wants and how to get it.

Surely people are lining up to purchase these amazing products.

For those who are naïve enough, Sharon has a website posted at www.Barriobathandbeauty.com to support her business model of making and selling personal care products. It's a GoDaddy Instant Page website, very much like an electronic business card with no internal pages. However, on the bottom of the only page, there's a link entitled, "Support Abused

Women." When clicked, it brings up one more link on the upper right corner. The text above the link reads, "Attend the Empowering Women to Excel Conference IV" and the link itself says, "Click here for the Empowering Women Conference information." An explanation of the Women's Conference can be found in Chapter Twelve.

During the production of the Barrio printed catalog, Sharon brought by several samples to use for product photography. The cap was loose on The Fight for My Love lotion, which spilled onto the table. It was a berry blend all right, smelling like rotten fruit bathed in musk oil. It took half the container of Lysol wipes to eradicate the smell from the office.

A legitimate financial advisor once asked Sharon how many bottles of perfume she sold on a monthly basis. She claimed to sell two hundred or so bottles, priced at $50 each. Funny, though, that the catalog of all the products didn't list a single item over $40. Based on her math, her income would then be around $10,000 a month. The reality, as is always the case with Sharon, was something vastly different. When she couldn't answer this financial expert's pointed questions, she made a hasty exit and never spoke to him again. He warned me then to steer clear from Sharon. It's some of the best advice ever given.

Beyond the perfume and body wash, Sharon takes advantage of her child's death in a truly bizarre manner. She tells certain people that Barrio was a victim of the local hospital and died because of malpractice. While that story in and of itself would be sad and horrible, Sharon's spin is much worse.

The complicated fabrication goes like this: "My baby was killed by those doctors. I got my lawyer to sue an' we won dis wrongful death suit. We won real big and now it's all good. I got $81 million and if you'll just do _____(insert expensive service request here), I'll give you $_____(insert a ridiculous amount of money here) in return."

This story is one of two primary lures she uses when running her operations.

Here's an example. Sharon tells someone she needs five thousand dollars to finish the arrangements for her women's conference. If she could just give her the five thousand now, because her name's on the line, when she gets her settlement funds freed up from the bank, she'll pay her back double the money in ten days' time, which is ten thousand dollars.

She plays on the sympathy garnered from the wrongful death of an innocent child to gain what she wants. What a terrifying tactic by a very dangerous woman.

The *Be Smarter than a Con* Takeaway: When someone plays on your sympathy, don't offer yourself in blind faith. It's still a good platitude to live by: Trust but verify. If you were told by a friend that she won a large judgment in a lawsuit, those types of cases make news, especially when the case involves the death of a child. Moreover, court records exist, usually as part of a public record that you can verify for yourself.

CHAPTER TEN
The You, Too Foundation

On the surface, the You, Too Foundation is an admirable charitable endeavor. Its stated focus is assisting battered and abused women overcome life's struggles. Sharon tells a story of mental and physical abuse from her past that includes the loss of her young daughter when explaining how she founded the You, Too Foundation.

Officially formed with the South Carolina Secretary of State in December, 2011, the You, Too Foundation lists itself as a non-profit organization. Very young in its formation, Sharon commissions an ink drawing depicting "You Too" and the tag line, "Women Walking Through Their Changes." An intricate butterfly with a woman of color in the center, the logo was attractive and relevant to her cause. She's always had a good eye for things that look legitimate.

Money for the Family Shelter. Money for Sistercare. A life changing donation to the Meals on Wheels program. The You, Too Foundation is the purported benefactor for these worthy charities.

It looks like the You, Too Foundation is a traditional charity in its own right. But, the formalized structure as a foundation is different from a charity in its work to support other established charities but not actually be one itself. While charity and foundation are often used interchangeably, in this case the money is to be generated and funneled to recognized entities in the region.

In May 2011, Sharon claims credit for the You, Too Foundation sponsoring a trip to the circus for a local children's group. Yet the You, Too Foundation never contributed anything to the outing other than showing up with a camera to take pictures of the Children of God's Church Youth foundation's activities to post as its own.

This foundation was only originated legally in December 2011, yet she used the name well before that time by holding two women's conferences, one in 2010 and one in 2011 sponsored by this non-existent entity.

She goes full bore with using the You, Too Foundation name as a means to further her endeavors from 2012 forward. She establishes a bank account for the foundation and writes checks for a variety of things to benefit herself, including marketing efforts for one of her other pursuits, the fictional Barrio Bath and Beauty line of perfumes and bath soaps. She wrote a check for almost fifteen hundred dollars in April 2012 for an order of catalogs.

The check bounced.

If the You, Too Foundation doesn't have enough money to purchase a small amount of marketing materials, how it planned to pay for a conference and donate to charities remains a mystery. Of course, the real plan was nothing related to its stated purpose. The real plan was simply paying for Sharon's living expenses.

Sharon engages a graphic designer to produce professional business cards for the You, Too Foundation, listing her as a motivational speaker and author. This card includes Sharon's Yahoo email address, her phone number, a toll free number and two web addresses for Encouraging Women and Barrio Bath and Beauty. The toll free number is intriguing; when you call it, it answers with, "Thank you for calling customer care. All of our representatives are assisting other customers. But, a representative will be with you shortly. All calls are recorded for quality assurance. Please hold the line and someone will be with you shortly." If you hang on for a couple of minutes, you get to enjoy some typical hold music and then, poof, you're disconnected.

As it turns out, the toll free number routes you to a call center called Teledirect for inactive numbers from a variety of phone companies.

Linda Wilson helped Sharon complete the application process for making You, Too legal, but once her involvement with Sharon ended, Sharon wasn't savvy enough to keep up with the renewal or reporting requirements of a true non-profit organization. According to the South Carolina Secretary of State's office, "Every charitable organization subject to the "Solicitation of Charitable Funds Act" must file an annual registration with the Secretary of State's Office within four and a half months of the close of their fiscal year. Additionally, every registered charitable organization must file an annual financial report with the Division of Public Charities within four and a half months of the close of their fiscal year. The financial report may be submitted on the Secretary of State's Annual Financial Report Form or on the IRS Form 990."

And while the distinction between charity and foundation is minor, as a 501(c)(3), the You, Too Foundation is not exempt from filings with the state and federal government.

Paperwork has never been Sharon's strong suit. A check of records in June, 2013 at the South Carolina Secretary of State revealed the You, Too Foundation hasn't renewed or filed the appropriate paperwork.

To pull off her biggest feat yet, Sharon needed a fresh infusion of cash. The You, Too Foundation plans the 2012 Empowering Women to Excel conference at the most opulent venue yet, the Hilton in downtown Columbia. As usual, funds were lower than what she actually needed to pull off the event. Remember, this conference was billed as a fundraiser benefitting Sistercare plus the You, Too Foundation initiatives.

Sharon began a confidence game with a new mark, Jeff Downs. The specter of Barrio's death loomed large in this con, with Jeff believing Sharon's daughter suffered a wrongful death at the hands of a large local hospital. She frequently mentioned her "victory" in the wrongful death lawsuit and the $81 million that had her set for life.

If only the bank would release her funds, she could

pay for the conference. Wells Fargo was holding up her money and without it, she was sure in a fix.

Jeff wanted to help. Her promise to provide him with one hundred thousand dollars didn't hurt, either.

A resourceful man, Jeff found a private funding source to provide a short term loan to Sharon, just to cover the immediate need for the conference. In late January 2012, Jeff struck a deal on behalf of Sharon and the You, Too Foundation to gain $35,000 in cash for her women's conference planned for February, 2012. Jeff explained to the private funder how Sharon was the beneficiary of a multi-million dollar lawsuit in the United States District Court in South Carolina. The money was only temporarily hung up and would be available to repay this short term loan soon.

The money was provided to Sharon and the You, Too Foundation on February 2nd so the advance payment requirements of the Hilton hotel could be met to hold the conference as planned.

Sharon effectively signed her life away when she agreed in writing to repay this loan in full by March 2nd, 2012. She further agreed to pay a premium and of course all court costs and attorney fees if the payment wasn't made as promised. For the average person, agreeing to repay a debt of $35,000 is a very big deal. That amount of money would be the equivalent of a nice automobile or a very modest rural home or an exceptionally nice mobile home. Bottom line: it's a lot of money for the average Joe.

By the time June rolled around, Sharon had not repaid the funds as promised. She also had moved and changed her phone number – Avoidance 101 in the

Book of Sharon.

The private funder filed suit in the Richland County Court of Common Pleas, as he'd had enough and wanted his money back.

In some cases, time heals wounds. For the South Carolina Secretary of State, time makes it worse. The staff at the SCSOS was quite interested in Sharon's continued solicitation of donations taken under the guise of supporting Sistercare and the Family Shelter. The longer you go without your documentation turned in, the more problems a charity can have. For the You, Too Foundation, April 2014 brings a formal suspension from the Secretary of State's office. They're cited for Failure to pay a fine for Delinquent Annual Financial Report (Charity) for year ending 2012 and Failure to pay a fine for Delinquent Registration Statement (Charity) for period ending May 15, 2013.

Perhaps "Women Walking Through Their Changes" means going from civilian clothing to prison orange. The You, Too Foundation sure seems to be headed that way.

The *Be Smarter than a Con* Takeaway: Charities are required to register with the government in all states. In many cases, the Secretary of State's office is responsible for administering charitable organizations. Yearly tax returns and corporate documents must be filed for the organization to maintain its good standing. In South Carolina, an annual list of Scrooges and Angels for registered charities is compiled to compare the charities that contribute the most to their stated causes and those who contribute the least. Further, an online search function is available for most states to determine if a charity or non-profit foundation is legitimate or not.

CHAPTER ELEVEN
Back to School Bash

Always held at an apartment complex off Garners Ferry Road, Sharon's Back to School Bash is an almost annual event. It's almost annual, because with Sharon, you can never be certain about anything actually happening the way she says it will.

Sharon's Back to School Bash is framed as a way for her to remember her roots and help single mothers who are struggling to get their children ready for school by providing free school supplies, such as notebooks, pencils, and an assortment of other goodies.

Speakers from the community offer tips, a picnic lunch is served and even the local sheriff's department shows up to talk about stranger danger.

On August 13, 2011, Carriage Place Apartments held it's first ever Back to School Bash, organized by Sharon Johnson. It's held two days prior to the first day of school and received media coverage by the local CBS affiliate, WLTX TV 19. In addition to the video story, the text of their coverage follows below from their website:

Columbia, SC (WLTX) - Some Midlands kids got some help heading back to school as Carriage Place apartments hosted a back to school bash, after seeing a need in their community.

"I wanted to give back to show that I appreciated it and that anyone out here can overcome anything," says Sharon Johnson.

Johnson says after writing a successful book about a nine-year relationship gone bad, she felt the need to help those who were there for her in her time of trouble.

"I lived at Carriage Place five years ago and I was down on my luck, I was behind on rent and they worked with me and really helped me," says Johnson.

Johnson, along with other sponsors, gave students a back to school celebration with free food and school supplies. Says Johnson, "People showed me they cared and that pushed me to keep going."

She says seeing a community come together truly shows that it takes a village to raise a child. "I dropped out of school in the 8th grade, had my first child at the age of 13. So I didn't have anybody to give me anything so for me that's a great thing," she says.

She said it makes her feel good to see smiles on people's faces. "It doesn't hurt to give and take the time to tell someone that you care," she says.

The story is telling in more ways than one. First, it says that Sharon, along with other sponsors, gave the free food and school supplies. The key part of that sentence is, "other sponsors." Sharon didn't have any money invested in this event, but was smart enough to conceive the idea and find a way to make it happen. Second, it says Sharon "didn't have anybody to give me anything." The idea of giving back to the less fortunate is truly admirable, but the concept of personal responsibility and learning to do for yourself is the bigger lesson here, but Sharon's totally missed it.

Her successful book about the nine-year relationship is anything but successful. As discussed in Chapter Three, The Fight for My Love is another weapon in her arsenal of propaganda she uses to create legitimacy for herself.

The second Back to School Bash was held in August, 2012. Sharon spent no money herself on the 2012 event, either. Linda went to the Bi-Lo on Garners Ferry Road and gave them the flyer that she created for Sharon's event, along with the You, Too Foundation's non-profit ID from the South Carolina Secretary of State's office, which, as you now know, is the entity responsible for registering and monitoring charities. It was kind of last minute, but Bi-Lo ended up supplying all of the hot dogs and hot dog buns for the event. "I went and picked them up myself and took them to her," Linda said.

"Ms. Sullivan purchased the laptop that they gave away. Talitha Long provided some food, like chili for the hot dogs. Tom and I went to Sam's Club and got chips, big trays of cookies, sodas, we bought all of that. Talitha had her family to donate the chairs and the tents and that big bouncy house," Linda continued. "There were some other people helping, such as The Carriage Place Apartments management, who donated some gift cards that they gave away, like to Wal-Mart. Sharon gave some of her Barrio products away, but it was nothing that she purchased."

For entertainment, there was a volunteer DJ and Ms. Sullivan was the hostess. Sharon gave her little speech. The media came out for that and she did an interview. She didn't have as many participants as she did the year before. There was a lot of stuff left over. Linda worked it and helped serve the food, along with her daughter and niece. "We gave out raffle tickets for the drawing. Tom did all the grilling for the hot dogs," Linda said.

The Second Annual Back to School Bash was somehow supposed to be a benefit for the You, Too Foundation. Tom, Linda and a few other volunteers had packaged school supplies for the kids, with typical back to school stuff that children need. In 2012, she had maybe sixty children attend with their parents or guardians.

"Sharon is taking all the credit for putting this event on, but she never gives anybody that helps her or provides any support any credit," said Linda. "The purpose of doing these events is to appear that she is this great philanthropist and she's giving back, yet she didn't give anything."

"No matter what she says, she hasn't 'made it.' A person from the outside looking in, it looks like she is giving back to the community. The real purpose, in my opinion, is to further her scam. Everything she does is well calculated to benefit her in some form or fashion," Linda concluded.

What's interesting is Sharon doesn't practice the idea she promotes. Instead of seeking school supplies by shopping or even taking advantage of the many actual school supply charity drives operated in the area, Sharon does a little back to school shoplifting. The approach is an oldie but a goodie. Do a run through Wal-Mart with the baby stroller, pick out random things, easily concealable. Hide them under the baby's things, escape without being caught. Come back a day or so later to "return" them, saying you've lost the receipt and want store credit. Anything garnered through this method is kept for her family's personal use, and not part of the Back to School Bash. It's not even needed for that purpose, since her sponsors covered all of the event expenses on her behalf.

Right along with the Back to School Bash is her involvement with the Family Shelter of Columbia. By inserting herself into their promotional video, Sharon's found yet another charitable entity to wrap around herself. Like her very own cloak of invisibility, the Family Shelter angle supports her dream of appearing to be philanthropic.

Directly from their video, Sharon speaks about her past. "I was here for two weeks," she said when asked how long she was at the Family Shelter. "Actually, I was a young parent, I had my first child at the age of thirteen. By age twenty-two, I already had three kids. We had no place to go, my mother put us out.

"I got a job at Burger King. When I came home from work one day, she had the kids on the front porch with their bags packed." The father was nowhere in the picture, so that wasn't an option for help, according to Sharon. "We walked to a restaurant, sat down and ate to try and figure things out. I got the phone book and came across Family Shelter. I made the phone call and she said if you can be here in twenty minutes, then we can help you and your kids. So, we walked from Two Notch Road to the top of the hill and we made it here."

Finding help in a desperate time of need is wonderful. When you're Sharon, you don't just appreciate it. You spin it for all it's worth.

The Family Shelter provides up to one hundred twenty days of shelter per family. Only two weeks went by before Sharon and the girls moved on to something better. And while there's every reason to be grateful for two weeks' worth of housing assistance, to hear Sharon tell it, the organization played a much larger role in her life. What led Sharon's mother to evict her with three young children is unknown. The relationship was problematic, to be sure, but it had to have gone nuclear for her mother to put her own daughter and grandchildren on the street.

"I've done a lot of things to help women in my life," Sharon explained in 2012 with her trademark icy smile. The Family Shelter was mentioned prominently, with her tales of setting up fashion shows and personally cooking food to take over to the residents.

"I cook for them a lot," she said. This benevolent behavior was never witnessed by anyone in the past two years and could have taken place before Linda Wilson's introduction to Sharon. The reality is more likely that it never happened at all. You know the saying, the road to hell is paved with good intentions. She may have even wanted to do something for the shelter, but never actually made it happen. Wanting to help a charity is great, but not doing anything and yet continuing to

tell everyone you meet how much you do for them is
beyond unacceptable. It's reprehensible.

**The *Be Smarter than a Con* Takeaway:
When someone's telling you a story and the smile she
has doesn't touch her eyes, she's likely telling a lie.
A fake smile is common body language of a deceiver.
A genuine smile will be on a face with eyes showing
crinkles and minor crows feet, open lips and teeth and
no look of tension in the jaw or shoulders. Related to
the fake smile is a stare or unblinking eyes, with the
intent to intimidate the person to whom the story is
being told.**

CHAPTER TWELVE
Empowering Women to Excel

On the surface, this concept seems terrific. Putting together a list of powerful speakers and gospel entertainment to promote women's success – this idea should make money and draw a crowd. "I created and designed Empowering Women to Excel to help women from all walks of life, to help inspire them and motivate them while helping them to open up," shared Sharon during a television interview.

The conference looks like a high value production, from the quasi-professional promotional flyers created in Photoshop to the slate of featured speakers, many of whom are well-known names. The old saying, "you've got to spend money to make money," is true. Sharon's willing to spend money on getting a suitable location, creating advertising and putting people in place to run a conference so she can bring in a sizeable haul from ticket sales. The money she's willing to spend, however, isn't hers. It's ours. One victim after another has given her money to keep this façade going and when it's over, she's nowhere in sight when it's time to pay the bills.

The conferences are a strong plank in Sharon's platform of deceit. She can gain years worth of credibility every time she's able to pull off another conference event. She puts all of her effort into getting the symposiums together, as they provide a fresh infusion of cash for her living expenses and fuel her ongoing cons with more propaganda.

Sharon's held these events since 2010. The inaugural event was held in a church fellowship hall at Bishop Mack's church with paper tablecloths and balloon decorations. Dr. Partridge's wife (Sharon's cousin) was the emcee. "I started out with seventy-five women and it was so powerful, everybody was telling me, 'you gotta do this next year, you gotta do this again,'" Sharon said.

The second attempt at the conference was called, *Empowering Women to Excel II: How to Fulfill Your Dreams*. Go big or go home was her philosophy with this event, as she turned it into a two-day affair with an opening reception featuring a talent and fashion showcase on Friday night, January 28, 2011 and the main seminar series for approximately two hundred attendees on Saturday, January 29th. Held at Spring Hill Suites on Lady Street in Columbia's Vista area, pre-registered attendees paid seventy-five dollars (and could have made that payment in monthly installments, according to the promotional literature) and on-site registrants paid a cool hundred to attend.

The guest speaker was LaShana Harmon-Goff, Mrs. South Carolina International 2010. Additionally, breakout sessions on single parenting, domestic violence, HIV/AIDS awareness, women's health and beauty/self-esteem were advertised as well. She even had an exhibitors area for anyone wanting a booth to market to her attendees.

The Christian angle was beginning to come into play with this second conference, as the registration form requested a church affiliation from registrants. And, the IJD Children of God's Kingdom Youth Foundation was listed as a sponsor beside the You, Too Foundation. Remember, the You, Too Foundation didn't officially exist until the end of December, 2011, yet it's listed as a sponsor in January that same year.

The 2012 conference, called *Empowering Women to Excel III: Know Your Purpose and Walk into Your Blessing*, purported to support the Family Shelter and the program for the event showcased Sistercare as well. As an attendee, you would be under the impression part of the two hundred dollar ticket price for your admission was being donated to these local charities. Further, you'd believe Sharon was a full time philanthropist and a Godly person.

Tickets were available for purchase through the conference website, by mail with a money order or in person with cash. Sharon doesn't take personal checks.

Programs for this year's event were pitched to Melissa for graphic design and printing. However, the quotes of a digest size publication of twenty-eight pages and two hundred and fifty copies must've seemed too expensive to Sharon, as she chose someone else to provide them.

The location was prime, high class space. She selected the Hilton in downtown Columbia and catered the affair with Ruth's Chris Steakhouse. If you've never eaten at a Ruth's Chris restaurant, you are really missing out on an excellent meal. This restaurant is expensive, and is the sort of place you might celebrate a special event such as an anniversary or graduation. Imagine the cost of catering an event of three hundred people with a full entree, sides and dessert from a place like Ruth's Chris. Not surprisingly, the total due just for the food was thirty thousand dollars. At a cost of one hundred dollars per person and a guaranteed attendance of three hundred, that is serious math.

The Friday evening meet and greet started at seven o'clock on February 10th, 2012 and the remainder of the event was held the next day from three to nine, to include the speakers, the keynote and the unbelievable, over the top dinner.

Sharon invited a well-known minister and gospel artist, Wess Morgan, to perform and give the keynote address. A pastor, singer, motivational speaker and founder of a non-profit alcohol and drug abuse recovery foundation, Wess Morgan's star has risen steadily over the past seven years. He has released two CDs of soulful gospel music and was nominated for a Dove award in 2011 for his single, "I Choose to Worship." He travels around the country for speaking engagements and concerts.

Sharon's fascination with Wess led her to invite him to speak at the 2012 conference. His presentation didn't disappoint; everyone was mesmerized by his message. His fee for appearing was several thousand dollars. Sharon worked out a deal to have Wess' fee paid by her loyal associate, Linda Wilson. She promised to repay her with significant interest, just for helping her make it happen with Wess.

Tamika Sims, an author and coordinator of volunteer services at Sistercare; Cynthia Hardy from OnPoint with Cynthia Hardy; and Jeffrey Lampkin of WACH Fox 57 and American Idol Season Seven fame all played a role on the second day.

Always thinking about the big names, Sharon contracted the You, Too Foundation to engage the speakers Omar Tyree and Sheri Riley for further star power. Omar Tyree is a New York Times best selling author and speaker from Charlotte, North Carolina. He has published a number of novels and at least one of his works has been optioned for a stage adaptation. Sheri Riley is a certified personal development coach and life strategist who works with celebrities, athletes, executives and high achievers. Her company, Glue Inc., has a list of well-known names as clients. CVS Pharmacy, The Atlanta Hawks, Nike, Champs Sports and many other familiar brands have all employed Ms. Riley's firm.

Besides the speakers' bureau fees, Sharon obligated her company to meet the technical ryder for each presenter, which meant she was to pay the flight, hotel and ground transportation expenses, along with making sure the accommodations were at least four star.

The deposits for the speakers were paid several months in advance of the February 2012 event through Linda Wilson's Paypal account, whom Sharon promised to repay. Linda worked closely with Sharon for a year as her business manager and set up contracted services on Sharon's behalf.

Sharon advertised the speakers' participation and made sure to get them to the event on time. What she didn't bother to do on time was pay the balance.

The contract called for the final payment to be made by the event date of February 11th. Sharon held the conference, so no claim could be made that anything was cancelled. The speakers bureau chased her via telephone, email and regular mail. She promised to pay them on ten separate occasions before she stopped communicating altogether. They're still looking to be paid.

In the spring of 2013, Sharon plans another conference called, *Empowering Women to Excel IV: Believe It and Achieve It – You are too Blessed to be Stressed*. Part of this name is familiar, as Sharon claims to have spoken at an event in Myrtle Beach previously called *Believe It and Achieve It*.

Initially, it was scheduled at the Medallion Center off Garners Ferry Road for May 25th. But shortly after that booking, Sharon said she forfeited the six hundred dollar deposit to move the event to June 1st at Brookland Baptist Church in Lexington County. The Medallion Center, however, had this conference booked under the name, "Out in the Street," which is the name of the magazine Sharon wants to publish. It was never intended to be anything other than her standard money-maker, the women's seminar.

When asked about the reason for moving the location, Sharon said, "better publicity." The real reason is more about hiding from her former publicist, to whom she owes money for a bad check.

The players in this latest iteration include Victoria

Rowell, from the Young and the Restless soap opera; Dianne Barrino-Barber, mother of the American Idol winner Fantasia Barrino; Domonique Scott from the TLC channel's defunct show called The Sisterhood that only lasted eight episodes; Amber Smith, a local entertainer in the Kenny Smith & Unleashed gospel group from Columbia, South Carolina; and Juneann Lewis, a real estate agent and internet talk show host from Atlanta, Georgia.

The promotional flyer had screen grabs from the web of photos of each presenter and claimed a portion of all proceeds will go to the Family Shelter. Advertised ticket prices are fifty dollars in advance, seventy five at the door. The option to make payments on your fifty dollar investment was available, too. Sharon always makes it easy to give her your money.

The same website as the previous year is utilized for soliciting ticket sales, ultimately directing the buyer to eventbrite.com to finalize the purchase. The site created was a basic templated website offered through a GoDaddy hosting account, maybe costing as much as five dollars a month to keep the site live. It couldn't have been much more; the site was incredibly basic.

In the weeks leading up to the conference, Sharon posts numerous teasers on Facebook and Twitter. Since it appears there's no money for a proper marketing budget, she utilizes the free calendars on the websites of major news outlets throughout South Carolina, including all of the television and newspaper sites in Columbia, Charleston, Spartanburg and others. The category for the event listing on every single post was, "Religious."

She also sends a press release on Victoria Rowell, which is noticed by WLTX TV, the Columbia, South Carolina CBS affiliate that carries *The Young and the Restless*. One of the on-air personalities there tweets, "Looking forward to having you in the Midlands next week, @VictoriaRowell." It certainly makes sense that the CBS station would interview Victoria if she were in the area, as *The Young and the Restless* remains the most popular soap opera on daytime television.

The week before the conference, a quick call to the Brookland Baptist Conference Center reveals the booking for space is still marked as tentative. If the rental fee hasn't been paid, the space will be released shortly.

"Tickets are selling out fast," proclaims Sharon on Facebook two days before the event. When asked directly how many tickets have been sold, Sharon replies, "I don't really know, I just know it's a lot."

The fun began the day before the scheduled conference, with a series of early morning text messages from Sharon.

"Call me 911111."

"911."

"Gm, Melissa, call me soon bf I get on the plane."

"Hello."

"Anyone hm?"

Sent between 6:19am and 7:30am on May 31st, Sharon tried feverishly to reach me. I grabbed my phone from the charger on the way to work, right at 8:00am. Intrigued, I called her directly.

"Melissa, I need your help!"

"What's the matter, are you hurt?" I asked.

"I need your help. I'm bout to board this plane to Atlanta and got so busy yesterday that I forgot to book Victoria's ticket. Now she's raging, blowin up my phone, callin' the church and everything."

"So how do you want me to help you? And why are you getting on a plane the day before the conference?"

"I need you to buy her a ticket. I don't have time since my flight is about to board so I need you to do it. I'm going to Atlanta to do something with Tyler Perry. I'll be back in four hours."

"Sharon, I can't buy her a ticket. Can't you do it?"

"No, I don't have time and now she's mad and I need to get it booked."

"Doesn't she live in Atlanta? If you're going there, just bring her back with you."

"She in L.A. I need her to have the flight information before she wakes up. Just book it for me."

"Can't you just call the airline and pay for it with a credit card?"

"You know I don't have no credit card. Listen, I got the money, cash in my back pocket. I'll give it to you when I get back, just go on and book it. It's all good."

"Well, if you've got the cash and you're already at the airport, just go to the ticket counter and pay for it. They'll take cash."

"Oh, well, yeah, I guess that would work. I'll text you, I'm fixin to get on the plane. Ok, bye-bye."

Interesting. Questions requiring immediate answers include why Sharon is going to Atlanta the day before the conference and why hasn't she finalized the arrangements with the keynote speaker well before now?

Efforts to reconnect via voice were unsuccessful, so I left a voicemail and sent her another series of texts.

"What up," she texted.

"Driving…just left 2 msgs with info on the ticket situation."

"No, on plane didn't have time to stop buy a ticket, had to boad (sic) plane."

"Sorry I missed you, I was saying you need Victoria's info as it is on her travel documents, like date of birth and social security for her ticket bc of homeland security regs. How much is the ticket?"

"$950, I'm in tears."

"Did you hear the voicemail about the other way to do it? When you get to ATL, call her or her mgr and get info for a wire transfer, send her the money and she books her own ticket."

"Ok, PR person taking over now."

Nothing else was heard from Sharon that day, even though a text was sent to see if she was able to purchase the ticket.

Finally, the day of the Empowering Women conference arrived. An early report indicated Sharon was having trouble with Brookland Baptist, as she told revelers at a party the night before she might have to find a new place to hold the conference. Doubt crept in that the conference would even happen at all.

The Victoria Rowell issue still loomed as unsolved. A tweet was directed to her personal account, asking if she was in Columbia, South Carolina for the conference.

No response.

As I was invited to attend, my guests and I continued

to get ready like nothing unusual was happening. Around 1:30pm, a Facebook notification popped up on my iPad with a post from Sharon. "We do apologize, The 4th Empowering Women to Excel new location is the Medallion Center 7309 Garners Ferry Rd, Columbia, SC. Please come out and be encourged to move to your next level. We appreciate your support."

Holy cow, she's moving the conference two and a half hours before it's supposed to start!

The pull of gravity was too great. Sharon returned to the center of her universe, Garners Ferry Road, to salvage this conference. Since she'd previously paid the deposit, the thought is she was able to talk the Medallion Center into reinstating her original reservation and moving it to June first.

Just to confirm, a trip was made over to Brookland Baptist, where four signs were posted on the entry doors, "The Empowering Women to Excel Women's Conference is no longer being held at the Brookland Banquet and Conference Center. Please use the contact information on your ticket for additional information."

At 3:00pm, Sharon called to personally update me on the location change. At a quarter until four, we arrived at the Medallion Center. A handful of people were there with vendor booths in the hallway to sell things such as fashion handbags, beauty products (but not Sharon's line from Barrio Bath and Beauty), books (but not Sharon's book, *The Fight for My Love*), and jewelry. Very few attendees had yet to arrive.

The registration table sported a super large framed portrait of Sharon in black and white, perhaps as large as twenty-four inches by thirty-six inches. The photo was older, as it showed her gold front tooth, the one she had removed in the summer of 2012. A discarded laminated poster of the conference flyer was lying on the floor behind the registration table, clearly not being used. Perhaps advertising the keynote speaker literally outside the ballroom, even though Sharon knew full well the lady wasn't coming, was just too much.

The young lady checking tickets mentioned that she didn't know how many tickets were sold. She was doing a friend from high school a favor by working the conference and had no idea who Sharon Johnson was or anything about the event. Normally, a well-run function has a list of attendees to check off the names as guests arrive. Sometimes, nametags are prepared, along with gift bags or at least a printed program.

Not in this case. No list, no nametags, no nothing.

We were finally led into the conference room at four twenty by Patricia Sullivan and Juneann Lewis began the program at a quarter to five. At the time, approximately thirty people were in the room, which was set for one hundred and thirty six. Alá Dollar Tree, the centerpieces were silver sparkle balloon weights, holding one to two black and silver balloons in place.

Sharon sauntered into the fete, wearing a white chiffon dress with split sleeves, a multi-layered gold and silver serpentine necklace and beige heels.

A few days prior, Sharon claimed she was wearing black to the event. Guess not. In Sharon's world, black is white, white is black.

She came over to greet me, giving me a chance to ask why the venue was changed. "You know how I told you what was going on with Victoria? Well, she called the church and they were telling her all my business, like ticket sales and everything."

"You're kidding, right?"

"No, man. I got mad and just cancelled right then." Sharon said as she walked away to speak to some of the other guests.

The content of the program was certainly unusual. First, Juneann's remarks about how successful and giving Sharon is led right into the next speaker, Domonique Scott. Also known as Pastor D, Domonique preached a sermon for almost an hour, wherein she called out a woman as a street walker and talked about drug dealing, among other things.

She was followed by Stormy Wellington of Atlanta, Dianne Barrino-Barber, Amber Smith and then Domonique Scott again. Somehow, the event devolved into a faith healing where women in the audience were wailing and speaking in tongues.

Seriously, speaking in tongues.

"Where are my wailing women," Pastor D asked. Right on cue, four or five women began to cry out, dropping to their knees in the front of the room and pounding the floor. A large woman circled the room, speaking jibberish while Pastor D yelled, "Jesus, Jesus, Jesus," for minutes on end.

To add a bit of levity to the proceedings, Becca began to yell back, "Cheez-its," every time Pastor D yelled, "Jesus."

You just can't make this stuff up.

The sit-down banquet dinner promised on the advertising turned into a homemade-looking buffet courtesy of Sharon's friends and Sam's Club. The

Medallion Center didn't cater, which was expected by the ticket buyers. Now, by the time the food was finally served, which was nearly seven thirty in the evening, a good many more folks appeared for the conference. The product of frantic phone calls from Sharon's good friend, Patricia Sullivan, and family members, the message was clear: come on down, there's free food and entertainment at the Medallion Center tonight! The type of crowd gathered was not the typical ilk you'd find at a women's conference. Young men, small children and babies, older men and women in various stages of formal to informal attire began to populate the once sparse ballroom.

A young gentleman was overheard in the foyer speaking to one of the vendors about how he was going to make a movie out of Sharon's book.

Wait a minute. Tyler Perry is supposed to already be making this movie. Very curious.

The NBC affiliate WIS-TV appeared to cover the conference, interviewing Domonique Scott, Dianne Barrino-Barber and Sharon, of course. This story ran on the news at eleven that night, another plus for Sharon's credibility.

The advertised keynote speaker, Victoria Rowell, never materialized. People had to be disappointed. And no mention was made of the Family Shelter, to whom a portion of the proceeds had been promised.

Toward the end of the event, a processor server appeared and served Sharon with a civil suit filed almost a year earlier. The claimant searched for her for eleven months, trying to serve the lawsuit for the money owed by Sharon for the 2012 conference. Today, he was successful.

The person who took the most podium time, Domonique Scott, seemed unhappy with Sharon when it was all over as well, as she was heard asking several guests if they had paid for their conference ticket or not.

Two days after the event, a late night tweet came in from Victoria Rowell. Finally, a response!

"The sponsor never sent my agent a plane tkt or pd for the appearance but continued to publicize me. Just AWFUL!"

Thinking the conference saga was over for the year was premature, though. A little over two weeks later, the manager of the Medallion Center calls Linda Wilson, as she knew Linda used to work with Sharon. The manager has been trying to get in touch with Sharon ever since the conference to get the final payment for the facility rental.

Along with Patricia Sullivan, who did most of the talking, Sharon somehow convinced the facility management to let her hold the event there without paying the full balance in advance. The previous deposit wasn't enough to pay the full rental fee, which was clearly more than six hundred dollars Sharon mentioned earlier. A sad turn of events for the Medallion Center, which was kind enough to work with Sharon by making last minute arrangements. Sharon's avoidance behavior is in high gear, running from yet another unpaid bill from the Empowering Women debacle.

The manager of the Medallion Center first met Sharon in November, 2012, when she came in with her publicist to set up an event to debut her magazine and present her latest book. Sharon talked about her new book series focusing on how women can learn to overcome abuse and said she'd be bringing out a title in that series at this event. Trying to include all of the old familiar stories into a single happening, she also said her new perfume line would roll out at the same time as the magazine and the book. The original booking was December fifteenth.

She paid the deposit, which was actually $350, not the $600 she said it was.

After that initial meeting, the publicist was not heard from again by the Medallion Center. The manager thought it was odd, but decided it wasn't her job to chase people down. If she was involved, the publicist would make contact. Otherwise, the manager was just dealing with Sharon. Or so she thought.

Sharon changed the date from December to January thirty-first, with the reason being her need to go to Atlanta with her agent. Two more date changes, first to February ninth, then to May twenty fifth, were her only communications with the Medallion Center management.

On Friday, May thirty-first, Sharon and Ms. Sullivan, her trusty sidekick, show up to salvage the event at the last minute, but it's now a different event than what was booked originally – the women's conference. "She bebops in with Patricia and said we want to do it here," the Medallion Center manager said. "I spent forty-five minutes to an hour with them and they gave me a flyer with Brookland Baptist on it as the location. She never did explain why Brookland was on the flyer, she just kept on about needing to have it here."

"Let me see if I can throw this together for you," the manager told Sharon. The event staff was briefed and everything was scheduled for the afternoon of June first. Sharon and Ms. Sullivan signed an agreement to rent the facility on behalf of the You, Too Foundation right then with a new contract so the previous deposit from last December could be applied towards the balance.

The full payment was due, as the event was less than twenty-four hours away. Sharon and Ms. Sullivan were to return with the money later on Friday, so the manager waited around until 7:30pm for them to show up and pay.

"I kept getting these phone calls every hour or so from Pamela, saying Sharon was at the bank, but it was taking longer because her money had to come from a special fund and the attorneys were working on getting the money released," the manager said. "I just didn't believe it would be happening like that on a Friday night, so I went home."

The next morning, the owners of the Medallion Center instructed the staff to either collect payment from Sharon's group or lock the doors and put them out. They had to either have the money to pay or the access to the building would be blocked.

When Sharon and Ms. Sullivan arrived, they were confronted for the payment. They wanted to write a check, but were told it must be paid with certified funds or a money order. Miraculously, they left and then returned with a certified check for almost the entire amount. The staff accepted the payment with a promise:

one of the big event sponsors would be there at five o'clock to pay the balance.

The evening didn't quite go as Sharon originally planned, with the surprise appearance of the process server. Never one to let bad luck get her down, Sharon and Ms. Sullivan used that incident to their advantage. The Medallion Center staff called the manager at home around 9:30pm with the news about the remaining unpaid balance.

The manager left her family at the lake and rode into work, attitude in hand. She challenged Ms. Sullivan about the payment, as Sharon was conveniently absent. Her response? "We had a lot of dignitaries coming here, including our big sponsor, but they couldn't get in because of the seven or eight police cars blocking the parking lot. Now, Sharon's downtown trying to get everything with them straightened out."

For the record, one Richland County deputy escorted the process server for approximately five minutes in the bottom half of the hour around seven that night. The parking lot was never blocked in any way.

"I was born at night, but not last night," said the Medallion Center manager. "I knew something was not right with the story about the police because it didn't make any sense at all why they would be here, so I made a point of having Ms. Sullivan commit to a time when the balance would be paid. She signed a statement agreeing to pay the balance by the end of the next day, Sunday, June second."

"I've been chasing Sharon and Patricia ever since," she sighed.

As it turns out, the Word of God Ministries holds

services at the Medallion Center on Sundays. Early in the negotiations, Sharon made a point to tell the manager she was planning on joining that church and even went so far as to attend a few services. They did offer her membership, but in order to accept, she would need to attend their orientation classes for new members.

Sharon never made a single class.

**The *Be Smarter than a Con* Takeaway: Get your money up front. Only make payment arrangements with someone who has a verifiable track record of on-time payments. Chasing a bad debt is hard, often fruitless, work. Don't put yourself in that type of situation if you can help it.

CHAPTER THIRTEEN
The Christian Angle

A Christian is by definition a follower of Jesus Christ, Lord and Savior. As a group, Christians are good and decent people. Christians fit the exact profile of Sharon's typical target – good and decent.

How can a person claim to serve God while simultaneously stealing from everyone, including family?

Sharon sent frequent texts to her intended victims, feigning sadness or distress when she didn't immediately get what she wanted. "Imma find another way to get it work out, to God be the glory, jus dnt understand," she texted as a part of a series of texts intended to cajole the recipient into action.

She likes to use references to God and the Bible in her cons. While running a confidence game on a prominent real estate agent in Charlotte, North Carolina, Sharon posts several photos of an executive level home for sale on her Facebook page with the caption, "He has His hands on me."

"The Fight for My Love is gonna be a movie. LOOK AT GOD, MY BOOK IS GONNA BE A MOVIE," Sharon proclaimed (again on her Facebook page), with the intention of convincing others of her legitimacy. But for some reason, that particular proclamation was removed from Facebook within the first twenty-four hours. It served its purpose quickly, which was for the potential benefit of someone she was targeting at the time.

She invokes the name of the Lord both in her written correspondence as well as in her normal speech patterns. She's attended enough church services to get the idea of what Christianity looks like to know the hot buttons to push when dealing with true Christians.

Promises to fund church buildings in the amount of a million dollars come easy for Sharon. She made a deal with a local pastor, who just happens to be married to one of Sharon's close relatives, for a loan. In exchange for ten thousand dollars, she promised to repay him with a million dollars to build the church of his dreams.

By involving ministers and the faithful, Sharon preys on those most likely to help her achieve her goals. Once she's gotten what she wants, she uses her typical tactic of claiming her money is being held up by the bank. Once her mark's patience has run out, she stops talking altogether, changes her phone number and disappears.

The trusting nature of the ministry is Sharon's favorite card to play. As her resources began to dry up, she sought out a minister at a United Methodist Church to design a cover for her magazine project called Out in the Street. This minister runs a business for media design and placement; he is also a motivational speaker and a person with a physical disability. Yet Sharon had no problem taking advantage by roping him into her schemes.

Even the ploy used to get back in the good graces of The Medallion Center for the 2013 Women's Conference used a connection to the Word of God Ministries. This church bought and redeveloped a large property across town from Sharon's usual stomping ground of Garners Ferry Road. As you may expect, when this large congregation moved to the new campus, not everyone was willing to make the trip. A smaller faction of members stayed behind and began to use The Medallion Center for their worship services on Sundays. Sharon conveniently added into her pitch that she was a member of Word of God to make a connection with the manager and get her way. Sharon's definitely not a member of this body, so her utilization of their name was clearly wrong but totally in character for her.

As her game has played out over the years, the reliance on Christianity as one of her "go to" talking points has become standard. So, it was very surprising that in late July, 2013, Sharon posts, "Yesterday was a day I'll never forget, I got save yesterday, Lord I thank u, I'm so Ready for this walk with God." If this statement is true, there's hope for her yet. It's just so incongruous for her to now claim salvation, when she's claimed it all along. How it's something new is unclear. While her personal salvation is between her and God Almighty, those around her would expect to see a difference in her demeanor and behavior if the saving grace of Jesus has found her.

This latest declaration is for someone's benefit. Everything she does is for a purpose and another part of her plan at the moment.

Those involved on the wrong end of her past schemes found something truly puzzling about her statement of new salvation. The basis for *The Fight for My Love: Final Chapters* is her story of redemption, showing how her personal turnaround was based in the Word and faith in Christ, bringing her away from abusers and a life as a drug pusher. If she only became saved in July 2013 and this story from The Fight for My Love was penned years earlier, one or both of these claims must be inaccurate. You can't have been saved years ago and then saved again just now. Once you've professed a belief in the resurrection and power of Jesus Christ, that's all it takes. Once is enough for a lifetime and eternity beyond. Real Christians know that.

Another sign of her insincerity is she has no known church membership. Even when Christians aren't very active in the faith, the presence of a particular church in the background is common. While you don't have to be a member of a church to be a Christian, if you are a Christian, fellowship with other believers is an important part of the worship experience. This dedicated fellowship is missing in Sharon's life. And while believers may not go every Sunday, you're usually going to either the same church or the same type of church, keeping with the same branch of faith such as Lutheran, Baptist, Methodist, Episcopal, Catholic and so on.

"Give a hand up and not a hand out," is a philosophy

of many good people in the community who want to help the less fortunate. Sharon tries to imitate these do-gooders with her own twisted version. The help found in churches across the South, and for that matter, even the nation, is varied and focuses on things like food pantries, clothing, resources for utility payments and programs for vocational and social help. Sharon's "help" is a cheap imitation designed to create a short-term windfall for herself and prop up her public relations juggernaut.

The cyclical nature of her stories means you'll come across the same concept in slightly different variations, based on her chosen victim. Christians have consistently remained one of her favorite populations to exploit. As 2013 drew to a close, yet another (yes, another) group of Christian victims was uncovered. Sharon duped an independent film company into agreeing to make a trailer for her book, *The Fight for My Love*, with the idea it teases a coming theatrical production of the manuscript. The deepest desire of her dark heart, Sharon wants her book to be made into a movie. No force of law, ethics, literary worthiness, conscience or nature will get in her way.

Ever pushing forward, she focuses on these filmmakers with a ferocious intensity. Their faith is obvious; their company logo incorporates a cross. As far as Sharon's thought process goes, it might as well be a bulls eye.

A script for the movie trailer was written by the filmmakers and a casting call sent out for local talent. The trailer was to focus on younger Chanda (Sharon's name for herself in the book), her grandmother Bessie and the older Chanda once she'd become involved with Jim, her ultimate love interest and abuser. All in all, eleven characters were to be cast and a small stipend was available for speaking roles. Rehearsals were planned for Thursday and Friday, with principal photography on Saturday at locations to be disclosed only to the players at practice.

To get to this point, time and money were already invested by the filmmakers. They were clearly the ones driving the bus on this project. But, they weren't alone. The third partner in the movie venture had a separate minor company in the same creative field, but wasn't an equal in experience or resources.

If you believe Sharon funded this effort to date, grab a glass of Kool-Aid and step aside.

The intention was to get as much work as possible for as little as possible from these Christian writers and producers. Promises of payment would lead to nothing but wasted time. Luckily, an emergency intervention was successful in convincing the primary filmmakers to end their association with Sharon. However, the third partner remained convinced and committed to carrying out Sharon's wishes for the project. Texts sent to the filmmakers were forwarded to the third partner, who promptly shared the messages with Sharon herself.

Not pleased with the kink in her plans, she left an indignant voicemail on my cell phone within ten minutes of the original text. If she was actually indignant and not just making the phone call for the sake of the third partner, she wouldn't have blocked her phone number. If she really wanted to discuss her supposed ego injury, you'd think she'd leave a number

116

for a return call. Or, more directly, call the office number, which she had. Instead, she has her daughter call within five minutes of her own call and ask for me. I was on another call, but Aneshia chickened out and only said she wanted to know what address we had on file for her.

The number given by Aneshia links back to PTA-FLA network, which offers flat rate, unlimited calling with no credit check or deposit. Perfect for a con artist and her family, Sharon and Aneshia signed up for this easy plan since they wouldn't want anyone to run their credit.

The filmmakers are daughters of a minister, raised in a Christian home, brought up in the church. They're not used to dealing with criminals. When they were told to do their own due diligence and search on their own for background information on Sharon, it was a totally new concept to them. Once armed with the truth, the women backed out of the deal. They're very lucky to have a potential disaster thwarted so quickly. Many others aren't so fortunate.

The *Be Smarter than a Con* Takeaway: "A malicious man disguises himself with his lips, but in his heart he harbors deceit. Though his speech is charming, do not believe him, for seven abominations fill his heart. His malice may be concealed by deception, but his wickedness will be exposed in the assembly." Proverbs 26: 24-26 NIV

THE CON GAME PLAYERS:
A COMPLEX CAST OF
VICTIMS AND CO-CONSPIRATORS

CHAPTER FOURTEEN
Player: Melissa Sprouse Browne

I first met Sharon Johnson and Calvin Jones at my office in West Columbia, South Carolina on January 10, 2012. We had been introduced over the phone by Taci Jones Bradley, Calvin's sister, earlier in the week. I remembered Taci as a former student of one of our businesses, the Real Estate School of South Carolina. Taci was aware of my graphic design business, The Marketing Division, which operates from the same building as the Real Estate School, and mentioned those services to Sharon.

At our first meeting, Sharon discussed her company, Barrio Bath and Beauty, and claimed to carry 42 items in her line of perfume and body products. She discussed her need for a website for the perfume company, as well as a program for an event she was having in February called Empowering Women to Excel. She asked me to quote production of three hundred programs, which were to be twenty-eight pages, self-cover. I provided the information and concluded the meeting.

As the date of the Empowering Women to Excel event was early February, I expected to hear from her on the program production, but didn't. I sent a follow-up email to Sharon's assistant Linda, asking about the project on January 31, 2012.

Sharon called after the event and we set a meeting at my office for Valentine's Day. At the meeting, we discussed creating a catalog for Barrio Bath and Beauty, to include printing and product photography and designing a cover for her book, *The Fight for My Love: Final Chapters*. These services were agreed upon and performed over the next couple of months. The total amount charged to Sharon through April 9, 2012 was $1,404.18. She paid with a check from her You, Too Foundation account to The Marketing Division and the check was returned by the bank for insufficient funds. When confronted, Sharon made the check good by bringing the same amount in cash to cover the check, saying there was a mistake at the bank that caused the check to bounce.

On March 30th, Sharon came to my office and said she had a secret she wanted to share with me. She claimed Tyler Perry had optioned the rights for her book and was going to pay her six million dollars and produce a movie about her life story. She said that once she got her money in line, she would like to thank me for the work I was doing for her by donating $300,000 to me personally and another $250,000 to my charity of choice, Senior Resources and the Meals on Wheels program. She seemed very surprised when I told her that wasn't necessary for me, but if she wanted to give something, I would appreciate her donation to Meals on

Wheels. As the months wore on, she would repeat this offer multiple times.

While a huge windfall would certainly benefit me personally, I just couldn't see it happening. I work for my money. If she wants to give money, let her give it to a group who really needs it. That amount of money would have eliminated every single person from the Meals on Wheels waiting list and allowed a tremendous expansion of services to combat senior hunger.

She told me she wanted to move to Charlotte and buy a house in Fantasia's neighborhood. Since I have a real estate license, she asked if I could help her buy a house in both Charlotte and Columbia. I told her I don't use my license very often, but would consider helping her whenever she got her money from the movie deal. She showed me a picture of a house on Bevington Lane in Charlotte and said that was the house she wanted me to help her buy. She only mentioned buying real estate a couple of times, so it was never pursued.

Next, in early April, a basic website was created to promote the book, *The Fight for My Love*. She was charged three hundred dollars and paid cash.
It isn't uncommon for me to be involved in real estate dealings, so I was in the middle of handling a remodeling project at a waterfront condo formerly owned by Bob Fulton, who was a local celebrity as the Voice of the Gamecocks for the University of South Carolina. Bob's estate was in the hands of his daughter in California, who had entrusted me to manage its redesign and rental.

Right before Bob's passing, he'd purchased a new living room set. Comfortable beyond words, his suede and leather sofa and love seat were practically unused. They were the only things left after the estate sale and the family didn't know what to do with them. I brought them to my office building, where they sat in the hallway for a few months, waiting on a buyer to offer the right amount to satisfy the needs of the estate.

Well, Sharon saw the furniture on her many trips to the office and declared one day she was buying both pieces. She gave me her ATM card and the charge for five hundred fifty dollars went through on the first try.

Two days later, her next payment for $1,124.50 was paid by Visa. This payment was for business card printing, purchasing domain names and line editing of the manuscript for *The Fight for My Love*.

From May 12, 2012 through May 23, 2012, time was spent on producing labels for Barrio products and purchasing a pack of ISBN numbers for the book, at a cost of $250 for the ISBN number purchase. The book was finalized, such as it was, and uploaded to Createspace for publishing. She had begun to talk about a company called Destiny Image as a publishing company she was interested in using, but never provided any additional information about them. As it turns out, Destiny Image is a real publishing firm, focusing on Christian authors. One of their famous names is author T. D. Jakes.

She claimed Destiny Image was so impressed with the work I did on her book that they wanted to give me an "award" and when the movie premiered, she wanted me to go with her to Los Angeles. She also mentioned Patricia Sullivan, her former publisher from Greenville, who had produced the last version of her book. She claimed to be at odds with Ms. Sullivan and discouraged me from contacting her about questions on her book.

On May 29, 2012, Sharon came to my office without an appointment and asked to see me. At this meeting, she told me she was working with her attorney and Bank of America in Charlotte to get a check for me and one for Meals on Wheels. But, in the meantime, she needed fifteen hundred dollars to send to Smith Publicity in New Jersey to get started on promoting her book.

"I need the money for Smith," Sharon demanded. Her insistence was absolute. "Mmm hmmm, I got to have a check today before I leave."

"Sharon, I don't have that kind of money just laying around. I would have to write it out of my business account, but would need it back right away."

"My attorney said he would take care of you in a couple of weeks on that, so to go ahead and write it out now so I can send it off."

"Can I speak to the attorney to get the information," I asked.

"No, he's in court. I just talked to him before I got here," she said.

"I don't understand why you have to ask me for money. Aren't you all set with your own money?"

"Everything's tied up right now. If you will help me out now, I will take care of you later."

"What's the legal name of this Smith company?"

"It's Smith Publicity, but just make it out to me. I'll put it in my account and the attorney will send it with his part up to Smith for me."

"You know I chase people who owe me, right? I hate someone telling me they're going to pay their bill and then they don't do it. You won't be like that, right?"

After getting her to sign a promissory note agreeing to pay back the fifteen hundred no later than June 8, 2012, she was given the check, made out to her personally. She cashed the check at a BB&T branch that same day.

And that, ladies and gentlemen, is the stupidest thing I've ever done.

A few days later, she asked me to look at a rental listing on the Consolidated Multiple Listing Service for a home in Woodman Farms. I printed the listing for her and she said she was going to rent that property because the reality show producers needed someplace nice to film her family for their upcoming show. She said her current home was just too small. On June 4, 2012, she invited me to see her new home, which was indeed the house in Woodman Farms. The home was furnished, but didn't have the type of furniture and accessories you'd expect from someone who was supposed to be wealthy.

She came to see me several times right after going to the dentist. She was having the dental work from her youth replaced and eliminated the gold tooth and bridgework for natural colored replacements. She said her producers advised her to change her appearance in that way to be more respectable.

Along the same time, she asked me to host a baby shower for her daughter Ceira Nicholas. I agreed to have the party at my home on July 14, 2012. For someone who said she had significant resources, I was very surprised when she asked me to go shopping with her for the baby shower at Dollar Tree. This store must be her favorite.

As the time approached for the baby shower, she talked more and more about her reality show. She claimed to be filming in various locations and also traveling to Los Angeles, Charlotte and Atlanta for meetings related to Tyler Perry, her movie and book. She said the reality show producer wanted to get some "raw footage" of her family and asked if they could film the baby shower. I didn't mind, so she said the camera crew would come on the 14th of July.

The week prior to the shower, right after July 4th, she said the producer, who is really her business manager, couldn't get his crew free to come and asked me to find someone who could film it for him. As the owner of an advertising agency, I have many contacts capable of filming television quality footage, so I made contact with Zero Gravity Project, who quoted $700 for one high definition camera and cameraman. When I told Sharon the cost, she said she'd get the business manager to find someone local who would be cheaper.

A gentleman did come to the baby shower to film, but he had a very basic handheld home video camera. He was clearly not a professional. What's more, he was her cousin.

Very little work was done for Sharon after that date with the last billed item on August 22, 2012.

She continued to mention the large donation she wanted to make to me and the charity, and sent an email on September 24, 2012 saying she had some issues at the bank regarding finances but everything has been worked out and she would have my payment that week. She said her accountant was preparing the payments and wanted the tax identification number for both the Real Estate School of SC and Senior Resources; both numbers were provided to her. I tried to give Sharon an out, saying that she didn't have to donate anything to anyone if she didn't want to, yet she insisted that she was definitely going to donate to Meals on Wheels the outrageous sum of $250,000.

In September and October, 2012 Sharon would stop by my office or call me on the phone to discuss her latest projects, which she claimed were going to be a women's magazine called Out in the Street and a video and perfume line with Fantasia, the singer. She called me several times, saying she was at the bank or an attorney's office, working on getting the money released. She said the problem was the IRS put a lien on her account because of a former cleaning company she had that didn't file taxes or report wages properly. She blamed the cleaning company bookkeeper and said it was taking her weeks to reconstruct the records for the IRS. But, as soon as it was cleared up, she promised to pay what she owed me plus a big donation for both myself and Meals on Wheels.

Based on her continued promises to donate a large sum to this charity, I invited Sharon to the Every Senior Counts luncheon on November 1, 2012 at Seawell's in Columbia. As a potential donor, I wanted her to see what the organization does for the community.

I was stunned by her attire. She walked into this business luncheon wearing a t-shirt dress clinging to every unflattering wave of fat, along with a gold knit cover-up that had a small hole near the left shoulder. She looked the part of someone needing help, not someone providing it.

At the end of the luncheon, she donated $100 in cash and promised to make monthly donations for the next year. As a member of the Board of Directors for Seniors Resources, I never saw anything further from Sharon come through as a donation. Finally, she at least did give something to the charity after months of promises.

On Saturday, November 19, 2012, Sharon called to set up a meeting, saying she had my money. I was at Roof Jewelers on Two Notch Road and she agreed to meet me in their parking lot. She pulled a wad of cash from her bra and gave it to me as payment for "what she owed." It was two thousand dollars in cash, a giant bundle of folded twenties, which I applied to her outstanding balance. She still owes several hundred dollars, though. My question at the time was, "how did she get that much cash?"

In late November, Sharon said she was planning an event called, "Out in the Street, A Mogul in the Making." She asked me to create a program for this event, scheduled for December 15, 2012. When I quoted her the cost of printing the program ($3,000), she said she would have some of Tyler Perry's people print it for her and that I didn't need to worry about the printing part, just to do the graphic design. (She also gave me a new phone number, saying it was her home number. This new number was my first experience in her phone number switcheroo.) By the beginning of December, she said the event was cancelled because they didn't have enough time to plan it properly.

In mid-December, I visited Sharon's daughter, Aneshia Jones, at Palmetto Baptist Hospital to see her newborn. Sharon was there and spoke to me about Linda Wilson. She said Linda was trying to borrow twenty seven thousand dollars from her because her house had gone into foreclosure. She also said Linda was bothering her and she didn't want to have any further contact with her. I was shocked to hear her comments about Linda, as I saw her with Linda on numerous occasions and knew they were together frequently.

In January, 2013 Sharon called me several times but I wasn't available whenever she called. We finally caught up on February 7, 2013 when she gave me her new phone number, again. That same day, I met with Jeff Downs, who presented me with a letter outlining what was known of Sharon's dealings at that time. I was told she had moved out of the house in Woodman Farms, as Jeff, Tom and Linda were looking for her but she disappeared in the middle of the night. As I know the owner of the rental company, I called to inquire about Sharon. Kym from Real Estate Consultants said they evicted Sharon because she was two months' behind on her rent. Sharon presented Real Estate Consultants with a check that was supposed to be from an attorney's escrow account to pay the delinquent rent, but the check had been altered and was really a starter check that was returned for insufficient funds.

It so happened that a current student at the Real Estate School of SC and a neighbor of mine, Kandi, said she had been hired as a stylist for Sharon by

Sharon's publicist and saw her at the Woodman Farms house a couple of months ago. Today, she disclosed that Sharon approached her last week about renting an apartment at the community where Kandi works as a property manager. Sharon didn't pay the application fee and was not granted an apartment. Sharon didn't try to rent in her own name, but rather offered up both of her daughters' names and social security numbers, as well as her company name, Dream Development.

Sharon called in early March, saying she has a job for me. She's ready to work on the magazine. Her propaganda must be running low, so she's ready to engage me. Little does she realize, I'm definitely engaged in her world, just on the side of the law. She talked about the book tour from her publicist and doing a perfume deal with Fantasia and the lady from Sisterhood, the TLC show.

Sharon kept saying she was going to show me her letter from Tyler Perry and the day she came to my office with the oversized orange fake leather purse, it was supposed to be in there. She rummaged around, but declared she must have left it at home. The propaganda folder wasn't present that day, either, but I saw it at the Woodman Farms house, Applebee's and several other places. She keeps a black leatheresque binder with her most of the time, full of purported contracts and deals. Amazingly, whatever you ask her to find in it to provide proof of the story she's telling you is never in there. "It must be at home," she says frequently.

All of the times Sharon called me and said she was at the bank, or at the CPA's office were total fabrications. She asked me for my company's federal identification number more than once, with the idea it was for either the financial institution or her accountant to prepare a check. But even the few times she paid me for anything, it was always in the form of cash, a personal check or a debit card. Never did she produce a Certified Funds or Cashier's check of any kind.

The program from the Dove Awards in Atlanta Sharon claimed to attend as a VIP was kept floating around in Calvin's ride. She took me out to the car and showed me the program and then a few pictures on her phone of she and Calvin in a hotel room somewhere, all dressed up. She stacks the "evidence" of her fame with these props and prays no one looks any deeper than her inky surface of evil.

The *Be Smarter than a Con* Takeaway: I was an idiot. Don't follow my example – take the time to check the connections potential friends and business associates claim to have. If you're involved in any type of charitable group, protect them from predators like Sharon. Her oft-repeated promise to donate to Meals on Wheels should've been taken with a grain of salt, but on the outside hope it would be kept, she was invited to meet the local leadership. Her lies remain an embarrassment for me, as I presented her as a real benefactor when she was most definitely not.

CHAPTER FIFTEEN
Player: Linda Wilson
◇◇◇◇◇◇◇◇◇◇◇◇◇◇◇◇◇◇◇◇◇◇◇◇◇◇◇◇◇◇◇◇◇◇◇◇

Linda Wilson came to be Sharon's right hand man and trusted associate through a convoluted set of circumstances originating from her ownership in a small publishing business. Her partner in this venture was Tom Blackstone.

Both Tom and Linda opened an enterprise called Create & Publish Company and had begun to seek authors for whom they could publish their books. Sharon and Ms. Sullivan already had *The Fight for My Love* manuscript to use however they chose, and it made for the perfect introduction to the principals of Create & Publish.

***

"I met Sharon Johnson in May 2011 at a business meeting where she was interested in the publishing business. I was told Sharon was an author, and I work with individuals who are interested in self-publishing. Sharon said she wanted to invest in my publishing business.

When Tom and I first met with Sharon, Andy Roland and Milt, we all got together with Sharon and Calvin. She wanted to get into the publishing business and that's when she said she was with the publisher, Ms. Sullivan. She claimed Ms. Sullivan took advantage of her, stealing her work, stealing her money and all of this here, so now she wanted to move on.

At the time, we actually presented Sharon, who was saying she wanted to invest, with the projects we had in the works right then. One of those projects was Michael Vick, another was with Kwame Kilpatrick, the former mayor of Detroit. During that time, she basically was interested in talking to Kyle, Michael Vick's manager, more than anyone else.

Tom and I gave her twenty five hundred dollars in cash in late May, right after we just met her. We believed she was being discriminated against and thought we'd help her. She was talking about investing a lot of money in our business, so it seemed like the right thing to do.

We started conversations and negotiations with Michael Vick's people and Sharon was a part of some of those talks. She made the commitment, talked directly to Michael's manager and promised that she had this money and put herself out there as being responsible for the upfront funds that were to be paid out to Michael Vick.

Sharon convinced Michael's people enough that they sent her a whole package of autographed memorabilia for her birthday. We would talk to him consistently, Sharon and I, sometimes once a week and sometimes twice a week. Sharon kept saying her funds were going to be in and so we kept having conversations to that end.

They had signed a contract with us and were just waiting for it to be funded. Sharon always had a reason or excuse about why the money wasn't ever there. It was the attorney, the bank hadn't released it, it was just tied up. This went on for several months, to the point where they just didn't believe any more and the deal ended up falling apart.

Sharon was the reason behind all of that. She talked to these people because she had a copy of their contract and kept stringing everybody along. The same thing took place with the representative for Mark Sanford, too. All of these people were on the table at the time and it was contingent upon Sharon doing what she said she was going to do with her money and investing.

People have asked my why I was so convinced she was telling the truth. It's because Sharon showed me a Wachovia bank statement in the name the cleaning service, which was supposed to be the company she had with Calvin, with a balance of $81 million on it. She said she'd won a settlement from the hospital for the death of her daughter, Barrio Jackson. She claimed her daughter had been misdiagnosed and treated for the wrong illness, which caused her death.

She said attorney Hammond Beal represented her in the case and it took seven years to finally receive her funds.

Sharon was upset that as soon as her money was

deposited, the Internal Revenue Service froze her bank account for a tax lien totaling thirty thousand dollars. She reassured me she'd definitely invest in my publishing business when her funds were released.

She told me a lot of people had taken advantage of her because they knew she didn't know a lot about business. She came across as naïve and uneducated, but determined.

I thought Andy Roland was her financial advisor and Sharon implied he had taken advantage of her and was trying to get control of her money. From that point, in good faith, I started helping Sharon with various things she was trying to do and teaching her about the publishing industry.

I felt compassion for her after she told me her story and wanted to let her know that there are still some good people in the world.

I worked with Sharon eight to twelve hours every single day. I used the various business contacts I had to help her with different projects, including the 2012 Empowering Women to Excel conference. I even cashed in an investment I had to pay Wess Morgan, the keynote speaker, in the amount of six thousand five hundred dollars.

I also started helping Sharon with her personal bills, such as rent, car payments, utilities and child support for Calvin, her boyfriend, all because she told me she had this money coming. I actually used my own money to pay Sharon's bills.

As soon as her money was available, she kept telling me she was going to give me some extra funds in addition to the investment in the publishing business, for helping her with all these things.

On numerous occasions, Sharon was going to show me her paperwork regarding the settlement, but she never once showed me anything. The only thing I saw was the flash of the bank statement initially and then nothing afterwards.

As time went on, there was one excuse after another about why her funds were not available. I would ask, "What is the attorney saying?"

"We have a meeting set up with the bank and the IRS to get to the bottom of the situation," was her usual reply. Sharon said her attorney at that time was Hammond Beal, the same attorney that represented her with her daughter Barrio's malpractice settlement.

Her responses started becoming more and more bizarre. She said things like, "they got everything worked out, the funds are going to be released on such and such date." When that particular date rolled around, Sharon used the excuse, "the IRS has put another lien on the account." This excuse was used at least three times. Once that excuse ran out, she said she fired her attorney.

I suggested she let me contact attorney Willie Gary out of Florida, since he specializes in these types of cases. She agreed and I contacted attorney Gary and explained the situation to him. He asked me if I'd seen the documentation about Sharon's daughter's settlement. I told him I hadn't but I would get her to send the documentation to him. Sharon told me her daughter in Virginia had all of the documentation and she would have her fax it over to him. Eventually, Sharon started talking directly to attorney Gary and I was no longer privy to those conversations except what Sharon shared with me.

The attorney didn't need me to speak on her behalf and he wanted to deal directly with her. I was upset the attorney took this position since I was the one who introduced him to Sharon. She told me she agreed and didn't want to have anything to do with attorney Gary anymore.

Supposedly, Sharon hired another attorney, Jeff Johnson from the I.S. Leevy Johnson Law Firm. After several months of more timetables and dates for the availability of funds, including purported court orders requiring the bank to release her funds and closed court hearings before federal Judge Margaret Seymour, she said she fired attorney Johnson.

During these times, when the funds were scheduled to be available on different occasions, Sharon did ask for my bank account information and told me the funds would be in my account by a certain time or day, but of course nothing happened.

She had me go over to Wells Fargo bank and wait because the funds were being transferred at that time to my checking account. I explained to the banker what was going on and they continued to check my account, looking for the transfer. The banker checked until the close of business but the transfer never came. I even spoke with Sharon a couple of times while I waited at the bank.

She told me her banker said someone was tampering with her account. Every time a wire transfer is set, someone goes in and cancels it. She later called me and told me to check my account because her daughter

Myesha called and said she'd received her wire for two million. I hadn't received anything nor did I show anything pending.

Things had started to get weird.

I later discovered attorney Willie Gary never told Sharon anything about me. The real problem was Sharon never sent the information to verify her settlement. I also found out attorney Gary concluded Sharon didn't receive any settlement regarding her daughter and neither the IRS nor Wells Fargo bank were holding any funds belonging to her. Essentially, the whole story was a fantasy and he had just moved on.

I also was later confirmed attorney Jeff Johnson has never represented Sharon. Never.

As things were starting to come to light for me, I think my subconscious was trying to tell me the truth. In the summer of 2012, I had a vivid dream about a big, scary snake that really turned out to be Sharon. I told Sharon about the dream and she had a big laugh.

In September 2012, Sharon said her friend Melissa was supposed to visit on a Saturday afternoon. When Melissa never showed, Sharon said Melissa couldn't come because she was at a party with her husband who had gotten drunk and was abusive to the point that Melissa was crying and had to leave. I was really surprised. I had met Melissa and she didn't seem like the kind of person who was living in an abusive relationship. But, I thought, "you just never know about some people." I later found out the true story: Melissa was working an open house at an assisted living community and was simply too tired to go visit after working all day.

In December 2012, I spoke with Myesha, Sharon's eldest daughter who lives in Virginia and serves in the United States Navy. She said she wasn't familiar with any settlement and certainly didn't have any paperwork regarding one.

It began to become painfully clear Sharon had been lying to me the entire time to get me to help her financially with all of the things she was trying to do.

At this point, my own home had gone into foreclosure since I'd been helping Sharon with her personal bills and not paying my own during this time. She kept telling me her funds would be released and I would be able to not only take care of my current home but to buy another one if I wanted to do so.

When things got really tight for me financially and I started pressing Sharon about what's going on with the release of her funds because I was in trouble with my home, she told me she had it worked out and not to worry about it. She told me she'd have the money for me to take care of my home no later than the end of January 2013. She told me the funds had been deposited in my account on Friday, right before the bank closed. Since it was the weekend, I asked her to text over the confirmation number once she received it from Ms. Sullivan since she was the one to initiate the transfer from Bank of America, yet ANOTHER financial institution in Sharon's world. I wondered why it was Ms. Sullivan who was initiating the transfer instead of Sharon herself.

I never got the confirmation. I asked Sharon again on Saturday, who said she sent the number, but again I didn't receive it. She said she deleted it from her phone and would have to wait again for the number from Ms. Sullivan. This conversation was my last with Sharon.

The next day, I found out she had moved from the house in Woodman Farms. She already changed her phone number. I found that she had a new phone number but didn't want me to have it. I was cut off. Finally.

I've learned a lot of things since I've been extracted from her world. First, Sharon preys on people who are of a strong faith because she sees it as a weakness she can exploit. Sharon talks about being a Christian, but she doesn't behave at all like those with real faith she seeks to abuse.

I think it's possible Sharon testified against both of her brothers and that's how they got life sentences for drug trafficking and possibly for murder. Sharon was complicit and she gave up something on her brothers to stop from going to prison. Sharon said her mother testified against her brothers. Sharon did admit to selling drugs in her past life.

Second, I saw a check Ms. Sullivan wrote Sharon for fifty thousand dollars. Sharon said Ms. Sullivan owed her for book sales. This check was a piece of disinformation she used to make us think she was a successful author. Carolyn Graham saw it, too. I didn't understand why she was working on what she billed as a sequel, *The Fight for My Love: Final Chapters* that needed so much editing if she'd made money off the first version. Wouldn't it have already been edited? If so, where was that version?

Sharon never signed the agreement with us for the publishing company; while I executed my portion,

Sharon never returned a signed copy. However, she kept it handy to show other players, such as Carolyn Graham, when looking to make herself appear credible. Her reason for not signing it was a supposed phone call from Andy Roland, her advisor, who wanted her to be in his presence whenever she signed agreements. Very convenient.

Sharon didn't want Tom to be too much involved in our dealings because he gets too excited and makes her nervous. She stays stressed out around him. What was actually happening was he was asking her too many questions and she didn't have any answers.

I also think Sharon had that cleaning business and after it closed, they were filing false tax returns, collecting income tax, but they never worked. She said the IRS was after her because they never filed payroll taxes.

Sharon has a routine of giving out phone numbers and having it ring to somebody she knows but she makes you believe you've been called from somewhere else. I was called from a number she gave me for Wells Fargo, but found out later it wasn't a real number for them. She could be using an app for Android like Caller ID Faker or www.spoofcard.com, which works with iPhone, Android and Blackberry phones. These apps will do amazing things, including letting you change the number that shows up on a caller ID, change your voice to be either a man or a woman and not use your own voice at all and they let you record conversations. An app like that's perfect for her.

There was a court ruling in 2012 that caused a legal precedent to be set across the nation that Caller ID spoofing is legal in the United States if it's not done with "the intent to defraud, cause harm, or wrongfully obtain anything of value." If Sharon's using it, it will be to defraud someone.

The *Be Smarter than a Con* Takeaway: Don't assume because you are a trusting person that's the case with everyone you meet. Even if that person was referred to you by someone with whom you have confidence, always check things out for yourself. Do your own due diligence.

CHAPTER SIXTEEN
Player: Talitha Long

"She just moved into a new house, we helped her move," Sharon said in July, 2013, about her friend, Talitha Long. This little tidbit was likely told to see where it would go. Sharon likes to tell people different versions of a story so when she hears it come back to her, she'll know who was talking. She provided this minor detail about Talitha as a test, waiting to see who repeats it back to her.

A hair stylist, Talitha is another Kool-Aid drinker when it comes to Sharon and her stories. Thinking Sharon is a cash cow, she hangs on for the payday she's been promised for years.

Talitha called Melissa in mid-February of 2013 to ask questions about redeeming a property after a foreclosure had been completed. I suspect she called to see if I was going to say anything negative about Sharon. After speaking with Linda Wilson, I found out the actual foreclosure concluded almost a year earlier.

In fact, Linda helped Talitha write a letter to see about changing the hearing date months ago. Talitha spoke to me about how her brother could possibly redeem the foreclosed home; she claimed to have been evicted last January, yet the house was sold in April 2012. I advised her to check the county tax records to see who currently owns the property.

Talitha seems to be a good person. The IJD People of God's Kingdom Youth Foundation is supposed to be her charitable activity as a part of her church's ministry outreach. Early on in the beginnings of the You, Too Foundation, this legitimate charity was mentioned as a co-sponsor of a children's circus outing.

She's a frequent poster of positive sayings on Facebook, copying a picture with an inspirational quote as her status update almost daily. She wants to believe the best in everyone. Her unwavering belief in Sharon's largesse continues even today.

Talitha seems to be on the periphery of Sharon's circle, showing up at events but never as a central part of anything. She was a happy attendee at the 2013 Empowering Women to Excel conference, sitting at the table with us, cheering on Sharon's own private circus of the stars. When the event turned into a full on religious uprising of sorts, she was in it just like the rest of them.

Frequently mentioned in Sharon's propaganda as her stylist, which isn't always specific to just hair, Talitha's name is bandied about with countless victims. It's doubtful she fully understands the extent to which her name has been used in a variety of con games.

When Linda first met Sharon, she mentioned Talitha

to her as her hair stylist. They were friends since 2010 and Sharon spent a lot of time with her, almost every day. Talitha is the person who introduced Sharon to Andy Roland. They went to the same church. Sharon had Talitha under the impression that she had all this money and that it came from Tyler Perry.

Talitha was giving Sharon money and helping her out by footing the bills whenever they went somewhere. Sharon had her thinking her money was tied up and she was waiting on it, but in the meantime, she needed things. She promised Talitha a million dollars and a house. She also promised to get a hair salon for her as well. Sharon told Linda that's what she was going to do to support Talitha for her loyalty and help. As time went on and Linda came in the picture, she didn't spend as much time with Talitha but she still interacted and did things with her regularly.

Sharon even convinced this woman to do her hair. For free.

Talitha was taken along on the trip to Charlotte to show the "evidence" of her wealth by visiting a house Sharon wanted to buy.

"You can tell Talitha anything, she'll just believe whatever you say," Sharon once told Linda.

When Linda finally discovered Sharon's true nature, she went to see Talitha in person and told her everything she'd found out about Sharon and that she was running a scam. "I just wanted her to open her eyes and see what was really going on," Linda said.

"Wow." Talitha's reaction to everything Linda said was incredulous.

The day after their meeting, Talitha called Linda

early in the morning and was adamant about not wanting to hear anything negative about Sharon. She had Sharon on the phone line with her, listening to her vigorous defense of Sharon's character to Linda. She went on so much so that Linda finally surrendered and hung up the phone with Talitha mid-sentence.

Talitha is a serious victim, too naïve to really understand the seriousness and the depth of Sharon's chicanery and deceit.

The *Be Smarter than a Con* Takeaway: You will never find the truths in life if you constantly keep your head in the sand.

CHAPTER SEVENTEEN
Player: Andy Roland

Andy arranged for the creation of the aptly-named company, Dream Development, for Sharon in late Spring 2011. Of course it was registered as a For Profit entity; with Sharon's business model, it was all pure profit, since she never had anything of her own invested in any venture, ever. Andy Roland operates a respected financial advisory business and is also affiliated with a religious organization, which makes him an ideal target for Sharon's machinations. Andy's frustration with Sharon is clear in his disconsolate recollection.

As a man and an individual who works during the day, he would miss a giant clue when Sharon has an associate call and claim Sharon's been admitted to a hospital that's found not in Columbia, but in the fictional town of Salem from Days of Our Lives, the long running soap opera on NBC. Sharon uses any information she can find to twist into her reality. Andy wasn't expecting to be conned, but the master pulled another caper and roped him into her bizarre plans.

***

I was informed by a mutual friend of myself and Sharon, Talitha Long, that Sharon received $81 million dollars from Tyler Perry for the rights of her book and to do a movie on her. This same friend said Sharon ran into some tax issues and the money was being held and that she may need the help of Capital Place Financial, our company.

I met Ms. Sharon Johnson over the phone in late 2010 and begin discussing with her the situation. I made several attempts to meet with her in November and December of that year and was not successful. I got a phone call in January 2011 from mutual friend of Ms. Sharon Johnson, saying she wanted to meet and discuss her tax issues.

I finally did meet with Sharon about these tax issues and she stated at that time she owed back taxes from a business she owned. She had her bookkeeper working on what was needed to get her taxes cleared up, but mostly needed help and advice on how to disburse the money she received, set up her business the right way and manage her money.

After hearing what she had to say, I told Sharon that I would set her up with my broker. I followed through and make the introduction for her to my broker to help her get a handle on what was needed to help her manage the money she received.

Sharon visited the office in February to give us a run down on all that was going on in her life. The conversation was she got $81 million dollars for her book, sold the movie rights and she had another book that was going to be published.

In that meeting, she also said she wanted to know the best ways to gift money to her family, contribute to her church as well as loan another family member (Dr. Partridge) money to build a church. She also wanted to get her business and battered women's foundation set up the right way. Ms. Johnson also stated that she wanted to do some investing, prepare a sound retirement and possible loan or invest in her current publisher's publishing company.

After that meeting, I was advised by my broker on what all was needed to do at the time to get Ms. Jackson on the pathway of success and that we needed verification of funds, along with a few other things. Ms. Jackson stated that she would get me those documents.

I met Ms. Jackson for lunch to pick up the documents. She at that time showed me bank statements showing $81 million dollars and would not allow me to take them for copies. However, Sharon stated she would fax us or bring back the bank verifications along with the other documents needed as soon as possible.

Well, I called Ms. Johnson to do a follow up after our meeting and to let her know what would be needed to start working with her. At that time, she stated to me she was in the process of buying a house and she would pay cash for it. We, in turn, asked her for the information on the house to make sure we would have it on file. The HUD-1 settlement statement was emailed to us for our file. (A HUD-1 is the document generated at a real estate closing that shows the distribution of funds to all parties and is created by the closing attorney with instructions from the lender, if there is one.)

About mid-February, we began to layout our plan to help Sharon accomplish her goals. In late February and the beginning of March, it was difficult to meet with Ms. Johnson due to supposed book signings and speaking engagements. In late March, we were finally able to get with her to finalize what would take place next.

In April of 2011, Sharon called our office to say that she wanted to invest also in a funeral home with her cousin, Carl McDaniels. She also expressed to us that she had some concerns with her current publisher. That same day, she asked that we help her find some land to build a funeral home or possibly purchase an existing building. Ms. Johnson stated that she would have her cousin call us to give us a run down on how the funeral home will be run and what would be needed to get it off the ground. Sharon insisted we handle all of this detail for her so that she wouldn't be stressed out.

The next thing I heard from her was that I should be on the lookout for a call from a local pastor that she wanted us to help get funding for his church. She also stated she was going to give this church two hundred thousand dollars toward their building project and we would get them a loan for the rest. She insisted we review all documentation from the church contractors to make sure they were not being taken advantage of.

The pastor contacted us and we sent the church our loan questionnaire to prepare to put a deal together.

In May, we found an existing building for a funeral home off of Parkland Road. We went ahead and made contact with the real estate firm to tour the building and talk figures.

We were also asked to contact the local real estate agent who represented Burnside Farms off of Garners Ferry Road by Sharon and her boyfriend, Mr. Calvin Jones, to potentially build apartment complexes.

Also in May, we introduced Sharon to a publishing company that was interested in reworking her book and offering potential ownership. We met several times with Sharon and the publishing company, where she verbally agreed to work with them. However, she wanted to be setup properly before she signed and invested in the company. Our next step was to make an appointment to meet with the CPA and discuss the overall Ms. Jackson situation.

It was at this point that, at our direction, the CPA set up Ms. Jackson's business, called Dream Development.

We also made arrangements with an attorney to handle setting up trusts for her family, an escrow account for the church she was going to loan money to for construction and a few other things. The publishing company sent a contract for Sharon to review for investment purposes and to layout her portion of ownership. We met with her to sign the contract, but she decided to wait until all of her other affairs were straight.

Again, we met with the attorney to handle and prepare to set up the trusts and discuss all the other legal things that needed to be done to accomplish her goals. Also, that day we'd made arrangements to meet

Ms. Johnson at the bank along with the attorney to set up all accounts needed for the trust accounts and to make preparations for disbursements to her church and Create & Publish.

The meeting with the bank was set for a Friday. An hour before the meeting, I got a call from supposedly a nurse at University Hospital (she didn't say which one) that Ms. Johnson had been admitted to the hospital. We had no choice but to postpone the bank meeting. After Sharon got home from the hospital she said she was going to rest for a few days and then meet to get things set up.

Ms. Johnson called a day later, saying the house she was going to buy she was going to give to her daughter and then buy another house in Charlotte. She also stated the Realtor® would be emailing me all the documentation on the house.

Sharon wanted to arrange a conference call with all of her daughters and her future sister in law to explain how the monies would be disbursed and what would be set up for them.

Our next meeting with Sharon and her family focused on a discussion about how they could save their family home from foreclosure and while there, Sharon expressed to them she would be giving them all ten thousand dollars apiece. A few days after meeting with Sharon's family, she stated she was ready to meet with the attorney to go ahead and fund the money for trust accounts, invest in the publishing firm, gift money to family members and donate to her church.

Along the same time, the real estate agent from ATR Real Estate contacted Sharon to rewrite her offer on the home in Charlotte and request proof of assets. Sharon forwarded all the information to us. Then, Sharon's cousin contacted us for the status on the building purchase for his funeral home. The CPA contacted us, too, for payment for setting up Ms. Johnson's limited liability company. For meeting to discuss the formation of the LLC, creating the business entity, the documents package, preparing the Internal Revenue Service Form SS-4 and securing the federal tax identification number, the CPA firm originally wanted three hundred and twenty five dollars, but because of our relationship trimmed the total to two hundred, which we never received from Ms. Johnson.

Sharon would commit to meeting and funding, yet never would supply the requested documentation and cancel almost every meeting. She wasted the time of a lot of professional people. Nothing made any sense.

The *Be Smarter than a Con* Takeaway: If you request documentation to verify a situation, but the person gives excuses instead of immediately supplying what you need, put on the brakes. Dig deeper into the background of the person and make an educated call on how to proceed.

CHAPTER EIGHTEEN
Player: Sandra Smith, ATR Real Estate

◇◇

This professional real estate agent had the misfortune to represent the seller of a fabulous home in the Piper Glen community in Charlotte, North Carolina. This neighborhood happens to be the home of Fantasia Barrino, which made it doubly attractive for Sharon.

The particulars of this true executive estate include six bedrooms, six and a half baths, almost seven thousand square feet of living space on a waterview lot with a pool. A hard coat stucco exterior, regular maintenance and extensive renovations called for an original list price of $1,750,000 in November, 2010.

Sharon nosed around this house for months. It was on the market and she wanted it so badly she could taste it.

Sharon ultimately wrote two separate contracts on this same property. The first was in the name of her cohort, Ms. Sullivan, in December, 2010. The second was in the name of Sharon's company, Dream

Development, in May, 2011. These transactions went so far as to have an appraisal, a home inspection and negotiations on the inclusion of the contents of the house (personal property) with the deal.

As you know by now, such an accomplished con woman as Sharon can pretty much worm her way into anything. Her alternate reality was convincing enough for the listing agent to let Sharon and her crew spend the night in this home valued at over a million and a half dollars.

Sharon promised the agent her proof of funds would be coming from her accountant and attorney, but briefly showed her the bank statement confirming her money on deposit was the $81 million everyone had been talking about. In fact, the primary purpose for the creation of this fake bank statement was to get this house. Bear in mind mortgage fraud is a federal offense. Using a doctored statement as proof of funds is beyond not allowed. It's criminal.

In a real estate transaction, several steps are needed to get from contract to closing. The appraisal, which is usually required by the lender, is an expensive item. The appraiser in this case would need to be the top license level, Certified General, as this property was valued at over one million dollars. Certified Residential appraisers can work with properties up to a million, but this one would've been out of reach. CG appraisers are more expensive, as they have the most training and education and can appraise virtually anything that's real property, be it residential, commercial, developed or raw land.

Once the appraisal has been completed, someone's

responsible for the bill. Normally, that person is the purchaser. But Sharon's not normal. Since this deal was put forward as a cash transaction, Sharon convinced the agent to order the appraisal for this fantastic home on a double lot. The agent engaged a professional appraisal firm in downtown Charlotte to provide a complete appraisal and the official Uniform Residential Appraisal Report (URAR).

As a real estate professional, Smith had plenty of long-standing contacts in the industry. Since she'd referred business previously to them, the appraisal firm graciously reduced their fee from eight hundred dollars to only six hundred. The appraisal was done based on the first contract of sale in December, 2010. But since Sharon kept hanging around, the agent didn't feel too pressured to collect the appraisal fee. She paid her vendor, like any good business person would do, and hoped to recoup the fee in the tremendous commission that would result from the sale of this home.

During the course of the second contract, Smith sent several communications to Sharon and her "team" in May and June of 2011. The first one was sent directly to Sharon and Andy Roland was copied:

"Hi Sharon,

It was wonderful to see you and I am so happy that everything is working out for you and your family. I believe things happen for a reason and am thrilled that your home is still available for you AND I am thrilled that I get to be a part of making it all happen!

As we discussed, I am catching you up on all the previous information for Bevington that

Patricia and I had worked on. I want you to understand everything, answer any questions for you, so that we can move forward and submit an offer to purchase with your new company name of Dream Development.

This information will arrive in three different emails – they are large attachments, so I need to break them up. This email has the original offer, which included terms of the contract and the list of personal items to be included. It also includes the appraisal.

The offer has been negotiated and agreed to $1.5M including the personal items with $14K in earnest money. However, the appraisal came in at $1.45M. After the appraisal came in is when Patricia was not able to provide funds so we did not negotiate to the appraised price.

The second and third emails will have the inspection reports. Let's discuss the terms of the contract once you have read this information."

After Smith sent the above message and the two others with the documents she mentioned, she sent two more missives to Sharon and Andy:

"Sharon,

You should have received three emails from me w/large attachments, let me know that you received them.

Also, after we have reviewed what I sent to you and you are ready to rewrite a new offer to purchase, I will need a few items from you at time of offer:

1.   Dream Development, LLC –

origination paperwork.

2. The document that proves you are the responsible party for Dream Development. You had said you are including Calvin on this paperwork, so he will then need to be a signor on the Offer to Purchase as well.

3. Proof of assets – either a current bank statement or a letter from your financial institution stating that you have in excess of the $1.45M in immediate, available liquid assets.

I am certain that the seller will ask that entire funds of the agreed upon purchase price be wired to McMillan and Terry (closing attorney – you can choose the attorney, this is just who I usually use and Andy seemed familiar with them) w/in 48 hours of the effective date of our contract. This money will be held in escrow until closing. I will forward the wiring instructions. Thanks!"

True to her word, Smith sent the detailed wiring instructions on June 8th. The law firm's trust account was ready to receive Sharon's funds to consummate the sale.

Sharon's lack of knowledge in real estate and closing requirements worked against her. She believed the flash of the bank statement and her typical give the run around routine with lawyers and accountants would give her enough traction and time to move into her ultimate dream home. She may have gotten to spend the night, but her tactics weren't enough to get her all the way in the house.

Perhaps it truly was, but I doubt the goal was ever to own this property. Rather, it was to take possession of it long enough to make an impression with her next mark or marks. Primarily, Fantasia and her manager were the ones Sharon wanted to impress, since she was trying to work a deal to develop a perfume line for the singer. If she could meet her and get to know her, Fantasia would fall under her spell.

Unlike other properties, this one was unattainable for the long haul. There'd be no moving in under cover of darkness and squatting for a month until the owner could have her evicted. No rental agreement to be had, as it was for sale and not for lease.

With funds never coming, the agent was stuck with the bills on the appraisal, home inspection and law office work while Sharon scooted away down I-77, back to Garners Ferry Road.

The consolation prize for Sharon was a series of photos she and her family took while in the house. Naturally, she posted them all on Facebook. The best one? A photo of Talitha Long with her jeans rolled up, lounging with her bare feet in the pool. Sharon's caption, "Get ur feet out my pool."

The *Be Smarter than a Con* Takeaway: Never deviate from your company or industry's policies, procedures and standard practices for someone you don't know. Unless you can verify through a third party the person's information, don't give your trust blindly. In this case, the bank should've been called to verify funds on deposit. Further, residential properties for sale aren't hotels; buyers aren't afforded the chance to "test drive" the house by spending the night. Possession of any sort isn't generally granted until the sale has closed.

CHAPTER NINETEEN
Player: Wess Morgan
~~~~~~

The object of Sharon's desire, Wess Morgan was unattainable for her primary goal of sleeping with him. However, she did find a way to use and humiliate him without the sex.

A popular gospel artist, Wess is the Senior Worship Leader and Associate Pastor at the Celebration of Life Church located in Hendersonville, Tennessee. His story is one of inspiration; rising from the despair of drug abuse and prison sentences to become a respected gospel singer and minister, his message carries an almost mesmerizing power. He's been featured on BET Gospel, TBN, The Word Network, Superbowl Gospel Celebration, The Mo'Nique Show and (most importantly for Sharon) Tyler Perry's production, *Laugh to Keep from Crying*.

In 2011, Sharon heard Wess Morgan perform at the Gospel Fest at Finlay Park. She told Linda and Tom she wanted him as her keynote speaker and performer for the next women's conference, planned for February

2012. Tom got in touch with Wess Morgan's people to inquire about securing his services for the conference.

Sharon had an unusual attraction to Wess. She fantasized about making love to him and even talked about marrying him. The fact that he had a family never had any impact on her plans or fantasies about him.

She planned activities around anywhere Wess was going to be. Stalkeresque, she began to communicate with him daily. Ultimately, she promised him ten million dollars, of which he could use eight hundred thousand for a custom tour bus. He was excited to sponsor a Recovery Fest for recovering drug addicts and alcoholics and to build a new church for the congregation pastored by his father.

Wess got busy on the plans for his new tour bus. He contacted a vendor and they created a design to suit his needs. His travel schedule is heavy, so having his own tour bus would make his life much easier. Once the plans were completed, he placed the order for the bus.

For the speaker's fee for the 2012 conference, Sharon got ten thousand dollars from Dr. Charles Partridge to help with all of the expenses. She'd also gotten some additional funding from a private lender for the main conference cost of the location and food as well. All of Sharon's promises to Wess were in the forefront of his mind when agreeing to perform at this women's conference. Keep in mind, she had promised him millions of dollars for a new church and a bus.

He came to impress and those who witnessed his show were transfixed by the power of his voice and message. Every eye on Wess, he was the best part of the 2012 conference by far.

170

The total amount due to Wess for his performance, including speaking and singing, was thirteen thousand dollars. In a practiced move from her standard shell game, she moves money from one to another, staying a step ahead of doom. Sharon was able to pay the upfront portion of his speaker's fee, which was only sixty five hundred dollars, out of the ten grand she conned out of Dr. Partridge. Then, Sharon used the remaining twelve hundred to pay the deposit to the Hilton Hotel. That money was just a down payment on the banquet hall. Not covered yet were the rooms and the food, totaling over thirty thousand dollars. Again, catering with Ruth's Chris Steakhouse is not for the faint of heart or wallet.

Sharon had a check for the balance of the sixty five hundred dollars ready the morning Wess left town, which she had delivered by Tom. Linda wrote the check at Sharon's instruction on the You, Too Foundation account. Sharon was running the story that her money was being held up and when Linda found out the check wasn't any good, she was mortified. Tom had Wess to hold the check and not cash it immediately. The whole conference and even the money that Jeff Downs got for her, Sharon was supposed to be able to handle, as her money was scheduled for release during this time period. Then, it was moved to after the conference, just the next week following.

Tom and Linda knew Wess performed in good faith and really wanted to do the right thing by him. This delay in the money routine was fairly new (for them), so Linda cashed in an investment for nine thousand. Part of this investment would be used for the sixty five hundred balance due to Wess. A thousand dollars was also given to Sharon to tide her over until the money was released next week. Linda wired the money directly to Wess, wanting him to have it in his account as soon as possible to make Sharon's bad check good.

Sharon's money never came through for Wess, so he had to find another way to make things happen.

The tour bus order was cancelled.

In 2013, Recoveryfest became a reality. Leading up to the late September event, Wess solicits donations to help his program happen in as big a way as possible. Had Sharon kept her promise, it would've been much easier to hold the festival.

The *Be Smarter than a Con* Takeaway: Wait until you have the money in hand from the source before spending it. The old saying about, "don't count your chickens before they hatch," is sage advice. Planning a large purchase is great, but be certain you have the means to pay for it before committing yourself and your finances to a creditor.

CHAPTER TWENTY
Player: Donny Brady

A small but important player in Sharon's overall con game, this young man has the dubious distinction of creating the infamous bank statement, showing Sharon's eighty one million account balance. It was just supposed to be "for a flash," Sharon said when instructing Donny on how to make what she wanted. When he was asked to perform this service, Donny was still a minor, just barely under the age of eighteen. However, his age doesn't completely shield him from the operation of the law, should they decide to pursue him.

Creating a falsified bank statement is wrong. Further, its illegality should be common knowledge. Donny was promised something big in exchange for his talents, but needed to utilize his common sense and realize he was being asked to do something that could cause himself and his family serious trouble.

The United States is a country with many laws.

While each state has its own set of regulations, the federal government has an ultimate authority expressed through a national code of laws. The salient section for this type of bank fraud is 18 U.S.C. § 1005: US Code – Section 1005: Bank entries, reports and transactions.

Perhaps Sharon should've read this section before asking for her fake bank statement: "Whoever makes any false entry in any book, report, or statement of such bank, company, branch, agency, or organization with intent to injure or defraud such bank, company, branch, agency, or organization, or any other company, body politic or corporate, or any individual person, or to deceive any officer of such bank, company, branch, agency, or organization, or the Comptroller of the Currency, or the Federal Deposit Insurance Corporation, or any agent or examiner appointed to examine the affairs of such bank, company, branch, agency, or organization, or the Board of Governors of the Federal Reserve System; or Whoever with intent to defraud the United States or any agency thereof, or any financial institution referred to in this section, participates or shares in or receives (directly or indirectly) any money, profit, property, or benefits through any transaction, loan, commission, contract, or any other act of any such financial institution - Shall be fined not more than $1,000,000 or imprisoned not more than 30 years, or both."

To recap, if you mock up a bank statement with the intent to defraud someone, you can be fined up to a million dollars and/or go to jail for up to thirty years. In Sharon's vernacular, "Wow."

***

"This is my statement to explain what occurred between me and Sharon D. Jackson. One day while I was visiting my mother, Carolyn Graham, in June 2011, I was approached by Ms. Sharon to create a Wachovia Bank letter. She knew that I was going to school for graphic design in Charlotte, North Carolina, and also the fact that I had some computer knowledge. The document created was only to be used as a flash (showing just a letterhead from the bank with a amount) to close on her house in Charlotte, North Carolina. Ms. Sharon promised to help me buy a car and help with my schooling by providing money for it.

I agreed because I was in need of the help. I used a graphic design program to layout the document and to make it look as real as possible.

When it came down to her assisting me with the car and school, she gave many excuses for not coming through with the funds. Unfortunately, I lost my car that I purchased regardless of her broken promises and eventually had to drop out of school.

Fortunately, I am blessed to have a supporting family. My mother has allowed me to drive her car until I get myself together. I am working so I can stand on my own feet. I have not seen or spoken with Ms. Sharon D. Jackson since everything happened at the car dealer where she was supposed to be purchasing a car for me, but instead somehow got my mother to give her money instead."

***

The elusive bank statement has been mentioned to many victims and seen by several. Sharon's very careful to not let anyone keep a copy. There are possibly several variations on the original bank statement. The original one exists in cyber space, as it was sent via text message from Sharon's phone to her eldest daughter, Myesha, in Virginia, during the height of the Linda/Tom/Jeff scam that lasted well over a year.

Creating a false document is also forgery, which carries its own set of penalties. Also known as uttering a false instrument, the crime of forgery is a felony in all fifty states. A charge of forgery is broad enough to include making and/or possessing a false writing in order to commit a fraud. As you'll see in Chapters 39 and 41, Sharon's no stranger to forgery, as she convinces two different assistants to help her create a fake accountant letter to use in her folder of propaganda.

The *Be Smarter than a Con* Takeaway: "Food gained by fraud tastes sweet to a man, but he ends up with a mouthful of gravel." Proverbs 20:17 NIV

CHAPTER TWENTY ONE
Taci Jones Bradley
∞∞∞∞∞∞∞∞∞∞∞∞∞∞∞∞∞∞∞∞∞∞∞∞∞∞∞

Calvin's sister, Taci, is a tough call. She clearly wants to protect her brother, but just how far she will go to do so is questionable. Her feelings about Sharon are also questionable. The friction is palpable between them; Sharon speaks of Taci with contempt, even mimicking her voice in a derogatory manner. While Taci talks about Sharon as you would discuss an embarrassing family member, she secretly ties into Sharon's grand agenda by working as an agent of misdirection and propaganda.

It's thought that Taci knows of a suitcase belonging to Sharon, filled with documents. Fake W-2s, 1099s, social security numbers and federal ID numbers galore populate this suitcase of fraud. Sharon never knows when she may need to "prove" her information when renting a new place (which has happened at least ninety six times in the past ten years, including the move happening in July 2013).

The allegiance Taci truly feels is known only unto herself; her behavior is different to the point that she associates with Sharon but seems uncomfortable about it. She is the link between Melissa and Sharon, making the crucial introduction in January 2012.

In the middle of 2013's steamy summer, Taci calls with urgency in her voice. She needs to see me, right away. We set the appointment for four o'clock. The following is her stream of consciousness from the meeting, as recorded in my office:

***

"Sharon had an event, somewhere on Garners Ferry. That Empowering Women to Excel was actually my motto. And what's she's always picked up is from everyone else. I work in nuclear fuel and she actually grew up with practically nothing. She and my brother, Calvin, had himself in a situation. He's a very dignitary person, he's a great person, and he's done got caught up in all this. When he got out, Calvin's an entrepreneur. You're used to business. One point two million is not a lot for a liability insurance policy. You have to have the coverage and I went to a very dignified lady who's over by Dreher High School. She's a private investor, a very rich white lady with an insurance company. Very dignified lady. A red flag had been raised when she gave my brother's social security number, because ours are so similar. We were raised in New Jersey and our numbers are just a couple off from one another. So, I put the insurance in the business and didn't realize that insurance was just enough of what Sharon wanted to get it started and didn't know that she wasn't going to continue to pay the premiums. This here was for the P&P Cleaning Service, that was Calvin's. My brother had the contracts with several apartment communities for students at Carolina. I was just very taken by how she went and demoralized my character. Which no one can actually demoralize someone really, you stand for the truth of who you are. I'm like, "how dare she."

Out of the all the thousands of freakin' dollars I had given her and my brother to have a place to live and I want to apologize to you for ever introducing you. It's because of the simple fact that's like you meet this person in their face, and you see who they are and then you didn't realize it was like all of the different, multiple personalities. To just play professional people, and I'm a minister, well I just cry on the inside because I didn't realize how ruthless she was to just go around and mischaracterize great people.

I feel like I'm a woman of ethics, integrity, morals, values and I serve with merit. And I hope this doesn't put a damper on me. You know how much this girl freakin' owes me? I'm about to lose things my own self because of her. I'm about to lose my apartment. I have a house in Georgia, of course. But, they move from pillar to pole. They'll stay in a place three to six months and then move. A lot of these people are older, elderly Caucasian people that she's taking advantage of in the past. Sharon and Aneshia came to my place about a month or month and a half ago. Aneshia knows better. I put her, her mother and the baby out. I picked the carriage up and put them out. I told them please don't come back here because this is where I serve, a place of humility.

They came for a visit and probably wanted something. Now, don't ever leave information around because they steal information.

Sharon destroyed my relationship with my father, on the Washington side of the family. Most of this side of the family are school teachers, doctors, lawyers, very credible people. And she just really said some horrible things about me to my family. They saw this eighty one million dollar freaking thing and to see that just really transformed their way of thinking, they thought there might be some serious jealousy on my behalf. That has never been true. Nobody who pays your bills the way I helped Sharon and Calvin, I never had any jealousy.

When I saw the book, the value of the book couldn't be that much. It couldn't be real. But you have to understand that the people who are in that circle, who aren't really used to seeing celebrities or hearing celebrities and when they hear that, they're flabbergasted because of the simple fact that they're thinking that you are this and that. That's the type of lethal and toxic thing Sharon did. It was distraughtful, demeaning and heartbreaking for her to have done me this way.

I was also stopped by a banker, who said your sister in law was nasty. When you guys meet and we met in a very public place and I felt out of place. I wasn't received. There was a lot of deception. In order for a deception to take place, that conversation would have to have already taken place itself. If you would've asked me, I would have told you. I would have told you.

When you meet someone who always wants something and characterizes somebody poorly and plays people against each other, that is so distasteful and tacky.

I didn't go to the event this year. I went last year at the Hilton. I paid at the Hilton. I've had five or six people, in fact if you look up Bible Way Church of Atlas Road, it a big church and that's my church family. Someone from there was saying something is going on and I've been taken advantage of. When someone messes up your good deeds, it just spoils it for everybody else.

It was with the banker lady, that I met, she really...

The celebrities that were here, Fantasia's mother, she will never come back again. Also, too, the Fantasia thing, I know when we used to go to Charlotte, I actually went by the home where she was shooting the reality thing and that was the neighborhood, Piper Glen, where Sharon was going to move. She actually went and stayed in those people's house overnight one night. I guess the Realtor® was persuaded, I don't know how she got to do it. You know, she could've left the door unlocked. Anything's possible. All the Mercedes and all that stuff, you know the agent's husband ran the Mercedes dealer?

I have followed the paper trail where she promised me one point five million dollars with an attorney on the phone and she had somebody on the phone trying to talk to me and I told her, "I'm not getting into this on the phone. I need to know who you are. And, I'm not quitting my job."

My grandmother is ninety years old. She and my grandfather worked hard in their life. They're property owners, very dignified people and this girl went and, talk about this, they're educators, they're Gamecocks. Two of my God children play for the team and little does my brother know, I never revealed any of that to she and my brother because I never wanted she and Ms. Sullivan to get in my circle. I want to protect people for their good deeds.

Ms. Sullivan is a voice for Sharon. That lady is so fraudulent, she is so fraudulent. I don't want to characterize someone when I really don't know them, but when I met her back in 2007, I had a Vera Wang gown on, this was my deceased mother's gown. She never edited that book, she put a face on it, that's all she did. Both of them went to amazon.com and got that little contract to do the book. And so here I am, thinking by meeting her with Ms. Sullivan, I'm thinking it could be real, because of her stance with the post office, as postmaster and everything. I read that book in fifteen minutes. It was so easy reading.

The banker said to me, "are you the one that stole from Sharon?" I'm like, "I've never taken anything from anyone, anyone. I'm a humanitarian."

It was so awful. I have paid their bills, before they moved into the house, not at the house in Woodman Farms. Nine hundred dollars, a thousand dollars, it wasn't a very big place, they lived in just a normal place. I guess I'm so hurt because my brother is so caught up into this, he's so into it, he's so blind to it. Whatever she says, he does. I don't know if he feels like he owes her or what.

I have given my brother money to pay their bills and she would take it and blame it on someone else that was in the house, saying they had taken it or stolen it or something. He would believe it, so I had to let them go. I had to completely disassociate myself.

I went over there to Duck Point today, and tried to get some answers but they weren't there. I am so hurt because of the people that are involved. She is going straight to hell.

The owner of Pine Terrace shopping center off Garners Ferry Road, Sharon moved into three or four different houses of that lady's. You can't tell me that's not taking advantage of a senior, elderly person. That is so horrible. She never paid the lady. She'd use different names, somebody else's face, like Ms. Sullivan or her daughters, to get the agreement and then they wouldn't pay.

I went over there today and knocked on the door, just to say, 'Can I have eight hundred and fifty dollars so I can pay for my place to stay?" I knew she was going to say, "I'll bring it to you.'

Her daughter left owing me four thousand dollars for the apartment. Huntington Place knows, because I went to a month to month, not knowing what I was actually going to do. And every month, I had to go over there and take it. So, I had to go and evict her and take my place back.

I haven't seen them at all, because I know Sharon's not welcome back at my grandparents house. Several of my relatives have just gotten their doctorate degrees, but I don't feel like they come to my aid like they should. I don't know if they're judging me with my brother and her, or what.

I was out of work for like six weeks, this is like my first week back. I'm in a situation here, Melissa. There's two things I came here for. One is to get back into class, the real estate class. So, it's been a couple of years now that I did this class before but I didn't finish the whole course.

Also, to what Mary had shared with me, is that the people at the Medallion Center wasn't paid. I remember that, ok, there was supposed to have been an event in April or May and she put a deposit down at that point. But, they actually went on her good word.

And this is the other thing that I don't know how to really say. And this is the second thing and I hope that this is not out of character and I hope that you're not judging me but I need some help for Remington Place. And I've already talked to the property managers there and it's like what my salary was, it was like thirteen hundred dollars a week and it's been shot down to less than five hundred and I could write you a check and pay it back in a couple of weeks. Because I have no one else to really go to that I could trust to ask or anything."

"OH, are you serious" I could barely get the words out. Did she just ask me for money? Now I'm truly speechless. What in the world do I say next?

"NOW I understand. Taci, I don't have anything to give you," I said.

"I went through my 401(k) to send off and pull money out. I've already talked with the managers and actually I just have to pay it. That's all their willing to do, I just have to pay it. My deadline to pay it was by yesterday. I have to pay a thousand and forty dollars and I actually sent off for it out of my 401(k). It has to go through an approval process before it can come to me."

"As an independent person, I don't have anything like a 401(k). I don't have it to give to you. I know Sharon has always thought that we are some kind of wealthy couple, but we're just small business owners."

"Unnhh, don't connect me with her! Don't connect me with her! It's ok, everything is ok as long as I can get back into the school. I understand, and you don't have to call the property managers for me. I have a personal relationship with them.

You just want to pay for where you live but you have things come up and want to do the right thing. I don't have AFLAC or the short-term disability insurance like you were talking about. I'll try to find some kind of way."

***

There are lots of problems with that visit from Taci. First and foremost, why she thought to ask me to loan her over a thousand dollars out of the blue was supremely odd. We'd had very little interaction over the past year and suddenly she feels close enough to ask me for a huge loan?

I think the visit was a test. Sharon was slick enough to get fifteen hundred out of me, so why not go back to the well and see if Taci could hit the jackpot, too.

The second problem was the claim about going to Duck Point. She already knew Sharon and Calvin moved. Just a few days prior, she led Tom and Linda on a wild goose chase to find the missing couple at a house where they'd supposedly moved out near Hopkins.

The third problem was her claim of being out of

189

work for six weeks. Linda saw her and spoke to her several times over the past couple of months. Never did she seem ill or even mention being out of work for surgery.

The fourth problem was her interest in the real estate class. She first attended five years ago and didn't complete the course. While the schooling is valid for a five year period, you have to complete the class in order to obtain the license. For someone claiming how important it was to get back into class, she never called back to schedule her attendance.

Taci was married to someone in Georgia, who has now passed away. That's how she got the last name Brannon. Also, she said she has a house in Georgia. Currently. She has also lived at the same apartment community for the past six years. Why would you live there if you have a house?

The property management company where Taci rents said she pays late every month, around the twentieth or the twenty-fifth. She always pays in money orders. She's told the management that she puts the income from her job into a pre-tax retirement account that she then withdraws every month through a hardship disbursement. The reason? She's evading the Internal Revenue Service. She's told the property managers she owes big money to the IRS, but they can't get it if she doesn't deposit it into her checking account or take it as regular income. Instead, she funnels it through her retirement 401(k).

**The *Be Smarter than a Con* Takeaway:
Fool me once, shame on you. Fool me twice, shame
on me. Knowing Taci introduced me to Sharon and
having endured a year's worth of her untruths, once
my eyes were opened, the con was over. Taci's hope of
convincing me with tears and a sad story could never
work. When dealing with a potential con artist, make
sure you're the smartest person in the room. Do your
research in advance. Having the facts ahead of time
makes the con easier to spot.**

CHAPTER TWENTY TWO
Player: Dr. Charles Partridge

A pastor. A relative. But ultimately, just another mark for Sharon's conniving machinations. A Christian leader, Dr. Partridge is trying to bring others into the Kingdom of God. And while a small church can reach the unsaved just fine, a large church can do so much more for His glory.

Fueled by the promise of a million dollars for his church, and then further bamboozled with the incredulous promise of two million dollars, Dr. Partridge agreed to provide money for Sharon. All the while, he waits patiently on Sharon to fulfill her word to him that his church will be blessed by her benevolence.

Dr. Partridge is married to Sharon's first cousin's daughter, Connie– she's Barbara McDaniels's child. He studied at a small college in Columbia, South Carolina. He became anointed by the Holy Spirit at the age of seventeen and has been involved in the ministry ever since.

As a victim, he is taken for a full thirty thousand dollars. Whether Sharon promises to give you two dollars or two million, the outcome's always the same. She's gotten what she wants, and you're left holding the bag.

***

"I gave Andy Roland twenty thousand dollars for Sharon's account. The twenty was first and went to Tony's financial company, as it had to be put into a trust that would be secure. That was supposed to secure the money from Sharon. Everything would be overseen by them and if anything ever happened to Sharon, it would still be available for us.

She was giving me, at first, five hundred and fifty thousand, and then the loan turned into a gift of one million dollars. Then it was two million. The original twenty from me was to pay fees associated with the distribution and management of the million dollars to me. It cost me twenty to get a million. What I didn't understand was if she's giving us a million, why can't we just deduct the accountant and attorney fees from that big total.

They said it had to be paid first. So that's what I did.

After having done that, Sharon called me before the event when she had Wess Morgan in 2012 a couple weeks before it was happening. She had to get the money to pay him before he could come and Linda Wilson, her assistant, was with her. They met me up at McDonalds near where I work and asked for ten thousand dollars.

Sharon wanted cash, but I got two checks for

them, made out to the people directly for whom it was supposed to be paying so I can keep track of it. I needed to have some way to track it so I can keep records of it. I told her the bank wouldn't give me cash because it was too much money.

She kept filling my ears with stories, like she didn't like the car I drove. "You're a man of God, you should have a nice car," she said. She wanted me to go ahead and buy a new vehicle, based on the money I had coming from her. The church would have the money to buy something nicer for me than my Nissan Sentra, but I was driving what I could afford at the time. I'm glad I didn't listen to her then, I would've had one more debt that was unnecessary.

I hounded her and hounded her and sometime in 2013 was when I got that ten thousand dollars back. She was making it sound like it would be all thirty thousand, but it was only ten. The twenty thousand I gave to Andy's company, that part was never recovered. Sharon said it was their fault and "they stole that money and why am I trying to blame her?"

That's why she didn't want to respond. She never gave anything back and is passing it off on Andy. "I'm trying to help him out," Sharon said. "Mr. Roland is an old man and he's sick, and I don't want him to go through nothin'."

I was trying to be patient. But she was delaying the process.

Just give us our money back so we can move forward, that's all I ever asked of Sharon. Linda called me and Investigator Hinson called me, everyone trying to tell me about Sharon's lies. It was a little too late.

Mrs. Sullivan gave me a check drawn on her own account for twenty thousand that said in the memo line, "for Sharon Johnson." This check was in early 2013.

It was no good. I put it into an account that our church has and it sat there for two weeks to a month and I had to talk to the bank people and see what could be done. The bank sent us a letter saying it was a fraudulent check. I showed the police investigator the check. Hinson has everything, the bad check and the two commitment letters from Sharon for the first five hundred and fifty thousand and then the million dollar commitment. Hinson also said it was a must he meet with me. Here it is a year later, I went down there and took everything, even took a day off, and there's been no response. He has my direct number, so if he wanted to reach me, he could. I even went down there a second time, took another day off, to take the information relating to Tony and those, and still nothing.

I had to borrow more money to complete our church building project because the process was delayed and then we had to pay our family members back for funds provided that we'd given to Sharon. Initially, my parents had to buy the property the church is on. We had to go through closing and then buy it back from them when we got everything set with our financing. We could've just bought the land, cash money, and been done, but we were in a bind because that twenty went there plus we had to keep doing the ministries where we were plus paying the note on the property where we were and trying to get the drawings done. A six month project at most took almost two and a half years. Things kept getting more expensive and it really put us in a bad spot.

Andy and Milt are playing the victim as well. I pulled them both together at our old location at a meeting Sharon was supposed to attend. Sharon started to turn around and leave before she even got there because she saw them there and didn't want to face everybody. I called and said to her, "You come back here."

They were pressing my wife and claiming they didn't know what kind of game Sharon's running, she's just doing this, that and the other. When Sharon came in, I said, "Now tell me what you just said."

They started lying. I told them, "I never hired you. Now, we're a small church, but I have enough financial sense to get us where we are now with the numbers we have. I just need you to give us the money we need to complete the project."

I guess he was trying to cover up in front of Sharon. But, I called them liars and told them to get out. "You have fifteen days to respond to us or we're going to the police department."

They never responded back to us.

I went off on Linda on one occasion because she was trying to defend her. I said, "I don't care. I want to talk to her and tell her I want my money."

I chalk it up as a loss and here it is she's calling me now to speak the truth.

I kept asking people how did Sharon get the money. All of a sudden, she was telling people she had this book Tyler Perry was making a movie out of it. I heard the Tyler Perry story. I also knew something about the daughter that died, but I didn't know exactly if she was using that as a ploy, too. From what I understand, the girl got sick or something, but I was told she had strep throat and it infected her heart and poisoned her. Other than that, I didn't know anything about it.

I'm just floored by everything she's done. My wife and I were talking and Sharon used to do this kind of stuff back years ago, but not to this extent. She disappeared from the family and the area. She popped back up and explained why she used to be that way. She was molested and that's what she was telling people and that's how she was marketing her book. The family was like, "how was this stuff happening but we never heard about any of it?" The first thing the family heard was when they read the book. A lot of the aunts were saying it's all a crock.

Sharon is known to have used her cousins' identities, getting them in bad financial situations and telling them lies like she did with us. There is one cousin that has the name Sharon something Jackson, the other one has a different middle initial and Sharon got her credit all messed up. She did a fraudulent thing back years ago, portraying like she was that particular Sharon Johnson. Sharon said was going to make it right and, to my knowledge nothing's ever happened, she's never made it right.

Throughout this whole process, she kept communicating with me on her always changing phone numbers. We even had a Facebook chat conversation in September 2013 where she is still telling me I'm getting paid back. In my last Facebook post to her, I called her a liar. She didn't like it, trying to play the emotional game with me, like a man of God wouldn't ever speak like that. I told her I wasn't taking her word for anything else. I just wanted our money back.

***

Throughout the saga with Dr. Partridge, Sharon kept up her story with him via text messages and Facebook private chats. From January, 2012 through October, 2013, Dr. Partridge received one hundred and twenty six phone screens' worth of messages from Sharon. Sometimes, the messages were supposedly sent by one of the other close confidants in her world, including her daughter Ceira and the fiancé, Calvin. There's a standard playbook by which she communicates with those already victimized. She knows the longer she strings along the mark, the better chance she has of getting away with her crimes.

Sharon's messages range from simple avoidance to the outrageous lies for which she's famous.

What follows is an abbreviated transcript of the texts between her and Dr. Partridge:

09/05/12

DP: Here's my address to mail the check.

09/10/12

DP: No check yet.

SJ: Ok imma call NOW

SJ: He said it was mail out Friday at 4:15pm

09/12/12

DP: Praise Him. Bird had the baby yet? Still no mail.

SJ: He call me earlyer, just sent him tex he send me the tracking number

DP: He is a handsome little fellow. Ok. So you have called to find out where it is?

SJ: IM on it

09/14/12

DP: No mail.

DP: Praise Him. I just wanted to let you know that I'm very hurt and disappointed. I trusted and helped you and I have been put in a bind.

SJ: Ur going be find please please be know that, im on it, im talking with them to over nite it again every one concern, ill here bk from them in few, im on it, Lord knows i am. Im calling resouce office now.

SJ: Gm, give me a call

DP: in the middle of an activity, will have to call you in 30 mins. to an hour.

SJ: Ok, know that not who im am, i want stop til some brake.

09/18/12

SJ: Please let me know about mail u should have it no later than wed, thanks

DP: Ok

09/19/12

DP: Again, I say that I'm hurt and very disappointed with this situation. I just want to know an exact date that I can get the money that we loaned you back and the money that Andy stole from us in your name? Thanks. Blessings.

09/20/12

DP: Praise Him. I wanted to know if you got my message from yesterday because I have not heard back from you.

SJ: Gm, dnt know what happen. Im disponted as we'll, and bn following up with it, i exspress to them how important this was for me. I dnt think they r lyeing. Dnt think it bn mail when they said, how ever im have reach out to some other folks to get avance pay for a project that im doing, and trying to get loan on hm in Nc, ill know some thing by Monday, know that trying to fix this, u help me, Lord knows i dnt have problem helping u. Now what Tony did was wrong, and i didn't know nothing about it, til yall brought to my intention, but he will never have nothing, it will get work out, it ant over til God say it over.
09/24/12
SJ: Hello hope all is well, expecting to hear bk from home mortgage every thing went well so i should get the loan, let u 4sure date by wed, Barbara found the loan folks for me a friend of hers.
DP: Ok
09/27/12
SJ: Gm hope all is well, i know something today, didn't hear nothing yesterday im reaching out to them today, have a conference call about the advance pay. one way or another ill know somthing, thanks for ur patients
10/4/12
DP: Praise Him. I pray all is well. I wanted to know if I'll have the money by tomorrow to pay the people. U checking, because I have not heard from you.

201

SJ: All is well, got aprove fax title yesterday, waiting on final call, today i should know, ill call u before 5 but i sent over everything they need

DP: Ok

SJ: Im on it, I am

10/5/12

DP: Praise Him. Is all well? Do you have a time for me to get the check or any news for me to give the GC?

SJ: No, not yet i bn call them about three time today, dnt what the hold up, when Barbara call them to ask how u go by get it done they told her it could take up 2weeks im trying to borrow ten thousand from some one. He said he get with me later, im really trying.

SJ: What the company, ill have fantisa manger to make it to them, if it a go

SJ: Did you get my tex?

DP: I did.

SJ: Ok thanks

10/17/12

DP: Praise Him. I haven't heard from you. I was trying to get an update.

SJ: Hello hope all is well, the house pass the inspection last week, wed im waiting on the money, as soon as i get in my hand im calling u, 4sure

DP: Ok

10/22/12

SJ: Hellow, imma call u in the morning, in middle of an interview. Check not here yet, but it should be here any day, just hold on we almost to the end, hang in there, thanks u so much.
11/8/12
DP: Praise Him. I left you a message. We need to speak.
SJ: Im sorry i didn't, call u few
11/16/12
DP: Mail yet?
SJ: Im sorry I got certify mail at the house today, mrs Sullivan ck my mail i know that's it, ill be back monday morning bk in atl, have two booksigning. Call you lunch time monday, favor ant fair
11/19/12
SJ: Leaving Atl, be hm round 3:30, call u when i get hm
DP: Ok. Sounds good.
12/20/12
DP: Congrats on new grand baby.
SJ: Thanks, congrats to u
SJ: Lol u will be shouting
DP: Thank God!!! Thank you!!!
SJ: In bank call u in few
DP: Ok. I'll hold up a few mins. then before we leave.
SJ: Ok
SJ: Going be here for min, I'll hold to urs, call u later
12/21/12
DP: Praise Him. How is everything okay?

SJ: Everything went well, cks b ready 28/29
DP. Ok, thanks. How is everything else with you and the family? I know the two grands are keeping you all busy.
12/31/12
DP: Praise Him. Is all well?
SJ: Hay dis Ceira she left her phone, have her call this nb when she get bk.
DP: Ok. U and the baby well?
SJ: Ya we fine, who dis
DP: Connie's husband.
SJ: Oh, she's in a meeting with dem attorneys people she should be here round 8 be sure to tell her u call.
DP: Okay thanks. Blessings.
 01/01/13
SJ: Happy New Year to u and family, it be couple more days, please hold on almost got it work out call u later. Evetything going smooth, have a conference call with network 9:15 talk later.
01/08/13
SJ: Imma need ur acct info wed At 2 pm I'll be calling u from the bank, u dnt give to me, I'll let you give to the banker so we wire into ur acct, thanks for your sooooo much.
01/09/13
DP: Praise Him. I have jury duty this morning so if I don't answer the phone, that is why. Connie has the info and should be available today. Thanks.
 SJ: Ok.

DP: Praise Him. I am out early. Did everything turn out well?

SJ: Yes sir, im sorry im all over the place, should be there tomorrow. I'll confirm in the morning, time reality people leave I'll give you a call.

01/10/13

SJ: Will show up in ur acct today

DP: Ok. Thanks. Is well with you? I don't want you stressing.

SJ: Thanks, im fine.

SJ: Congrats ck acct in the morning, it leave my tonite. Have happy life. Don't forget to left me up in prayer, pray that protect me from the enemies.

04/08/13

SJ: Hay I'm trying to find a Chase bank on phone with Barbara, trying find closest to Columbia, it's 2hr away.

SJ: Drove, 6hr for 4 day hold, smh

DP: Ok

04/11/13

DP: Praise Him. I have not heard from you. Is it supposed to be available today or tomorrow?

SJ: Gm, they holding it 4 days, i did it Monday, dnt have the paper in front of me.

04/18/13

DP: What's the reason today?

DP: What's the excuse today? I'm disappointed! Seems to me you're jerking my chain. Really not happy right now.

SJ: The loan was for 500,000 bc it was drawn

on out of state bank and the amount, it sometime
take lil longer to clear. I'll take u to bank with
04/30/13
SJ: Dr. Parriot, Sharon going to get everything
for you, today call us when you get off. This
Calvin, still in Nc, it's over 20,000 folks here.
She did event with Tisa and it was crazy with
pple.
DP: I have not heard from u.
DP: You deserve a Grammy or an Oscar because
you are good!!! Applause, applause, applause.
05/01/13
SJ: Dr. Parrtrige, dis Ceira dnt know if u heard,
my mom is lock up, they r trying to keep from
the media, charge simple assault, we bn Bond
court dis morning. I'll keep u inform.
DP: Ok.
SJ: Be out later today/morning, everything went
well
SJ: we r waiting for dem to release her, lawyer
said the lady may drop the charge. Thank God
dis is all crazy.
DP: Ok
05/03/13
SJ: GM, I've bn in hearing all yesterday, trying
to get this this charge drop, have to go bk today,
when get from there I'm coming to u. I've got
myself in mess, tried to fix one problem and
create another one, bare with me, please. See u
today.
05/04/13
SJ: Onway.

DP: How far away are you?

SJ: Almost there, Dnt move

DP: Praise Him. This 10 is real isn't it? No counterfeit business, right? I'm just asking because I don't want another shock like the check from your girl.

SJ: Lol, yes it is.

05/10/13

SJ: They change ct date til 23 of May smh, call later, have finish up.

05/11/13

DP: Praise Him. Gm. I didn't hear back from when will you be able to get the other 20 to us?

05/14/13

DP: Praise Him. R u going to be able to meet me today with that?

SJ: She's going get bk with me later today, soon as i know 4sure let u know, waiting on her call.

05/15/13

DP: No word yet?

05/18/13

DP: Praise Him. I have not heard back from you.

SJ: She haven't return my call yet, im work on some else, I'll call u when i work it out.

06/06/13

SJ: Wait on my folks to get in town, they not here yet, call u soon as they get here

06/21/13

SJ: Hello, wait for the cash, u first on the list

DP: Ok.

07/03/13

DP: If you have your phone off how can I reach you?

07/04/13

SJ: Happy4th, just call to confirm was i still good for the loan, they both said yes, on my way bk hm soon as i get to them to get I'll give u a call.

07/05/13

SJ: I'll call u when they get here, guess the rain hold them up, I'm waiting.

DP: Ok

SJ: Thank Lord, one just call say when it clear up they b here, not giving up, claiming this

07/12/13

SJ: The owner of the shop should be in 4/5 call u then

SJ: At shop waiting for the owner to, come shop close at 7, call u when it's done so we can meet. I tex u earlyer. Praying this is over today. See u later

DP: Ok

SJ: Dr. Parrtrige this Calvin. How r u, the man try to pull a fast one, but i work it out going bk, tomorrow, Nee call u in morning, she mad at folks but i talk to got it work out,

07/16/13

SJ: Calvin got work out, but owner wasn't ready to get them today, he put us off. And we not putting u off, been doing everything we can. Only for a couple of days, and we r taking a lost, for them but anything to get this over. Please give it couple of days. I'll call Thursday we r disappoint smh. Imma try another one in morning, not giving up. Call u tomorrow we try some other shop.

07/17/13

SJ: No luck today, Imma wait on the other shop, they offer more.

SJ: He ask us come bk in couple days, please know that we r trying.

SJ: Im trying so hard, to get this fix for me and u, Lord know i have problems, to my lights was off today. So no excuses i want fix this so i can focus on me and the thing im faceing. I need u to bare with, notice i haven't done anything lately cause im trying get pass this.

07/22/13

SJ: Good evening, first let me share my good news, i got save yesterday, best feeling in the world, I'll see u this week, Calvin told me u call with help of God i should see this week, in meeing now, but haven't forgot.

DP: That's a blessing. Ok.

07/25/13

DP: I need our money asap. I'm tired of all of these excuses. You said you are not I think you are but your actions are not helping your case. I'm very upset! I don't like for people to lie to me and then play games.

SJ: Wow, if u only knew, one thing 4 sure God know my heart, I'm doing everything i can think of, we still have the watches, no I'm not playing games I want this over badly, and u have bn great, in working with me, but please please

209

know I'm trying my best, i know how it may look but i care more than u know, imma get work out with the help of God.

SJ: Dr. Parriot, wasn't put u off, i was meeting people all week trying to do different events to get money, if i do event that's couple thousand dollars, we don't have money yet, Calvin went bk to work so we can our way, The Lord know how bad we r having it, I'm trying to hold on. I dnt want to owe u, or no one for that matter, everything we have is behind, everything. I just gave my life to God, a is for real about my walk. One thing i want to do is play with man of God.

08/01/13

SJ: Gm, going to a shop in Nc, pray for me im bn working call u this afternoon.

DP: Ok.

08/02/13

SJ: I think i got it work out, pray for me plz, I'm stay up here to see, praying it's a go call u sat evening.

08/03/13

DP: I think, don't spend.

08/06/13

SJ: Good afternoon, Ronald going to bring the cashier ck, today call u when he gets here.

DP: Ok.

DP: I have not heard back from you.

08/07/13

DP: Why is there always some kind of excuse or delay? Why should I believe what somebody said that calls me for you that I have never seen

or don't know whether you lied to them to lie to me. I've been repeatedly put off over and over again. I have not heard anymore about this money you're supposed to have, money from BB&T and I have not gotten our money from the church back. I'm not very happy at all. You are saying all the right things and doing nothing.
08/28/13

SJ: I'm sorry, not yet, but im still saying Monday, they have end of day and tomorrow.

DP: Ok.

09/01/13

DP: Praise Him. What time will we be meeting on Monday?

09/04/13

DP: I pray that you're not teasing me.

SJ: No sir, I have nothing to gain from that. I dnt go around hurting folks and causing habits in there life, and I want go in there acting ugly to cause problems in mind. When she call me this all behind us.

09/13/13

SJ: In bank. Gm, Today is the 5th day, and just have wait, never count weekn just the bz days they said 2-5 days see u next week u first.

09/17/13

DP: What happened to meeting today?

SJ: That's day I got from them, bf we left I sent u the message, and the date the computer gave them, I ask same thing she said that's date came from feral reserve

DP: Ok.

211

Now, we switch over to the Facebook chat.
09/23/13
DP: Praise Him. I tried to reach you this morning and your phone is disconnected.
SJ: Gm, it b working real soon I'll be in contact later today have Great day. See u later.
09/25/13
DP: Is there an update? You got me in a bad spot. If by Friday I haven't gotten at least the 20 back, I'm going to have to file suit against Ms. Sullivan for that bad check since they are taking their time with the case on Tony.
DP: This is looking like you are playing games. I want to give you the benefit of the doubt but you have not done anything you said. That is good. I'm disappointed. I'm still waiting on the call I was supposed to get the other night.
10/2/13
DP: You are still playing games but we need our money. You are making Linda and Tom look like they knew what they were talking about. It's sad you would do that to your family and a church.
10/8/13
DP: I guess it was crazy for me to believe that you were honest. I guess the joke is on me.
10/16/13
SJ: Gm, hope all is well. U have bn saying ugly things to me for the last two weeks, and I want respond bc it is so disrespactful and not true, i always respact u, as a person, a Man, and Man

of God, and far as steeling that has never bn me at all. U know i didn't even know u gave UR money to Tony, until it brought to my tention, not only do u know that but God know.

DP: You have not done anything you said you would and now you are trying to play the victim. Come on, get real. All I have to go off of is what I see. Talk about disrespect, wasting my time and not communicating is disrespectful. Giving our church a bad check, knowing it's bad, is disrespectful.

10/17/13

SJ: Okay, we family. Dnt want bad blood.

October seventeenth was the last communication between Sharon and Dr. Partridge. Her best solution to avoid "bad blood" as she calls it, is to cut off all contact. She hasn't been able to secure enough cash from a con to run her daily life and pay back her debt to him as well. A woman's got to have her priorities, right?

**The *Be Smarter than a Con* Takeaway: The saying, "It takes money to make money," is not applicable when someone promises you a gift of cash. The promised bequest of a million dollars was, on its face, outrageous and unbelievable considering its source. When Dr. Partridge had a gut feeling that he shouldn't have to provide any money up front, or ever, to someone who was supposed to be funding his endeavor, his feeling should have been heeded. While he did obtain a legal document outlining her commitment for the funds, he needed to investigate whether or not

213

this "commitment" was worth the paper on which it was written. The second lesson in this chapter can be gleaned from her communication style. With so much evidence of her educational level in her voluminous writings, there should be no doubt this woman was not a successful author. She comes across as barely literate, so her so-called success in the book world should be highly questionable. A book written at this level would not be a best seller or attractive to Tyler Perry.**

215

CHAPTER TWENTY THREE
Players: The Attorneys

Many people with Esquire after their names have been used by Sharon to further her con games. She favors high profile attorneys; the more public name recognition they have, the better. But in an interesting dichotomy, one of her go-to moves is referencing the "Atlanta attorney" or "my attorneys," none of which is named, ever. The menace of an action from any attorney is often enough to get her way, to a higher degree than you'd expect from the general population. From Linda's perspective, all of the attorney stories are linked together. She helps us navigate these troubled waters, showing how these professionals were used in Sharon's mischievous deeds.

***

Player: Attorney Hammond Beale

Hammond A. Beale, Esq. is the attorney Sharon told Linda Wilson that helped her get the settlement from the hospital on her daughter's wrongful death lawsuit.

Sharon was introduced to Attorney Beale by Carolyn Graham, one of her former assistants. Attorney Beale's firm, the Palmetto Law Center, P.C., was perfectly positioned for Sharon's taste, right off Garners Ferry Road. Their areas of practice cover personal injury; specifically, wrongful death lawsuits.

"When I first met Sharon she told me her attorney was Hammond Beale," Linda explains. "She said he helped her in her malpractice suit regarding the death of Barrio. (I later found out this story was a complete lie).

"Sharon had asked that we fax over a copy of the publishing agreement to Beale's law office for him to go over the agreement before she signed it. We did fax the agreement as requested. Later, we found out Sharon spoke with Mr. Beale regarding the fax, but never came back to discuss the matter."

"Sharon used Attorney Beale's name to have us believe he was the original attorney handling the release of her funds from the bank, which was Wachovia at the time. On numerous occasions, she made reference to Beale meeting with the bank and the IRS to try and resolve the matter. She would say everything has been worked out and the funds were scheduled to be released on various dates. This charade went on for several months."

"I eventually told Sharon I didn't know anything about her attorney, but he does not seem very competent and she needed to look at getting a different attorney. She later told me Beale suggested she speak with attorney Clarence Davis with Nexsen Pruett, a major commercial law firm in the Carolinas, because the situation was complicated. Attorney Beale had used Clarence Davis to work with him on Barrio's case previously, so they had a history of collaboration."

"We believe Sharon is now communicating with Clarence Davis. Attorney Davis has supposedly set up meetings with the IRS and Wachovia bank to try and get to the bottom of this problem. At the end, there were supposed meetings set up with deadlines to have everything resolved, but of course there was always some kind of delay or issue to come up to prevent the release of her funds."

"Ironically, in my research I found Attorney Davis has represented Wachovia bank on different occasions in various legal matters involving customers. I brought this to Sharon's attention as a conflict of interest. Because I was believing everything Sharon was saying, I didn't realize at the time this should have been a big red flag to me regarding Sharon's story."

"Sharon eventually used the conflict of interest on behalf of attorney Davis as a way to further her scheme by saying she decided to fire him because she didn't believe he had her best interest at heart and he was working on behalf of Wachovia against her."

Player: Attorney Willie Gary

Willie E. Gary's website proclaims him as "The Giant Killer" in explaining his reputation for successfully challenging large corporations in court. He has gained national recognition for his accomplishments. The Law Firm of Gary, Williams, Lewis and Watson is based in Florida and its principal member has been featured on at least a dozen network talk shows.

Attorney Willie Gary initially became involved

219

because Sharon kept telling Linda that her attorneys were going to release the funds on this date or that date, but whenever the day arrived, Sharon claimed the attorneys were telling her something different. Linda suggested Sharon let her contact another attorney who specialized in these types of cases. Sharon agreed and Linda called Willie Gary with Sharon's story.

"At this point I tell Sharon she needs to get her an attorney that specializes in these types of cases and someone from out of state who is willing to fight for her," Linda said.

She told the law firm about Sharon's tale of discrimination at the hands of the bank, and it was a natural fit for the type of case Willie Gary loved to argue. A large financial corporation withholding funds from the rightful owner seemed like his next big win.

Functioning as Sharon's mouthpiece, Linda started making arrangements to put Sharon and Mr. Gary together in person. But, Sharon starts to seem annoyed by Linda's actions and eventually, Sharon took Linda out of the loop to deal with him directly. Later, Sharon said Willie Gary didn't want her discussing anything outside of the attorney-client relationship. Then, she announced she wasn't dealing with him anymore because he didn't want Linda involved, which hurt her feelings. She wanted to show loyalty to Linda, since she was the one who brought Mr. Gary to the party.

The truth was Willie Gary wanted Sharon's proof of the settlement she supposedly received for the death of her daughter. "Sharon tells me her daughter Myesha has all of the paperwork and she would get it from her. Attorney Gary has made flight plans to meet Sharon

220

here in Columbia and she would have the settlement documents for his review at that time," Linda clarified.

Obviously, she wasn't able to provide the proof. Attorney Gary concluded there was no settlement and moved on. But before anyone else was aware of his withdrawal, Sharon makes a big show of having a back and forth with him via telephone. He's supposed to be blowing up her phone, wanting her to use a large portion of her settlement for a donation to an African American college fund in Florida he supports. She's not interested in any such charity, clearly not a supporter of higher education.

Sharon says he's trying to set up arrangements for her to get her funds, but she's never satisfied with what he suggests. If someone was helping me to gain control of millions of dollars, I'm sure I'd take his advice.

Linda continues, "Sharon tells me Willie Gary came to town, but he didn't want to deal with anybody but her and he didn't want me at the meetings. Mr. Gary then proceeds to set up meetings with Judge Seymour who is handling Sharon's case to have her funds released. A closed hearing is scheduled with Wachovia, the IRS and Sharon to determine why her funds had not been released and to agree upon a settlement amount for the money being illegally withheld. Sharon's delighted – all parties agree upon one billion dollars!"

"According to Sharon, Judge Seymour is so disgusted by this incident she awards another billion dollars to Sharon because of all the hardship she has had to endure! (I don't believe a Judge can even do that at a hearing where all the parties have agreed to a settlement). When Sharon told me that, I asked her how could the Judge do that and she said the Judge got everybody to agree to it!"

"Judge Seymour sets a date for the funds to be released; this date is about thirty days out. I say to Sharon, 'why would Judge Seymour not have your funds released immediately, this does not make any sense!' I asked her why attorney Gary didn't request an immediate release of your funds. She says she doesn't know and is just glad it's over!"

"We went through another series of issues and delays and the release date of the funds came and went at least ten times."

Linda later found out Sharon had someone call Willie Gary the morning of his flight (he was already at the airport) to cancel the meeting because she had to go out of town at the last minute.

Sharon continues her attitude of reluctance in dealing with Willie Gary. On the day she is to finally get her funds released, she refuses to answer the phone from Willie Gary. "She tells me he keeps calling her to meet him at the bank, but she doesn't want to have anything to do with him," Linda said.

"When she tells me this story, which is after the fact (how convenient) I tell her she needs to at least meet with him to get her funds released. She then tells me he left town and went back to Florida."

Players: George and I.S. Leevy Johnson, Attorneys

Unsuspecting pawns in Sharon's game. I.S. Leevy Johnson is a prominent attorney in Columbia, as well as the owner of Leevy's Funeral Home. His firm, Johnson, Toal & Battiste, P.A., deals with civil litigation,

222

worker's compensation, probate, federal entitlements and medical malpractice. I.S. and his partner George Johnson maintain offices in Columbia and Orangeburg, South Carolina.

Attorneys Johnson and Johnson enter the playing field after the departure of Willie Gary. After the delay in getting her funds released because of Willie Gary's successful negotiation but inconclusive results, Sharon goes to meet with Attorney Jeff Johnson, hiring him to get her elusive funds released.

Linda hears Mr. Johnson promised he would have the funds released within a couple of weeks. The word is Mr. Johnson meets with Judge Seymour to discuss the matter. "While all of these different scenarios are going on, I asked Sharon why couldn't the judge issue a court order immediately releasing your funds? None of this is making any sense."

Sharon uses these attorneys in a variety of circumstances, including a terrific tale involving a botched gift of cash to tide them over until the real funds could be released.

Linda arrived at Sharon's home one afternoon to hear she'd just missed Attorney Johnson. Sharon said it was a disaster and Linda should be glad she wasn't there.

"Why? What happened, Sharon?" Linda pressed.

"I.S. was gonna loan me some cash until he can get the funds straight. He was gonna bring over three hundred thousand in cash," Sharon said.

Because most attorneys keep at least three hundred grand in their offices, you know, just in case.

"Well, when he got here, Calvin saw he had only

brought one hundred and fifty thou in a bag and told him to just take that back. We don't need no half ass amount like that."

Because that's just chump change, anyway.

Sharon then proceeds to tell Linda how Jeff Johnson wants to bring Willie Gary on as part of the legal team because of his expertise in this area. So now, Willie Gary is back in the picture. Sharon says she meets with Willie Gary and Jeff Johnson at Johnson, Toal & Battiste and they agree to work together on her behalf.

"This dialogue with Jeff Johnson, Willie Gary and Judge Seymour goes on for at least a couple of months. Sharon later on tells me she believes Wachovia has Judge Seymour and Jeff Johnson in their back pocket and that's why her funds have not been released."

"She then tells me Jeff came to talk to her and said Judge Seymour wants her to pay her a couple of million dollars to get this matter resolved."

A senior United States District Judge based in Columbia, South Carolina, Judge Seymour supposedly heard one of the cases involving Sharon and her wrongful death lawsuit for her daughter, Barrio. This judge also heard one of the cases involving Tom Blackstone, which made her a known name to Linda and Tom. They knew she was a high powered judge, so the idea of her hearing a multi-million dollar case seemed totally plausible. But graft?

"I personally know Judge Seymour and I told Sharon it was hard for me to believe any of this about her. I knew her before she became a federal judge and she was always a very decent person and of excellent character. This situation was becoming more bizarre by the day."

Sharon draws this part of the con to a conclusion, saying she fired Attorney Jeff Johnson because he and Judge Seymour were working with Wachovia and it's a conspiracy to stop her from getting her money.

In June 2012, Sharon called me with a list of questions about what kind of things had to be kept in confidence by an attorney and in what circumstances could they disclose something about a client. She mentions I.S. Leevy and Jeff Johnson by name. She knew someone was on her trail and her brain was twisting around the scenarios that could bring her down. She asked the same question in different ways, creating a very frustrating, circular conversation.

Players: The Unnamed Attorneys

My attorney. The Atlanta attorney. My team. Any of these phrases is liable to roll off Sharon's tongue at any moment. After the Beale/Gary/Johnson attorney debacle, she claims her sister in Atlanta has put her in touch with an attorney there to help her get her money.

"In the beginning she would never tell me the attorney's name," Linda said. "She said he wanted to keep everything confidential until she received her money. I started pressuring Sharon to go to the media about her funds not being released. Tom suggested we get Al Sharpton involved to bring some national attention to the matter. This is when Sharon came up with this attorney in Atlanta. I think it was really an attempt to take the pressure off her to go to the media."

"Sharon told us the attorney in Atlanta was putting together a plan of attack to bring in Al Sharpton and go national with a press conference to get the funds released. She used what we suggested about Al Sharpton and the media against us to buy more time to stall."

Eventually, Sharon came up with a name for the attorney. She started calling him attorney Williams. "How many attorneys named Williams do you think there are in Atlanta, Georgia?" Linda asks.

Plenty, to be sure.

Sharon pitches the new attorney Williams as the person responsible for paying her personal bills and he was the one who had gotten her the home in Woodman Farms.

This scenario went on for several months.

"Williams supposedly came over to Columbia from Atlanta on several different occasions to meet with Judge Seymour, Wachovia and the I.R.S. She even said he had gotten a court order from Atlanta from another judge for Wachovia to release the funds. Attorney Williams supposedly went to Wachovia here in Columbia with the Georgia court order to get the funds. She had me to give her wiring instructions to send what she owed and had promised me. Of course, the wire never happened."

Keeping up the façade, Sharon tells everyone she's directed the Atlanta attorney to get cashier's checks for everybody from the bank. Sharon says he went to the bank, but doesn't specify which bank, to have around fifty checks issued.

Ready to play the Sharon runaround? See if you can keep up: "Sharon says the attorney went to the bank and was there waiting for the checks. He'd been there

226

since nine thirty that morning and at this time it was around three o'clock. She said he was going to have to come back the next day for some reason to get all the checks issued. I told Sharon it does not take that long to issue fifty checks, plus ninety percent of it is done by the computer. All the teller has to do is type what or to whom the check is being made out to and the computer does the rest. At the very most, it should have taken no more than an hour to an hour and a half."

"Sharon, your attorney is very incompetent and he is telling you things that don't make any sense because he believes you don't know any better," Linda told her, trying to look out for her. In the end, though, Linda should've been looking out for herself.

"Boy, did she really have me fooled. The truth is, she really didn't know how banking worked and that's why the things she said sounded so ridiculous. These crazy ideas were coming from her and not an attorney. By this time we had figured out Sharon was lying and didn't have any money and everything she told us was based on a lie."

**The *Be Smarter than a Con* Takeaway: A key lesson is learned from this chapter – don't tell lies about attorneys or judges. People in these categories have the means to strike back and don't appreciate someone tarnishing their reputations. Sharon's operation depends upon these powerful people remaining oblivious to her use of their names in her con games. If you hear repeated declarations about judges and attorneys from someone questionable, pick up the phone and call the attorney mentioned.

He or she will take it from there.**

CHAPTER TWENTY FIVE
Player: The Kandis

Kandi #1: Kandi Buttons

Sharon likes to tell you that when she rises, so will you. "I'm bringing people up with me as I go," she told a target once, meaning her fame would bring fame and fortune to those around her as well. Kandi Buttons is a prime example of this tactic's use.

A hair stylist and beautician, Kandi has fixed Sharon's hair for quite some time. She even accompanied Sharon to the BET Awards in Los Angeles, as a part of her posse. The speculation is that trip cost more than she expected, with the theft of cash from her purse. If only she had an idea about who did it.

Tagging along with the crew on the trip to Charlotte to view Sharon's new home, Kandi was in the million dollar house with Sharon's daughters and was even told by Sharon to start getting some ideas on the types of houses she'd like to have for herself.

The innocent belief in Sharon's benevolence has

this Kandi in a fix. She has heard over and over how Sharon was setting her up with her own salon and maybe even a house. She's afraid to not keep up with helping Sharon in case it really is true. The thing about promises is they need to eventually be kept, otherwise they're just lies and fantasy.

Kandi's managed to keep Sharon's hairstyle looking fresh while the suggestions of success and wealth grew stale.

When Sharon's working a con, she puffs herself out as larger than life. The team of quasi-professionals she claims to employ always includes a stylist. Sometimes, this reference can mean "stylist" in the grander sense of the person responsible for her overall look. Other times, it can simply mean the lady who does her hair. This beautician is almost always Kandi Buttons. However, it can occasionally be Talitha Long, since she also works in that field.

Kandi #2: Kandi Keeply

"My stylist is here somewhere," Sharon whispered to me while she straightened her gold-plated necklace, preparing for the television interview with local NBC affiliate, WIS-TV. Image is everything when you're Sharon Johnson. Having a stylist means you should be looking great and fashionably dressed when in view of the public. Somehow, Sharon didn't quite get that concept totally down. But boy, did she try.

"When Sharon's publicist hired me to style Sharon for a photo shoot, I went to her home in Woodman Farms to look through her closet to get an idea of what I had to work with," Kandi said. "I sure was shocked at what I saw. The clothing and furniture didn't match a wealthy woman. Everything was Payless, not Rodeo Drive."

Kandi picked up on the rental furniture right away and through the process of evaluating Sharon's closet determined her assignment was harder than she thought.

The home was a rental, too, but Sharon told her the attorney bought it for her.

For this particular photo shoot, Sharon needed three different outfits for the images planned for the promotion of her new perfume line, Simply Sharon. First up, the evening gown.

A deep blue v-neck number, this look showed off Sharon's ample bustline and her colorful Monarch butterfly tattoo, just off her left shoulder. Calvin couldn't be left out of this important promotional activity, so Kandi styled him to match in a blue/silver bow tie and tuxedo vest. The photographer positioned the happy couple at the doorway to the formal dining room, with Sharon looking as if she has just opened the door and Calvin walks up from behind to kiss the nape of her neck. The concept was Calvin was enthralled with how wonderful she smelled, naturally because of her signature fragrance.

Her hair and makeup were perfect. The addition of tasteful jewelry completed the scene. Sharon looks totally happy. She doesn't even need to be photoshopped, the smile was genuine.

The second outfit was a black jumper with a lace vest and a gigantic peacock blue leather belt. The dark color photographed well, slimming her profile a bit. Calvin ditched the tie for this setup, going with an

Oxford blue button down with French cuffs and a suit vest. Kandi had the con couple looking sharp.

The final outfit for Sharon's session was casual – black pants, orange camisole and a black lace shrug. She stands in the dining room, taking an important call, looking serious.

The photos, the stylist, the perfume line are all used to promote her agenda. "A few months after the photo shoot, Sharon came into my office at the apartment complex," said Keisha, who works a regular job as a property manager and takes stylist work on the side. "She wanted to rent an apartment for her daughter. Back when I was over at her house in Woodman, one of her daughters was living with her. This one was supposed to be for the other daughter, Ceira."

They had a brief conversation about the rental rates and the application fee, which was fifty dollars. Sharon wanted it waived, but corporate policy wouldn't allow Kandi to do so. "Something didn't feel right. Sharon wanted to put the apartment in Ceira's name and gave me a social security number to use. But, I never ran the background check because Sharon didn't want to pay the fee. I felt like she was running some kind of operation, maybe drugs, and was looking for a place to use as a front. I mean, why else would someone living in a house like Woodman want to put her daughter in a subsidized housing unit?"

**The *Be Smarter than a Con* Takeaway: If you're being paid to do a job, be sure it's something you believe in doing. Where Kandi Keeply went ahead and styled Sharon for the photo shoot, she knew in her heart

Sharon was a fraud. As a professional, she went ahead and completed the work for which she was hired, but failed to voice her concerns to the person who hired her. Had the publicist been made aware at that point, she may have chosen to drop Sharon as a client and save herself the eternally outstanding balance she now has.
**

CHAPTER TWENTY SIX
Player: Calvin Jones

The long suffering boyfriend, Calvin has been in and out of Sharon's private circle for years. They are a match made in Heaven, with his criminal past and ability to overlook questionable practices. They're linked permanently through their daughter together, Aneshia.

Calvin got an early start on his criminal career, with a charge in Richland County in 1987 for second degree burglary at the age of twenty-two. Between 1987 and 2000, Calvin was charged with several counts of burglary, arson and criminal trespassing. He pled guilty in all but one case, which was petty larceny and breaking into a car's fuel Tom.

Did I mention ARSON? Hide the matches because that's scary.

In and out of jail over a long period of years, Calvin has been out for at least the past few years after serving time for burglary. He's been with Sharon through thick, but not really thin. He often seems somewhat oblivious to her machinations and seemingly believes they're flush with cash, even if he can't always see it.

Jobless for most of 2012 and 2013, he functioned as Sharon's chauffer most of the time. He waits in the car while she conducts her business, whatever it may be. Rarely does he come in with her. He is the constant quiet presence, Sharon's rock in turbulent times. Well, except for those times when she's tried to cheat on him. Or lusted after someone like Wess Morgan. That doesn't count, does it?

Sharon's Facebook page announcement of her engagement to Calvin appeared in Fall 2012, "Calvin just asked me to be his wife." She planned a wedding for October. A specialty wedding boutique had a luxurious gown on hold for Sharon for a few months in late 2012. If she could only get her funds released, then the gown was hers.

Not surprisingly, the wedding didn't happen. That she's still married to John Stearman, an inmate with the Federal Bureau of Prisons, didn't seem to slow down her acceptance of Calvin's proposal, though.

A patient man, Calvin doesn't press her on anything – the marriage, the money, or the truth. As long as he can watch sports, eat and play the scratch off lottery tickets every day, he's happy. The frequent moves in the middle of the night should be a clue everything isn't right. He isn't too worried, as Sharon always comes up with a new or even an old place to stay.

His drug and alcohol use was frequently mentioned by Sharon. "I went to a meeting with him twice a day for quite a while," she said to Melissa while visiting the office. Dedication to one another makes the Sharon and Calvin relationship look stable from the outside. His supposed exclusion from the meat of her conspiracies could be a manifestation of her love for him, wanting to keep his hands clean of her criminal activities. The cunning of her plans could also be too complicated for his comprehension. Or, is he in the middle of everything, behind the scenes?

His sister, Taci, claims he has secured a legitimate job at the Michelin plant over in the Lexington/Batesburg area. The background check must've fallen through the cracks if he was able to gain employment with one of the largest tire manufacturers in South Carolina. It seems unlikely, but Sharon's clan has fooled people every day, so maybe Calvin has learned a few tricks from the master.

Calvin's name pops up in conjunction with some of Sharon's failed business ventures. While the P&P Cleaning Service was framed as Calvin's business by his sister, another one called R&S Cleaning also lists Calvin and Sharon together. It's in her main universe of addresses, right off Garners Ferry and Leesburg Road.

At almost fifty years old, Calvin's grasp of the life lessons sent his way is slippery. He barely holds onto his freedom by lurking around the periphery of Sharon's deals. Part of the same family as Taci, he has a number of successful relatives but no interest in holding down a regular job or pursuing a career. Instead, he goes along with Sharon every day, posing for photos when asked and driving her to the next stop in her game of the day.

Karen Johnson is Calvin's cousin. With all of the

mingling between the Davis and Johnson families, you almost need a road map to keep up with who's who. Calvin convinced Karen to secure a loan for Sharon. The loan proceeds were delivered, but Sharon didn't keep up her end of the bargain. She was supposed to not only repay the loan, but to buy Karen a home (for less than one hundred and fifty thousand, as mentioned in the fake accountant letter created by Sharon's assistants) from her settlement funds from the great and powerful hospital lawsuit she claimed gave her enough to live on for the rest of her life. Karen remains a Charlestonian lady in waiting, waiting for her payback like so many other victims.

**The *Be Smarter than a Con* Takeaway: "Ignorance is not innocence but sin," said Poet Robert Browning. Calvin is too close to not know the fault of Sharon's so-called truths. His ignorance, feigned or real, doesn't give him a pass on guilt. Don't get caught up in the euphoria surrounding a pitch someone's making to separate you from your money. Avoid your own ignorance by slowing down and postponing any decisions on requests for money or donations until you've had time to investigate. **

CHAPTER TWENTY SEVEN
The Rest of the Family

Player: Ceira Nicholas

The younger daughter of Sharon, Ceira is with her mother a lot. Traveling together, living together, they spend a great deal of time in the same space. She's very entertaining, with a great humor displayed in her many posts on Facebook and Twitter. She even professes her eternal bond of love for her mother online, "Aint a women alive that can take my mamas place. Sending a big birthday shout out to my leading lady. Words cant explain the love I have for you. Enjoy your day. Muah!!!!"

With Ceira, the apple didn't fall far from the tree. By the time the end of 2013 rolls around, she is in planning mode for her very own event, the Be You on Purpose Fashion Show.

Conceived as a new take on the standard Johnson family money maker, this event is sold as a fashion event for aspiring models. No experience necessary, just send your photo and information and your dream of walking the runway can come true. The catch? These inexperienced young women will surely need someone to teach them about the business and Ceira believes she's just the person for the job.

In early November, 2013, she takes a road trip with her sister to Charlotte. The sister does Ceira's makeup and they attend an open call at a well known modeling school in Mecklenburg County. Her Facebook post afterwards, "I guess Cover girl likes this face. My audition went great!!!"

The modeling school offers a program of instruction and a partnership with a professional photographer and agency for placement and representation. Dollar signs were in Ceira's eyes after seeing how much a person is willing to pay to break into the modeling business. Why couldn't she offer the same program in Columbia?

The Be You on Purpose Fashion Show was her ticket to the big time. Her mother's name wasn't on the advertising, but Sharon's influence was crystal clear.

Ceira creates a new Facebook page to promote the fashion show. She goes through several versions of the official flyer; all of them feature a prominent photo of a high heel shoe but the final image adds a headline font filled with gold glitter. High class, all the way. She lists herself as the Founder and showcases a personal photo on all of the advertisements.

Here's where the Johnson shuffle begins. The first few flyers list a venue called Charles' Place for the event. In true Johnson form, it's not actually where she thinks she's holding it. Bait and switch is in progress. The next flyers list the venue as the Booker Washington

Heights Cultural Arts Center, which is in the heart of Richland County. It's a reclaimed school, turned into a place for community events that's managed by the City of Columbia Parks and Recreation Department. This address starts to be prominently displayed on her Facebook page and the marketing for the show, yet the manager at City of Columbia never signed an agreement with Ceira for the rental.

"I met her once, but we never settled on a date and time. We already have a Department of Health and Environmental Control seminar scheduled for that day," said the Parks and Rec manager when asked about the particulars. She was shocked to hear her facility was listed anywhere, let alone on a website and ad flyers.

Model photos start to appear on the Be You Facebook page. First a few, then a couple dozen more young women are listed as Ceira's runway models. Sweet faces populate unprofessional photos, some of them selfies. Every single face represents a brand new victim.

A good fashion show is more than models and clothes. You've got to have quality entertainment. "DJ Phadded on the 1s and 2s" plus the emcee for the evening are all part of the total package. Tickets are only $20 in advance, including full bar and food for the evening. But don't worry, even if things get out of hand, "security will be on the premises."

The first clue this fashion show was falling apart was the lack of rental agreement with the city. The second clue was the emcee. This afternoon drive time radio personality had nothing about it listed on her twitter feed or the radio station's website. Two weeks out from the show, the emcee tweets about hosting an event on the same day in Charlotte. Clearly, she won't be at Ceira's soiree.

A week away from the big event, which was first going to be February 28th and then it was to be March 1st, (bait and switch, part two) the DJ posts, "Ladies, if you have a particular song you want to walk out to, inbox me." From this point forward, all activity ceases on her Facebook pages, including her personal profile page.

Curious about the outcome, I made contact with one of the younger models via a private message.

"Do you know how I can buy tix for the show?"

"The show has been cancelled," she replied.

"Oh, no! What happened?"

"I have no idea. Mike just told me today."

"Like cancelled forever or just postponed?"

"Maybe for good. The director of the show was not very clear with him. He got a text from her, not word of mouth."

"Maybe it's for the best. You'd think the show director could talk to people directly, but if not, then it might not have turned out the right way anyway. Sorry to hear you're disappointed."

"It's cool. Michael plans on putting on his own show soon anyway."

The complete disappearance by Ceira from her own event is classic Sharon style. Her plan to get tuition from her modeling students failed because of her inability to pay the upfront costs associated with the fashion show.

The biggest missing piece for the event was the

clothing sponsor. Runway shows generally showcase a designer or, at the very least, a department store or high end boutique. Never was any mention made of the clothing source. How odd it would be to have the models just show their own clothes. Even gimmick fashion shows have sponsors. No names were associated with Be You, other than Ceira and her fantasies. It was all about making a name for herself and getting paid. Her life philosophy is neatly summed up in her Facebook post from June 2013, "LETS GET THIS MONEY FIRST, FALL IN LOVE LATER!!!! #N DAT ORDER."

Holding a steady job has been tough for Ceira, so it's only natural she'd turn to the ways her mother holds so dear. A stint at a daycare, retail worker at Wal-Mart, caregiver for a home care company – none of these jobs lasted very long. And no wonder, as she would post while at work plenty of complaints about her current employer. "Bored, cant wait to get off," she writes. Taking a picture of herself in the mirror, she posts, "Headed to the trap. (Or her other favorite quote – Headed to the $$$$.)" A girlfriend asks, "which Wal-Mart you work at?" She posts photos of her handwritten letter received from her baby daddy and says she's just vibin' to Pandora, writing him back. While she's at work. Way to go, employee of the month.

Her name's used by Sharon to rent apartments and secure other goods and services, clearly with her consent. She goes wherever her mother goes, and they help one another make it from day to day. A tough, streetwise woman, Ceira is well on her way to living the legacy of Sharon's deceptive traits for many years to come.

Player: Aneshia Jones

Sharon and Calvin's daughter, Aneshia, seems to
be separate from her mother and sister's machinations.
Mostly. That is until May 2013, when she tells a story
straight from Sharon's fictitious world to her employer.

"Mom doesn't want anybody to know, but she's
moved to Charlotte," Aneshia said. "She's trying to get
away from Tom and Linda, plus they got her a house up
there anyway."

"Who got her a house," I asked.

"The network. They bought her a house and she
moved up there. But, she's gonna be back and forth for
a while to Columbia, too."

There's no house in Charlotte, or Columbia for
that matter, with Sharon's name on the deed. This lie
cemented Aneshia's involvement with her mother's
illegal moves.

Aneshia appeared to work hard and do a good
job for a number of months. However, the stress of
keeping up the fakery was too much on her, so she quit/
caused herself to be fired by making odd mistakes. For
example, her schedule to begin her shift called for her
to start working at ten o'clock in the morning. Instead,
she chose to go in at seven thirty, just because it was
better for her. Is there any job where you can change the
work hours on a whim, other than for someone who's
either in charge or self employed? Not likely. She then
simply stopped showing up for work.

Not as prolific as her sister, Ceira, Aneshia was
pretty active on social media herself. Her usual
comments were positive sayings and prayers for God
to bless herself and others. I was totally convinced she

wasn't like the rest of Sharon's brood until that fateful day when she ran that line about the Charlotte house past me.

During her pregnancy with her latest child, she suffered complications that called for total bed rest lasting several months. This forced period of leisure was served as an inpatient at the hospital where her sister Ceira gave birth. For a period of about three days, both daughters were in the hospital, just down the hall from one another. Linda and I were visiting at the same time and while Linda stayed with Ceira and the new baby, I went down to see Aneshia.

She was all set up, with cable TV, room service, her phone and computer. She had been there for a month already, clearly making herself at home.

"Wow, Sharon, you all must have great insurance for a hospital stay as long as this one," I said.

"Naw, we ain't doin no insurance. Aneshia's on Medicaid."

"How is that possible?"

"It's easy, she jus went down there and filled out them papers."

Medicaid is a program for the poor. If Sharon has the money she claims to have, how can she let her own daughter be on Medicaid? I wondered if Linda knew about it.

An hour or so passed and I was ready to go. Linda brought my purse down to Aneshia's room, since it had been in Ceira's room. Even though Sharon had been filling Linda's head with lies about my feelings for her, she was still kind enough to look out for me by taking care of my purse. I wish I'd asked her then if she knew about the Medicaid situation. Sharon wouldn't allow it, of course, since she successfully kept us separated.

Player: Barbara McDaniels

The popular lyric from The Monkees hit song from the late sixties, "I'm a Believer," is an apt description for Barbara McDaniels. While they are close and definitely related as cousins, Barbara didn't raise Sharon. But she follows her with devotion very much like that of a mother to her child.

A photo posted on Sharon's Facebook wall showed a triumphant Barbara shaking hands with the real estate agent. For all appearances, it was the image of Barbara taking ownership of the house Sharon bought her, just as promised.

So, why is it that Barbara doesn't live in that house? The photo was staged. The house wasn't purchased by Sharon, for Barbara or anyone else. Sharon hasn't purchased a home in her lifetime. Barbara and her husband still live in their modest home in Northeast Columbia.

Barbara puts forth a very public persona of praise and devotion to the Lord. There's no reason to doubt her faith. In fact, it's a very similar faith in her pseudo-child Sharon keeping her blinded from the truth.

Sharon asks Barbara for advice on whom to call for a mortgage loan. She also tells her about her plans and dreams for huge public events, book tours and the like. Sharon's so sincere with her plans, Barbara still believes them even after years have passed and nothing materializes as Sharon said it would. She banks on Barbara's naïve trust, since it's Barbara's son-in-law that Sharon cons out of thirty large.

**The *Be Smarter than a Con* Takeaway: Birds of a feather, flock together. This old saying, dating back to the 1500s and William Turner, gives you a hint about the nature of relationships. People who are close to one another share something, be it family ties or a point of view. Those of similar tastes congregate in groupings. In the case of this family, they share their knowledge of trickery and fraud to get over on those who trust too freely. **

CHAPTER TWENTY EIGHT
The Celebrities

If you're a celebrity, Sharon's interested in you. Of course, her favorite of all time is Tyler Perry. He's the key in over half her cons. But, hey, who is Sharon to play favorites? There are plenty of other celebrities that could be used in her games.

Her favorite thing to do is pick out new celebrities to target, sometimes as names to use in her propaganda or to actually target for a scheme where she can ensconce herself in their world for a brief period to get what she wants.

She throws around names easily, like my favorite, "Toya, you know, Little Wayne's baby mama. She's making a line of shoes for me."

These celebrities have been used by Sharon for years. Some of them are aware; most are not.

***

Player: Reverend Al Sharpton

If asked, Rev. Sharpton would have no idea who in the world Sharon Johnson is. However, she's invoked his name on many occasions to say how he defends her honor, ready to fly in at a moment's notice on her behalf. The discriminators at the bank, the unscrupulous attorneys – no one can stand up to Sharon's protector, the great and powerful Al Sharpton.

Except he's never heard of her. Ever.

When the heat was being turned up by Jeff, Tom and Linda, in August 2012, Tom and Jeff push Sharon on getting her funds released. If she can't make it happen on her own, with her legal staff already in place, then she needs to draw national attention to the situation. Who better to shine a harsh line on discrimination than Al Sharpton?

Sharon didn't want her antagonists to make the call, so she found a way to stop them. She claims her current attorney is flying her out to Los Angeles to meet with Reverend Sharpton in person. The timing works out so she's there during the BET Awards. As luck would have it, she gets to walk the red carpet with him and they make a plan for him to come to Columbia and sort out her problems with the bank.

On August 23, 2012, Reverend Al flies into Columbia and has a meeting with Sharon's attorneys and the bank. Or so she says.

Tom and Jeff find it odd they weren't invited to the meeting. Jeff is especially suspicious of the whole scenario, since Sharon doesn't have any photos of this red carpet thing and surely the local news would cover a national figure coming to town.

Jeff does a little cursory research and uncovers this headline from a Google posting, dated the same day Reverend Al was supposed to be in Columbia: "Rev. Al Sharpton & National Action Network Re-Iterate the Call for National Gun Control As Sharpton & Brooklyn D.A. Charles Hynes Prepare to Occupy the Corner Where A 13 Year Old Was Shot Last Night in Brooklyn."

Uh oh, he wasn't really here.

A little further looking turns up one more damning headline from the date he was supposed to be with Sharon at the BET Awards: "Rev. Al Sharpton & National Action Network (NAN) to continue NAN's Voter Engagement Tour in Cleveland, Ohio at Greater Abyssinia Baptist Church on August 14."

The one being taken advantage of in this pairing is definitely not Sharon, it's Al Sharpton.

Player: Fantasia Barrino

A promise of a perfume line featuring Fantasia's image with a signature fragrance, created by Sharon, was the lie told to worm her way into Fantasia's world. Known from her success as an actress and musician, Fantasia was the winner of American Idol's season three competition in 2004 and a natural mark for Sharon.

Sharon wants to be close to Fantasia in any way possible. Her business manager had a legitimate contact with Fantasia and his willingness to put Sharon into her circle was the beginning of an obsession. From wanting to live in her neighborhood, to attending her concerts and creating a product for her, Sharon's vision of her friendship with Fantasia knows no bounds.

She's over at Talitha's hair salon one day, getting her 'do crafted, when she hears a promotion on the radio that Fantasia's in town, at the radio station right now.

"Stop, I gotta go!" she shouts, jumping out of the chair and dropping the salon drape on the floor. She rushes over to Hot 103.9 and runs right in to see Fantasia. She has one of her handy minions take a picture, just a little more proof of her so-called relationship.

A concert in Florence was a close enough drive for Sharon, so she posts several pictures from the audience and even a one on one with her and the star.

The whole episode with the house on Bevington in Piper Glen also involved Fantasia, since the purpose was to live in her neighborhood. What's a little mortgage fraud among friends?

One of the more entertaining side notes to the Fantasia obsession was the fitness video. Sharon called five or six times in the summer of 2012 to explain why she was missing meetings with me. The excuse was she was still up in Charlotte, filming an exercise video with Fantasia. If you've ever seen an exercise video, the people on screen are in perfect condition and could kick your butt. Sharon's a hefty girl; she could no more exercise for an hour than fly to the moon. The rolls of fat would fly up in her face and knock her out. That's not the image you'd want in your video, I promise.

Fantasia has done a lot of projects, but an exercise video isn't one of them.

The perfume line was the main event in the Fantasia story. Sharon's bath and beauty operation was all set to produce and market a special fragrance to carry the singer's name and likeness. She had a detailed contract in her possession to set out the specifics of the arrangement. This document was not created by Sharon, but Fantasia's people, as it was legally sound and protective of her rights to the finished product and marketing. The caveat: Sharon was to put up one hundred thousand dollars of her own money for promotion and marketing. To launch a national brand, it takes a deep pocketbook. Sharon's self promotion made her seem like a good business partner.

When questioned about the timing of the marketing, she had no clue what needed to be done or in what order. For her to pull off the requirements of the contract, she'd need professional help. By herself, it was impossible. Perhaps she was thinking Fantasia's team would pitch in and take care of everything and still give her a cut. Why anyone would insert herself into this type of situation without the expertise or finances to make it happen is a real mystery.

When she lost her chance at Fantasia, Sharon moved on to Diane Barrino Barber, Fantasia's mother. She convinces the mother to sing at the Empowering Women to Excel conference in June 2013. Anything to hang on to her shred of connection with this celebrity, Sharon courts Fantasia's mother for her signature event. The nature of the audience was surely a surprise to Ms. Barber. If she was paid for her appearance, she is one of the lucky ones.

Player: Domonique Scott
"I'm so honored to be here today with a woman

who has overcome so much and is ready to make a difference in our generation, in our community. I'm talking about Sharon Johnson," said Domonique Scott as she opened her remarks at the 2013 Empowering Women to Excel conference. "She is a spit ball of fire and has not ceased to be a woman of inspiration in many ways."

Domonique looks like a perfect target for Sharon's next game. A quasi-celebrity, Domonique Scott was on the short-lived reality show on TLC called The Sisterhood. This show was a one season long look at the wives of Atlanta preachers, controversial in many ways and doomed to cancellation.

But no matter how short the show, Domonique aka Pastor D, was an actual reality show star. Sharon reaches out to her and sings her the usual hymn of falsehoods about her life. Pastor D shows up at the 2013 conference and gives an over the top performance. Toward the end of that evening, she was heard asking guests if anyone paid for their tickets. She was catching on to the reality of Sharon's show, which is no money for her, all for Sharon. Sharon should've treated her better; they were a better fit for one another as friends than Sharon even knew. They both allegedly used some of the same tricks for personal gain.

In late 2013, Pastor D was indicted by a Fulton County, Georgia grand jury on charges of submitting false information about a tutoring company with the goal of getting federal funds for the program. Marcus Garner of the The Atlanta Journal-Constitution reported, "A Fulton County grand jury charged Domonique Scott, one of the stars of TLC's 'The

Sisterhood,' with first-degree forgery and three counts of giving false statements, authorities said. Prosecutors said Scott submitted bogus documents purporting false assets and liabilities related to the ownership of a tutoring company that allegedly only existed on paper in an attempt to qualify for the federal Supplemental Education Services tutoring program. Scott sent to the state Department of Education a false balance sheet, a false statement of net income, a program summary showing a false start date for her company and a forged letter from a fictitious bank representing a non-existent cash line of credit, prosecutors said."

Player: Bobby Kristina and Whitney Houston's Mother

Whitney Houston passed away in February 2012, a terrible and tragic loss. Her name was in the news a good bit following her death, which likely gave Sharon the idea to include something about her in her cons.

Sharon claimed to have given her book to Bobby Kristina and also claimed to have lunch with Whitney Houston's mother during her visits to California and Atlanta, Georgia.

"That's where I stay when I go to L.A.," Sharon said about the Beverly Hilton Hotel, the site of Whitney's death. "Imma have to stay someplace else from now on." This landmark luxury hotel has a range of reasonably priced rooms and an entire collection of sixteen penthouse/king rooms and suites that must be booked verbally as the pricing is too dear to be booked online. It's possible Sharon could've afforded the three to four hundred dollar per night charge for a regular room. Possible, but not probable.

The reason for even mentioning the Houston family was top of mind awareness. Sharon wanted to be relevant and at that moment, an attachment to the Houstons was relevant. A true opportunist, she grabs whatever she can to make herself look to be part of the Hollywood rich and famous.

Player: Michael Vick

Professional football player Michael Vick is yet another celebrity name Sharon tosses about with familiarity. Sharon mentioned getting together with him when we met one afternoon at Applebee's on Two Notch Road. She was carrying her famous faux leather binder filled with her contracts and business deals – AKA forged and manufactured documents, just to make it look good – and was gushing with the details of seeing Michael Vick and his posse recently.

Linda and Tom were the reason Sharon even knew anything about Michael Vick, since they were originally working on a book deal with him through their company, Creative Publishing. This deal was in negoTiation at the time Linda and Tom met Sharon, so she felt like she had some true insider information on him.

In this state, a lot of football players get drafted to the pros. It's not uncommon to run into someone who's got a friend playing football in the NFL. Sharon craved notice by the rich sports players and saw her chance to hook up with Michael Vick.

"There was never any face to face with Sharon and Michael," Linda clarified. "She had a few conversations over the phone with his manager, but nothing ever came of it. I don't know what she was trying to get from him, that was never clear."

**The *Be Smarter than a Con* Takeaway:
Con game is short for confidence game; the criminal gains your trust in order to separate you from your money. Sharon tried to gain the trust of both Fantasia and Domonique Scott as a way to make herself look important and further her desires. **

CHAPTER TWENTY NINE
Player: Minister Lamont Bubba Potts

"So, you didn't get paid, either." A familiar refrain among those who've been engaged by Sharon to perform work for her, Minister Potts unwillingly became part of the Victims of Sharon Brotherhood. She was an unknown at the time of their introduction; a referral from a trusted friend that knew he provided typical advertising agency services, such as graphic design and media management. Sharon was looking for help with another of her vanity projects and made contact with Minister Potts for this purpose.

Curiously, the date she first met with the minister was April 20th, the very same day she met with Melissa to discuss her several graphic design projects. The crossover was intentional, as Sharon just wanted it done as quickly as possible, regardless of who provided the services.

Over the course of their brief relationship, Sharon disclosed her mental anguish at the injustice she's suffered at the hands of Linda Wilson and Tom Blackstone.

"Tom and Linda stole three hundred thousand dollars from me, it was devastating. I bout had a nervous breakdown over it," she whined. "The girls had to coax me out of a dark room a day at a time until I could get over it. I mean, it's not like I don't have any more money, it's just so hurtful what they did. That's why I'm so behind on getting my publicity out for everything."

As the Media Minister at United Church of Jesus Christ, Sharon knew he and his wife would be susceptible to her "walk with the Lord" spiel, the sad story of financial deception she'd supposedly suffered and her mission for empowering battered women to overcome their abuse-filled pasts.

When she met him, curiously without anyone from her usual entourage, the projects she had in mind were a press kit and the magazine, Out in the Street. At least ten different magazine covers for this fictitious publication have been designed by at least as many graphic artists over the past few years. Without fail, the cover features a full frame photo of Sharon, along with glowing titles proclaiming, "Sharon Johnson, Road to Success," "10 Steps to Financial Freedom," "Sharon D. Johnson, Author, Speaker, Editor in Chief."

Minister Potts created the latest cover, set to debut with the full magazine in May, 2013. "My magazine's coming out on May twenty-fifth at the conference," Sharon said in April, a month before the debut date. At one point, Sharon made some actual headway on producing this magazine when she was still working with Linda. With Linda's coordination, a couple of articles were written and photos obtained to print as feature stories in her inaugural issue. Other articles were in the works, but never finished.

"Everything on the cover I made for Out in the Street was a fabrication," Minister Potts said. "Sharon just asked for a mock-up, so I set some type to show her what a cover could look like. I was clear that it was for review only, yet it started showing up everywhere, including her Facebook page. Why she was using it when she knew it wasn't real I don't understand."

Since Sharon wasn't forthcoming with the funds for the design, the only part ever completed was the cover and the press kit.

The stated purpose of the press kit was to showcase her enterprise, Dream Development, LLC, as an overarching organization managed by Sharon that would be perfect for a reality show treatment.

In Minister Potts's capable hands, this six page, full color press kit was tightly designed, prominently featuring several poses of Sharon in business attire peppered throughout the layout. Its cover proudly proclaimed, "Author, Speaker, Entrepreneur & Philanthropist."

The next page described Dream Development. "Dream Development, LLC is the end result of many projects envisioned by CEO Sharon D. Johnson. Her vision was far reaching but attainable. Her mission was very clear to all. She would use all available resources to help others grow and reach their personal goals. Ms. Johnson began this journey by writing her personal story of betrayal and abuse. She shared this story with local shelters, colleges and young ladies in the area seeking assistance and advice. Dream Development has expanded to include two books: *The Fight for My Love* and *The Fight for My Love: Final Chapters*, Barrio Bath and Beauty Products, You Too, A Non- Profit Organization, Out in the Street Magazine and SAC Geer, Children's Clothing Line. In addition, Ms. Johnson is well known throughout the area for back to school events and her annual Women's Empowerment Conference."

Page three is a full biography of Sharon, told through the rose-colored glasses of another Kool-Aid drinker.

Following the page of unwarranted praise is a snapshot of Barrio Bath and Beauty, with copy pulled straight from the catalog.

The next to last page focuses on the You, Too Foundation. "You, Too is a support group organized to help abused and battered women cope with their circumstances while understanding that they are not alone. Many women feel they must live with verbal and/or physical abuse because they have no one to confide in or they are ashamed to let others know how they are treated at home."

The press kit concludes with the phone number for Sharon's business manager and booking agent, followed by listings for Patricia Sullivan as "Sharon's Personal Assistant," and Talitha Long as "Stylist." Sharon seems to be confused on these roles, though. Her stylist has been several different people, often all at the same time as she tells it.

"She kept wanting me to do more and more, but I

wasn't willing to proceed until I'd been paid for the work already finished," said Minister Potts.

He heard the garden variety diversionary stories from Sharon, including, "I'm in Atlanta, so I'll get you when I get back;" and "meet me at Wal-Mart on Garners Ferry and I'll bring your money then." Sharon blamed several money mix-ups on her hapless assistant. Based on the last page of the press kit created by Minister Potts, it's Ms. Sullivan. Sharon's blaming her uncoordinated payment schedule on Ms. Sullivan.

Right.

When he finally pinned her down about the payment, she slid over two separate checks. They remained face down until she left. The shock came when they were turned over by the minister: two starter checks drawn on Wachovia Bank.

These checks were written by Sharon in May 2013. Remember, though, the acquisition of Wachovia Bank by Wells Fargo was completed on January 1, 2009. At the time of their utterance, Wachovia checking accounts didn't exist. The minister knew better than to attempt a deposit, opting instead to call the toll free number on the checks for confirmation directly from the bank about their validity. His fears were confirmed – the accounts didn't exist.

He confronted Sharon at their next meeting. She was indignant, saying there's no way the money wasn't there. Her assistant must have written those checks out of the wrong account, and boy, "good help is hard to find!"

Her promise to make the checks good goes unrealized, with his billable time written off as a bad debt.

Sharon pitched this same Out in the Street magazine project to me in November, 2012. I spent time quoting the production costs with several printing firms and created a page ladder to get the project ready for design and layout. One thousand copies of a twenty-eight page magazine on gloss stock, perfect bound, ranged from $3,500 to $4,700. When it came time to choose a printer and get started, Sharon said she'd have Tyler Perry's people do the printing. I think the cost was a surprise, with her expectations being somewhat lower. She backed away from me on this idea, ultimately pursuing the minister for the exact same job.

Her plans for Minister Potts were bigger than just graphics, though. She wanted him to be a motivational speaker at the 2013 Empowering Women to Excel IV Conference.

Sharon claimed to know the minister from her church and added almost seven years to his age when asked to describe him. Even simple questions don't warrant straight answers.

The minister is physically limited and an outspoken advocate for greater accessibility in both public buildings and private home construction. Sharon's proclivity for taking advantage is not dimmed in any way by his circumstance and she treats him with disdain equal to her other victims.

The Christian angle is evident here. With Sharon comfortable in the knowledge gained over years of practiced cons, the likelihood of a true Christian confronting her or chasing her for payment is slim.

Minister Potts readily admits his Christianity and

deflects his involvement with Sharon by not wanting to unjustly accuse someone of wrongdoing. Perhaps if he had the full picture of what Sharon truly is, he might feel differently.

He was not a part of the program at the June 2013 women's conference.

**The *Be Smarter than a Con* Takeaway: Those who take advantage of the disabled can look forward to an eternity in hell. **

CHAPTER THIRTY
Supporting Players

Player: Robbie Donner

Robbie is a tangential player in the Sharon game, being engaged for the latest cover of her book. He really hit the target with his graphic design by using the broken heart as the centerpiece of the layout. It's simple, yet right on point.

Her employment of a known book designer furthers her claims of credibility, which after all, is the only thing of value in her world. Her fictitious concoction of the author/speaker/entrepreneur/philanthropist motif is a hungry beast, needing to be fed by a steady stream of propaganda. This book cover is yet another piece of hokum.

Player: Albert Fundley

Albert came into Sharon's world, courtesy of Carolyn Graham. A handsome man and a professor at Allen University, he was a pilot and ex-officer. "Not stable," came Carolyn Graham's initial assessment rather quickly. "He may be someone you might not want to deal with, because it could be he was running a con on Sharon, or she was running one on him, but it's impossible to be sure."

Carolyn knew him, but not well. Sharon knew him, too. As her date to a gang wedding, there may have been more to their relationship than anyone else could confirm. She was with Calvin at the time, yet didn't invite him to be her escort for the wedding.

His handiwork for Sharon lives on in at least two projects. First, the holiday catalog for Barrio Bath and Beauty bears his mark clearly on the back cover, "designed by Albert." Sharon seemed very proud of this catalog when presenting it to Melissa for a refresh in early 2012.

The work was amateur at best. It'd garner a failing grade in a sophomore level Photoshop class, with the worst clipping paths imaginable. (A clipping path is used to isolate an object from its natural background, making it easy to place onto a different background.) Low resolution images, different fonts on every page, floating pictures of Sharon's daughters and fiancé Calvin and multiple variations on the same toll free phone number make it a poor piece of graphic design.

This so-called catalog is printed on gloss paper and saddle-stitched, coming close to being a proper booklet but still falling short. The paper and print feel like it came off a printer or color copier, but definitely not from a traditional press. Staying with Sharon's formula, it's trying to appear grander than it actually is.

The second project was the video trailer for Sharon's book. The Fight for My Love: Final Chapters got the movie treatment from Albert's production of several scenes from the manuscript.

Scenes were shot around town, including Sharon's daughter's apartment interior and the apartment complex exterior. Video editing wasn't his forte either; so he'd better stick to higher education.

Player: Ruth Law

Mrs. Law is a victim, plain and simple. She's representative of all the many landlords who've had the misfortune to rent to Sharon and her family. Almost one hundred moves in the past, always running from eviction, Sharon packs up under cover of darkness and disappears. What makes Mrs. Law stand out is her success in obtaining a judgment against Sharon, in the amount of three thousand dollars, for the back rent and damages to her property. This lady is elderly and didn't deserve the loss and aggravation dished out by Sharon in her usual approach to real estate. Unfortunately, Mrs. Law won't see any benefit from her win in court. Sharon's not interested in settling her debts.

Player: Jake Fulsom

Sketchy, meet your twin. This gentleman has his own line of t-shirts, books on home buying, talent shows and more. Oh, did I mention he doesn't look like he's on the level? John shows up in the summer of 2013, right around the time Sharon takes over the bookstore at Columbia Mall. He's pushing his wares and she has him hold a home buying seminar in the store on a Saturday afternoon. If she thought he was bringing in a bunch of business, she was disappointed for sure.

His home base for the t-shirt business is the parking lot of a vacant store near the hood off North Main Street. Wait, near the hood might not be the best description; perhaps IN the hood is more accurate. Promoting himself as an author, entrepreneur and speaker, he's the male match for Sharon. They scammed each other, so this relationship was a wash.

**The *Be Smarter than a Con* Takeaway: Even if you feel like you're the only one who has been taken advantage of by a con man, it's worth it to report the crime. Tell the authorities, file a case and let your friends know. The momentary embarrassment will be worth it if your case can stop this person from hurting others, now and in the future. **

CHAPTER THIRTY ONE
Player: Mary Louise Corning

Mary Louise Corning is a wide-eyed innocent lady who speaks in a soft voice and matches her outfit with her precious puppy whenever possible. As an aspiring writer, Mary Louise found the idea of being a published author highly desirable.

Mary Louise fell under Sharon's spell, offering to assist her with projects and events so she could learn how a published author conducts business. Sharon never paid Mary Louise for her services; instead creating a sort of internship for her to work whenever she had time away from her regular job at the bank. Her relationship with Sharon lasted for several months. While under Sharon's tutelage, she was duped into participating in Sharon's over-arching con by recreating a fake letter from an accountant that Sharon used to convince others she had big money from a settlement on the way.

***

"Where I come from, she would have been beat down a long time ago. She would have been beat within an inch of her life. But, she has been taking advantage of people who have a better way about them than she does.

I asked a photographer I knew who took pictures of Sharon if she was taken advantage of by her. She said no, she wasn't, but she knows a lot of people who were. The photographer said she has paid me every cent I have ever asked for, yet everybody else I know of has been taken advantage of by her. Sharon wanted to have professional pictures to put herself out there as something she's not.

I met Sharon in early Fall of 2010, after I moved to Columbia in 2009. When Calvin came into the bank to open an account, he got to telling me how his wife was a writer. I'm an aspiring writer, so it was interesting to me and he started telling me how Tyler Perry had purchased her stories and was going to make movies out of them.

I said, 'Wow, she must really be good.'

Calvin said she was good and to keep writing and something will happen for You, Too. Sharon said later he was running his mouth too much when we met.

Calvin said she had to go and meet with Tyler Perry and by this time, in walks Sharon. I'm finishing his account and he introduces us. He tells her I'm a writer as well and she tells me about her book and how her life has changed drastically and she needs people she can trust. She didn't want any of her family to work for her because she didn't want them in her business like that.

She began to tell me, "Be careful when you get your

book published. On my second book, I went through a publisher but I self-published the first book. There are going to be other books as well. I just need someone I can trust to work with me, like a personal assistant."

"Really? Oh, I would be interested," I said. "Whenever I'm not at the bank, I can work with you."

She said she could pay me.

"I'm not worried about getting paid because when I work with you I'm learning about the book business and publishing."

"No," she said, "I don't want you working for free. Let's set a meeting and talk about this. I'm dead serious. People I trust, I'm taking them with me. If I move up, they're moving up. Think about how much you'd charge for your services."

Gee, I think it would be a privilege to work with an author. Naïve, stupid me, Lord have mercy. We made an appointment for like, three to four days later. I run home, tell my best friend and partner, I tell her all about Sharon. She looks her up online and found something and said this could be for real.

I'm calling my family in Detroit and Illinois, saying "I'm going to be a personal assistant to this up and coming black author and it's a way to get my work out there." Oh, my Jesus.

I had been feeling pressure from my friends and family to do something about my work. I hadn't always believed that I had the gift of writing, I'd been chicken about it. Maybe she can teach me and give some pointers.

For some reason, my aunt told me to not read Sharon's book. My aunt told me to stop reading because she thought it would affect my writing and my voice. Gabriella, my best friend, read the book and she was cursing! I gave it to Gabriella to read and she kept saying, "Tina, this is bullshit. This is bullshit! Who in the hell published this? If somebody is getting published writing like this, then YOU are a superstar."

Well, I wanted to ask Sharon about Tyler Perry after I heard Gabriella's comments, so I did. Sharon reiterated that he had purchased all of her books (two books, one coming) and was going to be working with her on a movie about her life. All of that equaled eighty one million dollars.

What sent up the first alert was Gabriella's reaction to the book. Now that was a silent alert. I paid attention because she and her daughter are avid readers. They eat books, I'm talking about big, thick books. They can tell if someone really had a writing talent, Gabriella and her daughter could. "Mary Louise, be careful," Gabriella kept saying.

I thought at first it was her being overprotective. She has always been an overprotective person, especially where I was concerned. "Once I get my stuff published, you'll see that this is God blessing me and everything will work out, Gabriella."

I drew up a work contract with Sharon, and we both signed it. She's telling me my first piece of work with her was to contact Talitha Long and let her know that money was going to be deposited into her account. Believe it or not, she had me contact Calvin, too. And Ms. Sullivan. She had me do it this way: "This is Mary Louise Corning, Sharon's personal assistant and I'm calling to make you aware of funds that will be deposited into your account."

I typed up letters to Calvin and Talitha to that effect and mailed them. But, one of them came back, but I can't remember which letter came back. If you put on a formal face, but you're supposed to be familiar, it seemed to just be furthering the deception. Gabriella thought it was odd, but hey, I just work for her and I'm not really going to question it.

Even though I called her, I hadn't met Ms. Sullivan yet.

The accountant letter was another job she had me do. I didn't think I was doing anything illegal. I used to be a graphic artist, so I knew how to do that. I doctored it. I took the accountant letter Sharon gave me that had very specific amounts on it and removed them, put the letter together and copied it and made it look like the original letter. She said it was strictly for the purpose of her family going in her belongings and she didn't want them to know what they were getting.

What Sharon gave me was an actual letter, not an email version of the letter, to work from. My version talked about people and no numbers at all. I gave her a printed document to use, just like she asked me to do.

All of this all occurred before Sharon's birthday in October 2010. I went to her birthday party at Embassy Suites. I stood up like a dodo bird after the initial people spoke and was all emotional about what a great person she was and said I was going to stick by your side and I'm really proud of you. She and anybody that knew she was scheming must have been rolling in the floor in their minds, just laughing.

That was the night I met Ms. Sullivan. Cold and

impersonal, but professional. Sharon told her, "Mary Louise writes as well."

"Oh really? Well, give me a sample of your work and we'll go from there," Ms. Sullivan said.

"Gabriella, get down here and get down here QUICK. Bring me some of my work."

Gabriella brought my work over and I gave three pieces to Ms. Sullivan, who is supposed to be a publisher. The first was part of a book I'm writing and the other two were from other projects. I don't have them back to this day. She never made any comment, ever. I called her several times. And she didn't return any of my calls. By this time, Sharon started complaining about Ms. Sullivan and said how Ms. Sullivan treated her like an idiot.

One day Sharon had me over at the Alexander Pointe house. She wanted to go for a walk, so I said ok.

"I don't know what I'm going to do. I found out that Patricia Sullivan is ripping me off. She wants control over everything. She wants to control the house in Blythewood, the house in Charlotte and she wants me to put the homes in her name. She wants to pick out all the furniture, and have total control over my life. She wants me to take all of the gold out of my mouth," said Sharon.

"Is Ms. Sullivan gay? Does she have a thing for you?"

"No, I don't think so."

I told her she was crossing the line and this was beyond what a publisher does. She began to tell me how Ms. Sullivan charged her for so many books. And then, she was hustling, making up her own perfume, candles and all that other mess. She was making scented candles to go with the fragrance set. She showed me perfume, lotion and that one candle.

We're walking and talking and she's telling me how upset she is and then Patricia (Ms. Sullivan) calls. Right then, I don't know why it wasn't another clue for me, but she lied on the phone to Ms. Sullivan right in my face. She told her she was out of town, but she was in Columbia. She said she was way out of town, like in Charlotte, but I thought, hey, we're in Columbia.

Then, she goes, "Oh, you did, you heard from Mary Louise ?" She holds the phone out for me to listen and said, "I told her to call."

I didn't hear Patricia say this, but Sharon said Patricia said "I heard from your personal assistant and her funny little voice."

I didn't hear that from Patricia, so it could have just been Sharon saying that. "She's got a funny little voice, trying to be all professional."

Then, I decided at that second I wouldn't work with Ms. Sullivan. If someone could say that, I told Sharon then and there, "Can you get my work back please, since I think I will go the self publishing route?"

Sharon said she would, but she never seemed to have a chance to get it back. Ms. Sullivan never returned my calls, even though I left several messages. According to Sharon, Patricia was going to put it in the mail back to me, but it never came. I'm afraid Sharon's going to use it as hers in the future.

I was over at the Alexander Point house for a couple of hours and Sharon said she didn't like that house. "You know, I bought this house and I don't like it." This is after the birthday party. "I just don't want to be here."

"What is wrong with the house, Sharon? What's wrong with it? It's a nice house."

"Listen, that money is coming through and you wouldn't believe the people I have pulling at me. Everybody wants something and I just can't do it. I have to go hide. A lot of times, I just sit here right upstairs and peek out the window because I'm trying to hide from people. I just don't want to be bothered. I just don't want to be here. I don't know what I'm going to do with this house," she said to me.

"There's another house in Charlotte, in Fantasia's neighborhood. I'm neighbors with Fantasia and I've met with her a couple of times," Sharon said.

I told her to give the house to her children, but Sharon said they don't want it, either. One daughter, in Virginia, has a family and the other two daughters don't want it.

"Maybe I'll just sell it. But, hey what are you and Gabriella doing about where you're staying?"

"We're going to move."

"Really? Why don't you move here? I would rent it to you. I'm living in Charlotte or Blythewood, so what does it look like for my personal assistant to live in a trailer?" Sharon asked what I could pay and how would seven hundred dollars a month be?

I said it's too much, so how about six hundred?

"I'm going to go through my Realtor® so they can draw up the papers and the rent would go towards the purchase of the house," Sharon told me. That lie went on until she came back with a picture of a house that she claims was hers in Charlotte and said it was the house she just closed on.

"Tell Gabriella that I'm not going to rent this house. I'm giving it to you."

"You're kidding, right??"

"No, I have to set up tax shelters because I have been in trouble with the IRS because of not paying taxes properly on employees of a business we had."

She kept on, "What do I need with all of these houses?" She took me to a house that she said was Calvin's house, but it was hers but she let him stay there. It was in a subdivision near there. Calvin came out of the house, so he was inside. It might have been Talitha's house, I'm not sure.

"If you don't want this house, I'll buy you another one, the choice is yours. When I get all of this paperwork straightened out and the IRS releases the money, I will get everything done."

That sounded good.

In December, we went on cruise, Gabriella and I, so in the latter part of December, Gabriella went into the convenience store, bought a ten dollar lottery ticket and won two hundred thousand off a single ticket. Gabriella and her daughter were crying uncontrollably when I came home, Gabriella couldn't even speak, she kept waving this thing. My knees got weak and I just went to the floor. It was real and I went to Miami for Christmas. Gabriella got everything straight with the lottery folks, got her money and then blessed her family and me. She said I was her best friend and Gabriella insisted on getting me a new car. I took it to show Sharon and said, "look at what God has done for me." I told Sharon that Gabriella has come into some money and now, I know you said you'd give us the house, but if I could pay anything on it, I would.

We already started packing and I told her to let me pay a year's worth of rent. Now, Gabriella won the money in December of 2010. So, we packed up, and Sharon's like 'ok, fine, let's go ahead and do this.' Every time we needed to sign the papers, something would come up, which was fishy. Now, she's doubling back and covering up with another lie. She didn't want to sign, so she said, "Now, I've told them to get this all together. Just forget them and I'm going to give you the house."

She was moving to Charlotte in Fantasia's neighborhood and we're approaching the Empowering Women's conference in February 2011. Sometime before that, she asked me to bring Gabriella over to the Alexander Pointe house to show it to her.

She sat us down in the kitchen and began to tell us people are ripping her off because she's wealthy. "I'm tired of these people trying to rip me off and take advantage of me. They try to rip me off and I just don't think that's right."

This chick stands up and says, "Let me show you something." She brings out this bank statement.

"It just doesn't make sense, and they're holding up my funds and my name is at stake here. People are not doing right. Look at this," Sharon said. She brings out this statement from Wachovia, an actual bank statement. The format was different than my bank, but all I saw was eighty one million. The statement didn't have transactions, but it looked more like the second page of a regular bank statement from like BB&T.

She said that she was five thousand dollars short and needed the money. She'd tried to borrow it from a man who told her, "you want $5,000, I will give it to you but you'll pay me back $40,000." She didn't say who the man was, and I asked if he was a loan shark. My cousin in Detroit used to be a loan shark, and he doesn't even have rates like that!

"My name is on the line and I'm not paying that kind of money." She just sat there, looking at us.

I told Sharon that he doesn't want to give you any money and that man is ripping you off big time. She said, "I need the five thousand dollars for the conference." Before I knew it, Gabriella had agreed to give her the money. We usually talk about everything concerning our finances. But before I knew it, Gabriella said, "he's asking you to pay $40 for the $5, but if you give me $10,000, I'll give you the $5,000."

Sharon said, "Really? If you give me the $5,000 for the conference, I swear to God I will pay you back the $10,000."

Gabriella said it was a good investment and I was silenced. My immediate thought was we have to draw up a contract. Let me draw up a contract, everyone signs and it will be notarized.

Gabriella withdrew cash from her own bank, which was Wachovia, and gave it to Sharon.

"You'll have this back in fourteen days," Sharon said. This was the latter part of January, 2011. "I promise you, you know I'm not that type of person, I'm not dishonest and you will have double this money back," Sharon said.

The contract was signed inside of the Woodforest

Bank on Garners Ferry Road and was of course taped by the bank's security cameras. The first meeting we had and everything else that happened at the bank should've been filmed.

Calvin's account with Woodforest came and went quickly, like a feather in the wind. Sharon has a charged off account with them, but I'm not sure about Calvin's.

Sharon said her daughter Myesha was getting some money from a 401K that she could use. We thought she might be using that to pay us back.

I went to the women's conference Sharon was having and the chick actually asked for two hundred dollars more.

"Can you call Gabriella?" Sharon asked. I told her she'd have to talk to her directly. Sharon said one of her vendors was mad and we gave her that money to help the problem.

The February 2011 conference was at Springhill Suites near the Publix grocery store downtown. She was using me to look good. Outside of the conference, I rolled up in the new car Gabriella bought me and she told bystanders that I was the banker and, "You see what she's rolling in."

In April, we started this chase dialogue with her, asking where is the money. She came up with this fantastic story of how she's going to Atlanta to tape this Monique show with Tyler Perry. She comes back talking about how rude Monique was but never could come up with a date for when it would air. We figured out it was a lie.

Going into the summer, Gabriella being mad as hell is an understatement. By now, we found out the house situation was a lie. We didn't have the money back from Sharon. Money was running out and I was sick, needing to see a specialist but couldn't. Then, when she brought Linda Wilson over and said this is really going to happen, I said all I want is the $5,000 back.

I left messages on her phone, told her she was a con artist. She's having the conferences to empower women but the only thing they'll learn from her is how to steal from people. You will never run from God and He will unleash His wrath on you.

I knew I wasn't going to get the money back.

We went to the Alexander Point house and rolled up and saw the sign on the lawn, it was a For Sale sign. The house was vacant, so vacant. The cement block was blocking the driveway to prevent people from parking in the driveway. We saw it and called Sharon that night. She was talking about how she was sick in the hospital and her blood pressure was up and she was on the psych ward because so many people were running her down about her money. We told her, "You need to meet with us right now."

She met with us at Rush's on Garners Ferry. Gabriella was mad as heck and Sharon showed visible nervousness that night. We sat across from her and she knew I was more diplomatic and calm than Gabriella, who looked like she could throw you through a wall. Sharon spun some more lies and I heard for the first time about Linda and Tom's publishing company.

Sharon said she was about to buy Tom and Linda's company. "If you just be patient with me, it will work out. I had to go ahead and move out of the house, and that got messed up and I'm going to buy you a new one.

If you'll be patient with me, I'll be good to you. I'm working with these people now," Sharon pleaded.

She was about to go to Atlanta and meet with Michael Vick and his people.

Sharon called me months afterwards (the last time I saw her with Linda was in the summer of 2011) and said she was coming into some money from a seminar and she would just keep giving it to me along the way to pay on her debt.

After Sharon didn't pay me the money, her relative would come into the bank and she wouldn't speak. She did eventually say to me that Sharon's being influenced by some bad people, but I said I think Sharon's the bad seed.

By the way, I made the flyer for the women's conference. I never got paid for any of the work I did. She never paid me anything, ever."

**The *Be Smarter than a Con* Takeaway: A lot of unhappy events befall lottery winners. In this case, by telling the con artist they'd come into money from the lottery, they were setting themselves up as a target. If you are lucky enough to win the lottery or gain an inheritance, keep the news to yourself and hire professionals to advise you on your funds. A good tax attorney, licensed investment advisor and CPA will go a long way towards properly securing your financial future. **

CHAPTER THIRTY TWO
Player: Jeff Downs
The Diary of Deceit

∞∞∞∞∞∞∞∞∞∞∞∞∞∞∞∞∞∞∞∞∞∞∞∞∞∞

Jeff Downs is a good man with a giving nature. He was convinced to help Sharon through his friendship with Tom Blackstone and Linda Wilson, both of whom had been woven into Sharon's life of fantasy. Through elaborate promises of high returns on his investment in Sharon's Empowering Women to Excel Conference, Jeff provided exactly what she needed – cold, hard cash. He made the conference happen, furthering her guise of generosity towards women in need and the belief that Sharon was a Christian benefactor.

The following is from Jeff's hand-written journal during the time of his involvement with Sharon. Jeff had already committed tens of thousands of dollars to her for the February, 2012 conference at The Hilton in downtown Columbia when he began his journal entries.

***

On Sunday, April 29th, 2012, I heard from private sources and a high ranking official at Wells Fargo Bank that he could find no record of an account with eighty one million at the bank and no sealed orders of any kind with any large amounts as per the Federal Court of South Carolina.

On Monday, April 30th, I began to investigate on my own and on Monday and Tuesday I visited the attorneys George Johnson and Hammond Beale. Neither had represented Sharon Johnson in any action. (I suppose they both could have been untruthful, but I doubt it.) I also spoke with Judge Margaret Seymour at her office by phone and she knew nothing of either the You, Too Foundation or Sharon Johnson.

Next, I spoke with attorney Willie Gary via his international cell phone and he reported, "chasing around with Sharon Johnson and her fantasies, but there was nothing there."

The two ladies at the Hilton Hotel and the Ruth's Chris steak house had no knowledge of any other parties (namely, the attorney George Johnson and Judge Seymour) trying to pay for the You, Too Foundation conference.

I made contact with Marshall Cain of Wells Fargo Financial Services and the current manager of the Wells Fargo branch on Assembly Street and they knew nothing of Sharon Johnson. Nothing.

On Wednesday, May 2nd, I spoke to Tom and Linda about my findings. They were at the USC Law Library and were very upset with me and continued to defend Sharon and the eighty one million settlement. Even more so, they defended the $1.5 billion award for racial discrimination payment from Wells Fargo. They assured me, for like the two hundredth time, the money was there and would be released soon. Linda had seen the accounts and could get copies of the statements to confirm everything.

On Thursday, May 3rd, Tom asked me to meet him at BoJangles and was still very upset with me. He wanted to know if I stood by my stories of my investigation, as their follow-up (and Sharon's) with the people I had talked to showed none of them knew me or had ever talked to me, even though I had visited and talked to them all in the last seventy-two hours. He was going to cut me out of most the money I was supposed to receive, which was some $2.2 million, because I was disloyal to Sharon after I had raised some $200,000 for her.

On Sunday, May 20th, I visited Tom at his apartment and we sat in the car and had a very friendly conversation for about thirty minutes at which time he again told me he would get me a bank statement confirming Sharon's funds. I gave him $80 in cash since he needed to get some food for his grandchildren. I have been helping Tom for years, since he is such a close friend. On Thursday the 24th, we met again at BoJangles and Tom again confirmed Sharon had the money. But, if they gave me a copy of the bank statement to prove it, I wouldn't receive all of what had been promised because they had lost faith with me. Also, Sharon had moved into Woodman Farms into a huge rental house and she had about $8,000 worth of dental work done.

My moving company was not called to move her

because of the lack of trust. We'd moved her twice before for free! Yet, NOW they didn't want to take any more money from me? (After several hundred thousand, they developed a conscience.)

The money she had and was spending came from her "new" lawyer who has been at the Hilton going on three weeks, "getting her money." What??

Was Linda taking over the negotiations with the new lawyer? They were to meet at the Hilton on May 29th in the afternoon. That was called off and moved to Thursday, May 31st because Willie Gary would be in town. Really? This is getting more far fetched and deceitful with every passing day and lie.

Each lie adds to the web to move the story play to the next week. This play has been going on for more than a year. Tom and Linda are totally bought into Sharon, even though I have supported them for over four years. They've painted me as the disloyal, untrusting partner even though I furnished the entire operation for more than a year since Sharon came into the picture.

The whole thing with Sharon appears to be a fantasy built on lies, deceit and now conspiracy and fraud to solicit funds. She seems to build one lie on another as in a play or maybe writing a book.

But now she has money that she says is coming from her present Atlanta attorney (who has no name) until the funds hit. Maybe she has some settlement money and isn't telling. Also, she has said she's being offered a movie deal for her new book by some well-known producer.

Questions are: as smart and savvy as Tom and Linda

are, how could they help perpetrate this hoax for over a year and not see through it or at least question Sharon's stories while at the same time using my funds, but keeping me away from Sharon? Why was Calvin kept out of the loop? What is the motive for doing all this deception? To have a big birthday party, to save the You, Too Conference, to not have to work, to get to visit Wess Morgan, to get new teeth, to be a big wheel, to cover one lie with another until the layers pile up in this fraudulent solicitation and conspiracy to commit fraud, all using the death of a child as cover. It doesn't get much lower than that and again....WHY? Why do all that?

On June 1st, Tom reports the meeting with Willie Gary and the Atlanta attorney didn't happen (of course) but Sharon said the Atlanta attorney wanted to wait until next Tuesday. This delay until next week has happened more than thirty times. Sharon's story is that the Atlanta attorney has been here over three weeks, with his family coming over on the weekends, to get this issue settled. What?

Sharon is spending money from somewhere (the Atlanta attorney?) and can't give Tom cell phone money to keep his phone on and help with his rent after I have paid hers many times.

It's June 4th and Tom says he talked to Sharon and she is going to give up a copy of the bank statement. I may lend him a phone.

Tom says we will have the statement from Sharon today.

It's June 8th and I've asked again twice for the bank statement. No go.

On June 11th, Sharon and Linda are going to Virginia to meet with media folks on Monday to go public. Calvin is driving.

The three left at four in the morning from Columbia on the way to Virginia. They will meet with the media reps for the first time at 4:30pm today. They will return to Columbia on late Tuesday afternoon or Wednesday. This smells fishier and fishier.

The next day, Tom reports the group will be back on Wednesday and they're meeting again with the media folks today. Tom is now near the end of his patience and is getting very wary of Sharon. I think Linda is, also.

June 13th brings news from Tom; the group is on the way home and everything went well with the media folks. Her "lawyer" still says he will have her money by late Friday. They may be too "tired" to talk about things today. Sharon now has Tom back on the belief wagon and here goes another week, which now totals over fifty.

Two days later, I met Tom at the library on Parklane. He said Sharon had talked to her Atlanta attorney and Willie Gary. "They called her and she decided to take the call," Tom said. "They" related Sharon would have her money next Wednesday. If not, then Sharon was "going public." This is the most fraudulent situation I have ever heard of. Sharon keeps on giving the parties involved hope when it's all her lies. She has let Tom get evicted, he's spent hours and days buying them all cars, houses, and plane tickets besides milking me out of money, money, money.

Linda is up her ass so far, she can't see the light. Sharon will get charged with conspiracy and fraud, as she lives pretty well in Woodman Farms.

On June 19th, Sharon is promising money will be in Wednesday the 20th. She has promised several folks they would be paid by Friday. Sharon is also going back to Virginia to be with her daughter who has a brain defect and has seizures and goes into a coma. She, Calvin, and her other daughters are there to be with her.

It's Tuesday and Tom called. He wants to get "Occupy" and others to demonstrate at the bank on Friday if nothing has happened. He and Linda are trying to get this organized and obviously they believe still. I hear Sharon's daughter is going home from the hospital and Sharon wants to get back to deal with the bank and the demonstration. No more mention of any attorneys, including "Atlanta no name," Willie Gary, Jeff Johnson…even though "Atlanta no name" was supposed to be here since the first of May at the Hilton.

The 20th came and went. Through Friday, nothing happened except Sharon got a call from the bank to come in at 3:30pm on Friday. It didn't happen, of course. The meeting is now put off until Monday.

Also that day, Sharon had a meeting set with Mrs. Rogers at Wells Fargo on Assembly Street for 1:00pm. I wait in the parking lot for thirty minutes. No Sharon. Also, letters with her situation are supposedly faxed to Wells Fargo execs out west and to the branch managers at Wells Fargo on Assembly Street and the main branch downtown. Tom is desperate and he believes. This smells worse and worse. Who is ever going to check and verify Sharon?

The following Friday, in the evening, Tom said Sharon went to the bank and the lady told her to push on and she would get her money. "Atlanta attorney," Sharon and Linda are to meet Wednesday morning to go public. I spoke to Jennifer Rogers at Wells Fargo – nothing. A Susan Rogers used to be at the Main Street branch, but she's gone. Tom said letters had to be faxed from Sharon's phone and would happen today.

June's almost over. Tom and I agreed with the texts that it was of greatest importance that Linda meet the "Atlanta attorney" with Sharon and have input and confirmation into the ongoing process. Tom said they met and the attorney went to Wells Fargo to demand that they give her the money by Monday at 9:00am. Supposedly they met at Sharon's house and were meeting again this noon. They were said to have a petition signed by Al Sharpton, etc. and the public outcry would begin Monday unless the money was available. Tom said they were going out to dinner tonight, Sharon, Linda and the attorney. He feels strongly that it's happening.

July 2nd, this is getting stranger. Tom is saying the "Atlanta attorney," Sharon and her children flew to LA and walked the red carpet at BET network awards with Sharpton and that he got a big award and he was going to Wells Fargo headquarters on Sharon's behalf to secure her money. Her "Atlanta attorney" is paying for all of this, plus her home and expenses. What?

What is going on here? It's possible that she has had some original settlement money for weeks and is trying to stiff Tom and Linda and everyone she owes. Just my opinion, we'll see.

July 5th, will sign deal with Al Sharpton on July 6th. He will have the money in two to three weeks. Verify through Facebook, etc. the activity of who is where and when.

Jump to July 12th, Tom says Sharon had a twenty minute conversation with Al Sharpton himself. Would have the money by August 1st. Let's call a meeting to go over anything verified.

I hear on July 20th that Al Sharpton is coming to Columbia on Sunday night with his people. Don't know why.

Two days later, Tom cursed me out for speaking to Martin McFadden who does carpentry for us. His wife Barbara raised Sharon, I think; they're cousins. Tom said nobody knew Sharon had moved to Woodman Farms. Why is everything secret if this situation is legitimate? Tom said Al Sharpton and the "Atlanta attorney" were now to arrive at 6:30pm to go to the bank on Tuesday July 24th. Why go to the bank here when they were said to be working with the Wells Fargo headquarters in San Francisco?

On the big day, Tom texted me about finding him a job and he'll report on the other later. He's selling Kirbys door to door 15 hours a day to show his probation officer he has work. I didn't hear anything that day besides the message from Tom.

On the 25th, Tom said Sharon met with Sharpton and the "Atlanta attorney" and that he wouldn't have to work after next week. She wouldn't tell more, "because of all the talk going on," meaning me. This has got to come to a head soon, as Sharon is living pretty good and all other parties are tapped out. What are Tom and Linda thinking, still believing?

The last week of July, Sharon tells Tom it's going to

be this week and she'll call him so he can quit work.

August 2nd, papers signed to insure of no additional lawsuits. The next day, Tom needs $100 for the weekend, as he sold five Kirbys but doesn't get paid until Monday. With all the latest, no mention of Sharpton or the "Atlanta attorney" and where Sharon is getting the money to live. Linda is spending almost every day with Sharon and Calvin, so she has to know something. If this last attempt fails without happening by August 6th, we must meet to get to the bottom of this bullshit.

August 7th, the "Atlanta attorney" supposedly called Sharon last Sunday and told her he and Al Sharpton would be flying in Tuesday or Wednesday to finish the deal. He also supposedly told her she would have her money in three or four days and things would be changing fast for Sharon. She should let Linda handle everything and be a buffer to family and friends. Linda is spending days, all day long, with Sharon. I think Sharon is telling Linda all this stuff to keep her pumped and under her spell – almost captive, like a slave. Why are they not questioning?

It's Tuesday again and the "Atlanta attorney" and possibly Al Sharpton were flying in today to go with her to the bank to get her money. The first time I heard this line was June 2011, but with a different attorney. Bank trip is supposed to happen Friday, August 10th.

"I'm sworn to secrecy, but just left a meeting with Sharon and Linda and should have fantastic news by Tuesday morning. Pray over the weekend," advised Tom on the morning of the 10th. Waiting…

August 14th, Tom called and said Sharon had talked

with or met with Al Sharpton for 30 minutes the evening before. Sharpton was telling her life was going to change with all of the wealth and she should be careful how she handled it. He wanted to get his team to give her some "no obligation" advice as to the handling of her affairs. Sharon agreed.

Sharon said Sharpton said he handles Beyonce and other big names.

In the same conversation, Tom mentioned a Georgia judge, but I'm not sure why. Either way, the money should be available Friday or Monday. Again. Where is the "Atlanta attorney" and wasn't Linda supposed to be representing Sharon in these meetings? Apparently, that hasn't happened, not even once.

How is Sharon paying rent of over $3,000 a month plus expenses for this large home?

August 17th, text from Tom saying everything is good and very close.

August 19th, phone call from Tom, same message as the 17th.

August 20th, text from Tom saying, "this week." My reply, "I'm patient, but it's been sixty weeks and I'm getting sued by the private funder for her You, Too Foundation loan and a lawyer." Tom writes back that he understands and everyone is hurting.

NO, EVERYONE IS NOT HURTING. Sharon is living large in Woodman Farms.

August 24th, met Tom at McDonalds, where he said he's still confident; although if it doesn't happen by Tuesday evening, he agreed that we have to do something. He and Linda agreed to a Wednesday meeting to get real if nothing has happened.

I believe less and less because Tom was saying Al Sharpton had been calling Sharon four or five times and they were coming to Columbia Monday afternoon to finish the deal. He also thought it was a done deal and the only hold up was how much I. S. Leevy Johnson and Jeff Johnson were getting out of the deal.

His comments sounded contrived and made up to me. This whole diary I've recounted (taken as a whole) what almost appears to be the rantings of a deluded and deranged person writing a fairy tale and screwing the people who have been helping her.

August 27th, Tom called. It's our week.

August 28th, I texted Tom to ask, "Is AS here and are they going banking?" Tom replied they were going to the bank at 9:00am tomorrow, Wednesday the 29th, and they had met late Friday and settled everything. First, I have heard the Friday thing. Tom also mentioned an order?

I'm now at the main branch of Wells Fargo on Main Street on the 29th. None of our parties showed at either branch. No word late in the day. Tom still believes. Set meeting with Tom and Linda for after Labor Day if nothing happens. LOL! We WILL be meeting after Labor Day.

August 30th, Tom said he thinks we'll have the money on Tuesday. That's probably the two hundredth time we've heard we'll have the money on any given day. He also said we'd meet Wednesday if the money isn't here. He said he and Linda would be taking over handling everything then. Fourth time on THAT story.

We move our meeting to Sunday because we'll have the money by then.

September 5th, Tom said it's the best chance it's ever been and will call late tonight. He didn't.

September 6th, Sharon wants Tom and Linda to sign documents drawn up by the "Atlanta attorney" concerning paying taxes on any money disbursed. He really believes the money is here and Sharon is about to disburse it.

September 7th, Tom and Linda plan to meet with Sharon at 1:00pm to give her documents they drew up and to sign documents from Sharon's attorney. Where is this attorney? Have they met him?

September 8th, Tom reports what happened on Friday. The bank was supposed to give a two million dollar advance to Sharon, to Linda and to Sharon's daughter. But for some deep, dark reason, the internal transfers weren't made by Wells Fargo to Sharon and Linda. However, the two million was sent to Sharon's daughter in Virginia. It was not an internal transfer, but to a different bank. The "Atlanta attorney" and Sharon were very angry and report they expect this to be rectified on Monday, so everybody should have money by Wednesday. Linda has been spending each day with Sharon and has spent several nights. She is reported by Tom to be in the middle of all this activity and able to confirm its validity.

It's possible all of this information is coming from Sharon, who is pulling the wool over Linda's eyes, as she is still star struck and very naïve and afraid to ask Sharon for solid evidence for all these stories. I hope these are only my thoughts and they're unfounded.

September 10th, Tom reports Sharon would be going to the bank with the "Atlanta attorney" to get her

305

money on Wednesday. She would be getting cashier's checks and taking all of her funds out.

The next day, Tom reports Sharon is in fact going to the bank Wednesday morning and have them issue forty-two certified checks to all of the people she has promised to pay. I thought, what about the two million that went to Sharon's daughter last Friday? This still smells.

September 12th, Tom tried to call four times. The news is Sharon's youngest daughter had a baby and Linda stayed up at the hospital with Sharon for the night. The cashier's checks are supposed to be written already and Al Sharpton is back in town with the "Atlanta attorney." The daughter in Virginia still has the two million, Tom says.

September 13th, Sharon's with the attorneys now and they are grilling her about all the money she's giving Linda. Tom says they might have to let the judge know because Willie Gary was pushing it. BS! Anyway, they are getting certified checks either this afternoon or in the morning. I got a text at nine in the evening, saying no news and we would hear something before noon. BS again.

What happened to Al Sharpton? My thoughts: this is now eighteen months old. The stories are repeating themselves. It's been six months since I talked to Linda in person and nothing has changed. How is Sharon living without money while the daughter has two million from last Friday? BS.

We'll see what tomorrow brings, but it looks like we are another week down the drain.

September 14th, texts received: 1. will call by noon.

2. will call between three and five hopefully with good news. 3. Haven't heard yet, will call. Tom calls, "did you get my texts? I'm very nervous but I believe we are finally at the end of this." He continues to believe.

Let's see what kind of bull she comes up with this time. Lots of drama, no action, another week passes, number seventy-seven.

At 7:30pm, Tom called and said Sharon got her two million, but Linda did not get hers and therefore he didn't get anything either. They (Sharon and/or Linda or banks) are worried about Florida and Tom's case there. BS.

Linda is supposed to get her money on Monday and give Tom his as well. He says he will make a copy of the check for me and then give me mine on Wednesday. I already said let's see what kind of BS Sharon comes up with. Well, I just related it because none of the BS is confirmable as is the case with all of the stories of the last eighteen months.

September 15th, Tom called and says she got her two billion, not two million, and the checks will be cut Monday, forty seven of them, including five hundred million for Linda and the same for Tom. What??

This goes back to the original story of the judge and billions. I want it to be true, but it seems way out there. If it's not true, it is the most cruel, vicious, conniving, treacherous, subjective, crooked, underhanded, demonic plot ever.

September 17th, at 3:30pm, Tom called and is waiting on Linda to call him when she had her check. Then he wanted to borrow money until the checks cleared. Does he have proof? Certified funds?

At half past six, Tom called and now it's Sharon's fault the checks weren't issued. She was supposed to pick up the checks at 11:00am, but she was with her daughter and granddaughter and got to the bank late, which was at 2:00pm. Her contact person was in a meeting until after 5:00pm, so Sharon didn't get the checks. She said the "Atlanta attorney" and Jeff Johnson were pissed because they didn't get their money. But, all is well as the attorneys will bring her the checks tomorrow morning. Tom said Sharon got her two billion last Wednesday, but the bank put a seven day hold on it. A hold on their own certified funds?

Tom was going to ask me for more money until his cleared. So, you want my money when you have a certified check in your hand? My final thought on this situation is I hope and pray it is all legit, but it makes no common sense.

I asked Tom why FL people try to stop Sharon from giving him money, as he owes them. He said, "you don't understand, they just want to keep me from having all that money." It's the same playbook as the last eighteen months. Stall, stall for another week, which is number seventy-nine. I'm looking to see if any kind of check will ever be produced.

September 18th, Tom called and said they, meaning the attorneys, were at the bank getting checks. They were supposed to go at 11:00am, but Sharon dissed them. I questioned about the certified bank checks, but Tom said it wasn't like that. The bank, (which bank?) Wells Fargo, put a hold on money that Sharon has. (Or, did he mean that she had moved it to Bank of America and they put on the hold? On certified funds from a major bank?) This is all making less and less sense. What about her having all her money?

Now Tom says they were going to make some money available today in spite of the hold. As this saga continues, the stories and excuses begin to repeat. We were in this same place a year ago with a September 9th deadline for money.

What about the two million that went to Sharon's daughter? What about Al Sharpton? It's all questionable and we haven't seen one shred of confirmation or verification. This smells of unlawful solicitation of funds. Fraud. Criminal conspiracy to defraud. Who makes up a story about losing a child to gain sympathy and solicit money?

How is Sharon living seemingly at ease, while everyone around her goes broke? Where is the money coming from? Her expenses in Woodman Farms have to be at least $4500 to $5000 per month, just for the house.

The FBI, the State Newspaper, UPI, a court suit, IRS, slander cases from I. S. Leevy Johnson, George Johnson, Hammond Beale, Clarence Davis, Judge Margaret Seymour, Judge Joe Anderson, Al Sharpton, and the BET guy – these cases could all be made. At 8:30pm she says, this is the best I've heard yet, that the Florida people showed up and tried to talk Sharon out of giving Tom and Linda the money. Now it's one or two million, not five hundred and fifty million. Sharon wouldn't budge.

"Wells Fargo has got W.G., M.S and all knowing her business." I can't believe this statement from Tom. "George Johnson is behind it because he didn't say anything. But, the attorney has it under control and if

309

they don't get checks, it will be made public in a big way."

September 19ᵗʰ, Linda and Sharon went to First Citizens Bank, which is the first time I've heard this bank mentioned. They were told they could get Sharon's million this Thursday and the rest of her money would be available next Wednesday, the 26ᵗʰ. So, Tom says they will get $100,000 and they will give me $10,000. In the next breath, he wants $240 that I don't have to pay his phone bill. Then he says that his and Linda's money might clear before Sharon's. This makes no sense and it's more bullshit.

At 2:15pm, Tom calls and said Sharon and the "Atlanta attorney" were meeting at 2:00pm. Then he was gone abruptly. I text, "Sorry I couldn't help with your phone bill. My money is gone, my business is gone and I'm driving for $9.00 an hour." At 4:00pm, he wants me to back him up on the phone bill in case we don't get money tomorrow.

September 20th, I hear the "Atlanta attorney" isn't leaving town until Sharon has her money. He is getting her checks today at 4:00pm at First Citizens Bank. The story gets murky here, but bottom line, she will have all her money off hold next Wednesday and Tom will give me some tomorrow out of the advance. It will be thousands.

At 8:00pm, Tom says the "Atlanta attorney" is now going to get the checks for Sharon, forty seven of them, remember, from Wells Fargo in Atlanta. They already have them ready and they will deliver them on Friday. Then, what about First Citizens, who has $2.3 million of Sharon's money? Sharon claims now First Citizens is giving her an allowance of $50,000, of which she'll give half to Tom and Linda and also something for me. This is the most convoluted, confusing, cloudy crap I have ever heard about banks and banking. It could be truth, which would be stranger than fiction, probably from a deranged mind.

The next night, Tom called and said the girls (Sharon and Linda) weren't going to be able to get the $50,000 from First Citizens until Monday, which I had suspected.

On September 22nd, Tom says the "Atlanta attorney" is meeting with Jeff Johnson in the morning and he will have all the checks to deliver to Sharon. Tom said he was calling Bank of America on Hard Scrabble Road to let them know he wouldn't be bringing a check today. I think this admission shows he and Linda don't have a clue and are being led around by the nose. Monday will be interesting.

September 24th, I had a long day. Around 11:00pm, Tom called to report the "Atlanta attorney" never came to Columbia with the checks, didn't call or anything. Tom thinks he is coming back to town on Tuesday.

September 25th, at 10:30am the "Atlanta attorney" is with Jeff then coming to meet Sharon. Linda has been with Sharon every day, all day for the last thirty days. Sharon "feels bad" that Linda and Tom don't have their money and it's been held up for so long. She's going to give them something from hers at First Citizens.

I went to Drew Wellness Center to see Al Sharpton and Jim Clyburn. They left before I arrived. Funny, Sharon never mentioned that Al would be here nor did she attend. Could it be because she doesn't know the guy?

At 7:00pm, Tom repeated some of the same things from earlier and added Sharon's money would be liquid on Wednesday. Checks should be handed out or transferred via wire Thursday morning.

It's a new day and Sharon's meeting with the "Atlanta attorney" and taking Linda with her to get checks. Tom thinks the holdup was Jeff Johnson and the "Atlanta attorney" wanted to get their money straight with Willie Gary. Unbelievable.

It seems the "Atlanta attorney" wants Linda at this afternoon's meeting so as to make sure Linda is played up to because Linda and Sharon are a package deal for all of the future stuff (is Willie Gary behind this ploy?).

Later that night, Tom calls, which is very confusing. The lawyer was holding the checks until all of the attorneys agreed on the money. First of all, lawyers don't pay clients, clients pay the lawyer. Next, Sharon's hold on the money by the bank is now ten days instead of seven. Why would Wells Fargo put a hold on these monies after almost two years, while it was their own money?

October rolls around and Tom thinks it is happening. The "Atlanta attorney" and his family are here for the weekend and want to get this cleared up before 1:00pm. Sharon's going by First Citizens to see if her money has cleared. I feel the BS is going to new depths.

October 2nd, it's really out there now. Tom said the lawyers had to get a judge to take the money out of the checks and pay them direct. Now all the checks are going into First Citizens into Sharon's account. Linda has an account there and Tom is opening one with $150.

Sharon will transfer to Linda and then Linda to Tom.

Tom couldn't open his account because it's a Tennessee corporation. They're getting those papers in tomorrow. But, Linda is going to go ahead with the money to her account tomorrow. Sharon is getting the check from the "Atlanta attorney" tomorrow. They didn't do all of this today because of Calvin. They didn't want him in on all the details. Tom and Linda are getting separate checks.

Bullshit. This stinks.

All of these stories sound like the same stories we have heard for sixteen months. "The lawyers have the checks," has been said six or more times in the last three weeks. To date, no paperwork of any kind to substantiate anything has been seen.

October 3rd, I texted Tom with, "have you seen the checks?" He called with something about the attorneys are trying to talk her out of giving Tom and Linda the money. This is the same crap from a year ago. He then said they were meeting at 2:00pm to work out the money some other way. Something about Wells Fargo's money and First Citizens' money. Where are the checks? Can't someone at least get a look at them?

The next day, Tom says they won't get their checks because the attorneys talked Sharon out of giving them all that money. So, we won't see checks unless... what? Where is the check for the loan on the Encouraging Women's conference and the one for me?

Anyway, Sharon is getting something from her First Citizens money and will give to Tom and Linda two million today and will then transfer the rest tomorrow. They will be meeting at the bank at 2:00pm. Tom also said First Citizens filed a complaint with Wells Fargo about not funding Sharon's money at First Citizens and the president of First Citizens had called Sharon personally to say he would have everything straightened out at the 2:00pm meeting today. Again, BS!

At 5:05pm. Tom calls and says, "I've got good news and bad news." The bad? Wells Fargo didn't honor the check sent to First Citizens. So First Citizens filed a formal complaint with the FDIC and of course First Citizens' big wig said that should not have happened. BS! Anyway, Sharon went to Wells Fargo to get the checks made out to all her recipients and they gave her an envelope. When she got to First Citizens, she saw it was from Wells Fargo, one check for $2.3 billion, supposedly all of the money they owed less paying the two lawyers directly.

Bullshit.

First Citizens will now hold the funds five to seven days (again, the same bull) but they will give Sharon a percentage on Tuesday, which will be another week gone. Tom says the paying of the attorneys proves it's real.

My side note: I would like to be wrong but this is the biggest crock of shit I have ever heard. We will see what happens before we go in heavy and blow this up. What about going public? We have documents, witnesses, Al Sharpton and yet she's still living at Woodman Farms, unaffected.

They don't want Calvin to see any of this mess because he knows it's crap.

On October 10th, Tom called to say Sharon and Linda were going to First Citizens today (not yesterday as reported) to get a draw against the big funds of $100,000 for Tom and Linda to split. He promised me $5,000 or ten percent of what he's getting, after I've given him one hundred and ten percent of the money I had available for almost five years. He also said the big money was now coming next Thursday, October 18th because of some holidays and the holds they put on funds. BS.

First, let's see what happens on the $100 million, as I believe she has some money from somewhere, but if it happens, I believe that will be all she'll give Tom and Linda and she'll just keep on making up stories on the big settlement for as long as she's allowed to in her fantasy world.

Tom called again. Sharon would be going to First Citizens on Friday to get the draw against her funds in order to give them $100,000. We're suspicious, but Linda went in the bank meeting with Sharon for the first time. So, every other time Linda has insinuated or claimed she was there for a meeting (bank, attorney, Al Sharpton, etc.), it was untrue.

On the twelfth, Tom said Sharon and Linda would go to First Citizens at 2:00pm today and get the money with the rest of the funds to be available next Thursday. But, he also said First Citizens didn't have to give her the front money. This leaves the door open for more smoke and mirrors and delays. Lies, really. There are interbank transfers and these are immediate. All these seven day, ten day, fourteen day holds on bank checks and funds between major banks have been lies from the beginning. The point is Linda wasn't asked to be there last Friday. Why not?

It's the fifteenth day of October and Sharon's gone to First Citizens. It seems her person was out, so she picked up Linda and went back to get money. At 11:15pm, Tom relates she couldn't get any money. He said he was researching the banking laws and they would have to give her all of her money on Thursday. All BS! Tom thinks Sharon gets information mixed up and confused. She's not confused, she's lying and treacherous. She has outsmarted and deceived almost everyone, but mainly Linda and Tom. My prediction, which I hope is wrong, is that Sharon has some money from somewhere, maybe even a much smaller settlement. The vast majority of this bull from the last eighteen months is made up, fantasy bullshit and she is irreparably damaging and defrauding many people. "I'll be shocked if she doesn't have that money on Thursday," Tom said. I will be even more shocked if she does. After all, I've heard hundreds of broken deadlines and promises.

Later on the 16th of October, Tom called to explain how Thursday would work with Sharon getting her money. Sharon and Calvin would go to the bank to do something – get checks, give Calvin money, or just to be sure it's there. Then Sharon goes and picks up Linda, they drop off Calvin and go back to the bank to get Linda and Tom's money. My opinion is this appears to be a way to have two narratives: one, Linda doesn't really know what Sharon and Calvin do at the bank and, two, Calvin doesn't know what Sharon and Linda do at the bank or who is getting what.

This scenario gives Sharon complete control of all the stories to all the parties with no way for anyone to prove or confirm any parts of any story. It's been that way from the beginning. Sharon's stories are what everyone has accepted. She has ruled by deception, lies, fraud and dishonor using Linda and Tom's greed and friendship with unconfirmed stories to rule them like slaves. She destroys lives for her own ego, vanity and desire for power over others. It's simply slavery. I can only hope I'm wrong and if so, may God forgive me. If I'm right, then may God forgive her.

Here we are on October 18th and it seems Wells Fargo didn't honor their cashier's check to First Citizens. Big surprise. Also, the First Citizens people and the "Atlanta attorney" supposedly knew about this situation three days ago. So, the "Atlanta attorney" already got the Atlanta judge to issue an order to Wells Fargo to wire the money immediately (yet there's a two or three business day hold on this transfer?). BS.

I sent Tom a hot text about the one hundred and twenty nine times Wells Fargo has supposedly not met a deadline. Let's ask some hard questions:

1. Did Sharon give $2 million to her daughter?
2. Can we get Al Sharpton to go public?
3. Why are we broke and Sharon is living in Woodman Farms?
4. Does ANY of this make sense to you?

He immediately called back, all huffy about me getting four to five times my money back. He also made reference to maybe taking over all of this from Sharon and getting the money. Same old shit, different day. Bottom line, it will all happen Monday.

What is Sharon's motive? Why are Tom and Linda drinking the Kool-Aid?

Later that day, Tom reports that the money should be good on Monday or Tuesday and if it wasn't, his parole officer, Mrs. Dowd, said if he doesn't catch up on his restitution payments, very soon he will go back to the Florida jail. So, is he playing the sympathy card with me, setting me up for more money or is it just BS? He has had money for the restitution payments, but it's always behind.

October 22nd, Tom wants me to call Mrs. Bowers and tell her that I'll get him the money for his back payments on his restitution, $750 by Friday afternoon. He is very sure money will be available tomorrow as the "Atlanta attorney," the Atlanta judge and First Citizens have all said so. Tom's trying to buy a little time. I called and left Mrs. Bowers a message at the parole board. Sharon keeps saying, "it's all good," and adding to the outlandish story. They are still buying it. Unbelievable. If she's making up this stuff, it would be the lowest, most rotten act a human being could inflict on another and supposedly a close friend.

October 23rd, Linda was with Sharon all day and they said the bank had until midnight to get the funds into her account per the order. So in the morning, they are gonna go and try to use the debit card that goes with Sharon's account to see if the money's there. What?

Why not go online, call the bank or go into the bank and check on the funds? If it's big money, the bank would be running to her! If she went online, Linda could see if there really is an account with money. I smell a rat.

But, using the card… it could be a card on any account. It's about over. Charles will find her with the suit papers. All of these delays have been used by Sharon from the beginning.

The next afternoon, I get a text that Sharon and Linda are at the bank. Then it gets deep; the money wasn't there and will be available on Thursday and the three (now it's three?) attorneys will be at First Citizens Thursday morning and they will get everything straightened out so that Sharon can get her money, pay the attorneys, pay others and the saga will be over. If that doesn't work, Tom has a Plan B that we'll go to. I must get a meeting with Tom and Linda to go over all of this from day one to now, especially since I've been served by the lender for the note Sharon and I signed for the You, Too Foundation's conference in February.

October 25th, Tom said the attorneys didn't meet this morning but were meeting tomorrow and would have information on the release of funds Friday afternoon. Plan B is something about Tom and Linda standing up to Sharon and either going public or getting documents showing the money. My fear is that they don't know what I know, so she'll accuse them of being disloyal and throw them under the bus in an indignant rage. So, I'm gonna call Tom back and tell him we need to meet before they meet with Sharon.

He called me before I could call him and said he had great news. Gloria Allred had taken over Sharon's case and had been working on it since Wednesday. She'd have her money for her next Tuesday.

Same story, different day.

This is the biggest bullshit, ever. How could Gloria Allred be in Columbia and nobody, like the media, know? It's just more BS. Another week gone.

October 26th, Tom said Sharon is at the bank with Gloria Allred. Gloria says the "Atlanta attorney" is crazy and doesn't know what he's been doing. Gloria says she'll have the money by next Tuesday.

"If you buy me a hamburger today, I will pay you on Tuesday." – Wimpy, from the Popeye comic strip. Sound familiar?

My opinion is Sharon was getting a little cornered and thought Tom and Linda were fixing to put her on the spot with Plan B, so she came up with the Gloria Allred angle.

October 29th, Tom called to say Gloria Allred flew back to Columbia this morning and had some documents to present to the bank to free up the money tomorrow.

October 30th, Tom says Gloria thinks the case is so messed up by the "Atlanta attorney" that she must get a judge to write some new orders to correct the mistakes and it may take the rest of the week. Tom's Plan B is to get Jim Clyburn to use his influence to get the money released. My opinion is Sharon won't let anyone look over her shoulder because of what they might see. So, she'll drag out the Gloria BS and then come up with another one. I'm wondering if Linda mentioned to Sharon last week about Clyburn, therefore, presto! Here comes Gloria Allred.

November 2nd, Tom says Sharon has a deposit slip from First Citizens and the money will be available on Tuesday. Sharon was calling people she owes to let them know they would be getting checks. Linda was going to try and confirm this by seeing the deposit slip.

November 3rd, Linda hasn't been with Sharon yet.

November 5th, Tom says if it doesn't happen Tuesday, then Sharon will have to show the settlement documents to the bank to prove the money. BS.

The next day, Tom says the money will be in the account by midnight Tuesday or they are meeting with Sharon Wednesday night to get the money or bring this thing to a head using the lawsuit against me, Sharon and the You, Too Foundation as part of the leverage.

On the seventh, Tom and Linda told Sharon about the suit from the lender for the women's conference loan and she was "upset." We should have the money today or Thursday A.M. Sharon was also calling people again.

November 9th, Sharon was at the bank, ready to get the money. The attorneys are gone and it's all over. She will have all funds available next Tuesday or she will have to turn all of the files over to Tom and Linda.

Tom has Clyburn ready to go. The showdown is either the money or the files.

Was Linda with her for any of the bank stuff during the past ten days? No. No. No.

Has Linda seen anything concrete to verify any of this BS?

November 13th, Tom says Sharon was going to the bank, but Calvin was driving her and Sharon and Linda don't talk money in front of Calvin. Why? Because Calvin knows Sharon is full of shit.

So, they set up to go back to the bank, just Sharon and Linda, on Wednesday to get the money.

November 14th, Tom says they are going at 10:30am to get money. This is like a broken record.

Sharon asks Linda to help with disbursing the

money. Later in the morning, they changed the time to go until 2:00pm. Tom calls and said they actually got there at 3:15pm and it was too late for wire transfers. So much bullshit.

Calvin was with them again, so Sharon goes in with the manager and leaves Linda and Calvin in the lobby while she does business. Afterwards, Sharon says the wire transfers will be done in the morning and she'll get confirmation then. Still, no one has witnessed anything proving anything Sharon has done.

It's tomorrow again and Sharon and Linda are supposed to go to the bank together. This doesn't happen but Tom thinks it's all very close because Sharon and company are looking to buy cars and are ready to do it at least by tomorrow.

November 16th, Tom is beginning to sound frustrated as Friday rolls around and out and nothing happens. Not much (none, actually) explanation this time. Tom says Sharon is very disappointed, as she was looking for the money today for sure! Tom says Sharon is not living large and has been served an eviction notice at wherever she lives in Woodman Farms. If it doesn't happen Monday, Tom and Linda have agreed to meet with me.

Three days later, no money. Tom says he will confront Sharon after we meet on Tuesday.

November 20th, Tom calls up and we meet and he tells me some info about the confirmation of funds. The only thing Linda ever saw was a statement showing the $81 million and two Wachovia letters stating that Sharon did have money for a car and house that she was looking at buying.

We decide he will go see Sharon, call me on speaker phone and I would angrily rip him and Sharon and threaten legal action and jail.

We do this! Don't know the effect yet. But so far, nothing.

**The *Be Smarter than a Con* Takeaway: Don't co-sign on a loan. When you're considering putting everything you hold dear on the line for another person, you need to be sure you know what you're doing. As a co-signer, you are still liable for the debt if the original borrower defaults. The risks far outweigh the benefits. The lender will sue you, the co-signer FIRST, since your credit is obviously better than the original borrower. If his or her credit was that great, he or she wouldn't have needed a co-signer in the first place. **

CHAPTER THIRTY THREE
Player: Carolyn Graham

Carolyn Graham fell into the web of deceit orchestrated by Sharon in 2009 through a planned meeting at Wal-Mart on Garners Ferry Road. A friend of Carol's thought Sharon could help with her book. Recognizing talent and naivete, Sharon used all her charms to convince Carol to help her, instead of Sharon helping Carol, as was originally intended.

Carol was engaged by Sharon to write the original letter from the fictitious accounting firm called Robert and Company, CPA, PC. The firm was supposedly based in Marietta, Georgia, the location in close proximity to Tyler Perry's studio in Atlanta. In any good con, the devil's in the details.

The letter was written in August, 2010 and read as follows:

"Dear Ms. Johnson,

Congratulations on your success with your book, The Fight for My Love. Your steady progress and hard work is a result of your many accomplishments with this book. But the one that stand out is your success in getting the book out to the public, which I know was difficult at times. Your drive has long been known to many of us and I am elated to see you receive the nationwide recognition you have earned because of your years of diligent work. You have made many contributions to charities, along with being a motivational speaker, assist with battered and abused women, and countless achievements in your life. This is a beautiful example of unselfish love. As your accountant, I am proud of you.

I look forward to working with this substantial amount of settlement for {7} million dollars. That you received for selling the copyright of your book, The Fight for My Love. However in our last meeting, we talked about the distribution and investing some of your funds. It was discussed that you will give your children and grands, along Calvin Jones an undisclosed amount. You would invest {1/2} million dollars to Talitha Long for a hair salon, Andi James {10} thousand dollars, Pearly Gaston {6} thousand dollars, and Karen Jackson, a house for under {150} thousand dollars.

Please come in and meet with me on Friday, September 3, 2010 to read and sign your final agreement plan to release your checks. Again, it has been a pleasure having you as my client, and I look forward to doing business with you for many years to come. I enjoyed reading your book as well.

Sincerely,
Robert Goldmand, CPA"

The above letter is exactly as presented to Sharon, errors and all. Sharon's review of this letter concluded it wasn't good enough for her intended use, so she sought out another accomplice to continue working on the content until it read the way she wanted. Since Sharon's level of formal education is quite low, you can't help but wonder what parts of the letter were deemed unsatisfactory. I suspect she asked for explanation for some of the more unusual words. Other than the inappropriate familiar tone in a so-called business letter, the language is a sure giveaway the letter isn't legitimate. A professional would never use the term, "grands," in place of the proper "grandchildren."

The brackets were used to give Sharon the chance to change the amounts in the distributions to fit whatever particular con she was running at the time.

***

When I was writing my book, I called a good friend of mine, Joyce, and said, "I need some help. Do you know anyone who can help with a book I'm writing?"

"The only person I know of is Sharon Johnson, she wrote a book," Joyce said. She was Sharon's friend and got her phone number for me and also was going to give my phone number to Sharon.

Sharon called me pretty quick and asked to meet at Wal-Mart on Garners Ferry in Richland County. We met and for some reason, I had made a cake, a coconut cake, that I brought for Sharon. When I first met her, she was giving me some tips on the book she had written, called *The Fight for My Love*.

She autographed the book she brought for me and I wrote the date and time. It was August 5, 2009. I signed Carlene beside my notes of the date and location, since I sometimes go by that.

The next time we met, she asked how much I charge for my cakes. After talking for quite a while, we got to be pretty close. We would meet at Ruby Tuesday's on Garners Ferry or have lunch at Lizard's Thicket. When I met Sharon, she was staying over there off Leesburg Road and Garners Ferry.

A local newspaper carried an article on Sharon's book. This official book review made quite an impression on me. It talked about how Sharon, had overcome her struggles to be an author, role model and CEO of P&P Cleaning Services. She sounded amazing.

I would meet with my editor at Panera Bread regularly. Sharon was supposed to come and pay this lady for me. Calvin came in and then walked out and Sharon never came over, talked to me or my editor. I didn't know what to think.

She called and wanted to get together. I picked her up and we were driving down Main Street one day, and she was going to help me with my book. She had called someone, I don't know who. She was going to give me ten thousand and it went up to a hundred thousand during the course of the conversation. The person on the other end said, "Your friend will really love you." I could hear the person talking to Sharon through the phone.

She told them to add my name to the list, and I said it was Carolyn Graham!

Sharon then started telling me about her publisher, Patricia Sullivan. Somehow, this led to me telling Sharon about this guy, the man who produced a trailer to promote Sharon's book, *The Fight for My Love*. He wrote a treatment and then worked on the filming. Sharon would spend hours with him.

Sharon really liked him. She even took him with her to a wedding last year and she didn't take Calvin. It wasn't the sort of wedding I'd expect her to attend. It was a ghetto wedding, like a gang banger wedding. I was there, too and I told Andre if he wanted to stay at the reception he could, but "this isn't my cup of tea and it ain't my morning coffee." So I left. I was afraid because there are certain places you don't go, you don't put yourself in harm's way, not on purpose.

Spruce Creek Villas, where one of Sharon's daughters used to live, the guy used for filming part of the trailer for the book. So, he was definitely doing something for Sharon, to go to all that trouble. He became very aggressive and was inappropriate with her.

Sharon acted like she was all into Andre, and doing her perfume line. I was buying the alcohol for making the perfume from Snow Drift Farms, the company that sells alcohol for homemade perfume and my niece taught Sharon how to make it.

Anyway, Andre moved back to Georgia after Sharon promised him money and never paid.

I got invited to visit her at the house that was new construction, at Alexander Point, right off Lower Richland Boulevard. I think she was only there a few months. Sharon told me attorney Hammond Beal wrote a letter to give to the real estate agent about something to do with the house, but it didn't make much sense. That's the house I used to go to and meet her at a good bit.

When we went to Virginia in December, 2010, this Alexander Point house was where she was living.

Now, there was a visit to that house when I gave her two hundred dollars and I saw her with a white guy in a pick-up truck. It was to give to the white guy because she said she needed it. They were arguing and it looked intense but I didn't hear the conversation. She said the guy was trying to keep her in the house, but she wanted out and wanted to move to Charlotte. Calvin's sister said Sharon was in that house illegally. I didn't understand why she wasn't supposed to be in it or why his sister would say such a thing.

What got me was that house didn't have a refrigerator, which I thought was strange. So maybe she wasn't supposed to be in there after all. If Calvin had been working construction and had a sub-contractor's key to the houses for his builder employer, they could've just moved themselves in. Calvin knows more than you think he does on all these schemes. He's a weasel, right in there with Sharon.

330

When I met her, she was on Wingard, then at Alexander Pointe, then went to apartments off Green Lawn, then Deer Park, then Woodman Farms. I don't know where she is now. She has moved a lot.

I then met Ms. Sullivan. She had me to send my work to her and I sent it Certified Mail. She would share with Sharon the flaws in my writing, instead of telling me what to do directly to fix it. Ms. Sullivan said my work was a bunch of junk, which was very hurtful. You just don't know what it was like.

When I went to Virginia with Sharon, we used a rental that I had because my car was wrecked. I shouldn't have taken it out of town but I did it as a favor to Sharon. Sharon and Ms. Sullivan convinced me it would be ok. If you don't watch yourself, these two can get you. Ms. Sullivan belittles you, makes you feel like a nobody. She was really on me. So I felt like Ms. Sullivan had gotten me into this trouble and I wanted to wrap my pink phone charger cord around her neck.

Ms. Sullivan was all about Sharon and was kissing her ass. She just sucked up to her. When Sharon had that thing at the Marriott, the Empowering Women to Excel II conference, she was all over her.

I saw a check Ms. Sullivan wrote Sharon for $50,000. Sharon never cashed it; she just carried it around with her, saying Ms. Sullivan owed her for her books.

Later, Sharon gave me a bad check, drawn on Sun Trust Bank, on November 26, 2009 for $50 for two cakes, right around Thanksgiving. Sharon told me to go downtown to cash it, so I rode down to Main Street. After trying to cash the check, Sun Trust said it wasn't any good. Finally I got her to meet back at Landmark Square right on Garners Ferry, and she gave me $40 cash. She gave a nonsense excuse, just saying something to throw me off about why it happened and didn't pay the rest of what she owed, she just shorted me the $10. I never turned in the bad check to the authorities, though.

I started to question myself, wondering why was I so gullible.

Sharon said she was really busy, as she was supposed to be doing a tour with the singer Yolanda Adams in 2010. She had to get ready for the tour. But she did find time for us to do some things together that year.

I went with her to Virginia again and she spoke at the National Head Start Association Parent Awards Banquet. The program for the event had a glowing biography of Sharon that read:

"Sharon D. Johnson is a successful author and speaker from Columbia, South Carolina. She began her life's journey as a young parent who relied on Head Start to provide care for her children and to enhance her parenting skills. As the young mother of four girls, Jackson participated in training programs and established a lifelong relationship with her Head Start family service worker. Presently, Sharon Johnson is a business owner and the organizer of You Too, a nonprofit organization that helps women and families who live in local shelters. She meets with women on a regular basis to discuss issues such as domestic abuse and support systems. She is a sought after speaker with an inspiring story marked by determination and perseverance."

During her remarks, Sharon said her mother gave her brother away to a stranger walking past on the street. She further played on their sympathy by saying she only had to pay twenty dollars for her rent but she was so poor she couldn't even pay that.

The crowd was mesmerized by her. She had people on their feet! People were coming up afterwards and hugging her.

Sharon had a lockbox full of money at the end from book sales and her speaking fee. This book signing is on Sharon's Facebook page. She had a booth set up and it was listed under HYPD Publications, which belongs to Patricia Sullivan.

She was supposed to give me some money for taking her there. She said by the time we get back, the money will be there. Didn't happen.

I guess to make up for not paying me for the Virginia trip, Sharon wrote a check to pay my power bill to Tri-County Electric Cooperative, but the check was no good. This was December 23, 2010. The checking account was closed. Thanks to Sharon, I'd have no power for Christmas. Plus the power company charged me a fifty dollar NSF fee.

When I look back on it now, I can see what she was doing. When she was in hot water with someone else, she would come running to me. She'd say, "let's go out to eat," or "let's go somewhere." Whenever she would say, "I'm coming to spend time with you," she wanted something from me.

If you give her anything of your own personal items to borrow, you will never get it back. She took my hammer and my ladder from the Alexander Point house where I had let her use them. Also, another example, this lady gave me some outfits through Sharon. Sharon was supposed to give them to me, but she said they didn't look like anything so I never got them. I think she sold them.

She was also supposed to help me get my book published and have a lot of book signings for me. Even the lady at the Holiday Inn Express on Garners Ferry, she was the lady that knew Sharon and she was supposed to get with her about the book signing event for me, but it never happened.

In March, 2011, I gave Sharon three hundred dollars in cash for her to take me to Las Vegas. She was going to give it to Ms. Sullivan for myself, Sharon, Talitha Long and Ms. Sullivan herself to all go on a trip to Vegas. She said Ms. Sullivan had a travel agency and could book the trip for us. I wanted to go to sell my books, but they were all just going for pleasure. My son has a sister that lives in Las Vegas, so it all fit in for me to go and I could visit her while there. To this day, I don't know if anyone ever went on the trip. I know I sure didn't. Sharon gave me a nonsense answer about why we didn't go. I just know it didn't happen for me.

Of course, I asked Sharon about getting my money back. "Now, you know when you book these trips and don't go, you don't get all of your money back. You'll have to call Patricia Sullivan, since she booked it," Sharon said.

I left a message on Ms. Sullivan's recorder and told

her I'd talked to Sharon and I was requesting half of my money back. I never heard back from her at all, either.

A couple of months later, Sharon invites me and some of my friends and Lena the film lady out for dinner at Ruby Tuesday's. She had money sticking out of her pocket book! She treated us to a big dinner, which was nice. Now I think it could've been the money Tom and Linda had given her to help her out a few days earlier.

When we get to June 2011, I gave Sharon a check for six hundred dollars for a car she was going to buy for my son. This was money Sharon said she needed and she was going to put that money back in my account plus some.

"But Sharon, I don't have that much money in my account."

"Don't worry about it. I will put the six hundred dollars back in plus more," Sharon said.

I think she conned me into check kiting, which is illegal. She knew it would take a couple of days for the check to hit the account and said to not worry because it would be back in the account by then. I later went to the bank and put a stop payment order on that six hundred dollar check, hoping I did it in time.

When I was at the dealership, Sharon had my son to meet her there and told him she was buying him a car. She walked off with me to the ladies room and I asked her for the down payment on the car. This is what's crazy – after an hour or so, Sharon said she didn't have the money right now and told me, "Do what you have to do." But she promised again to take care of it.

By taking advantage of my son like that, I thought

that was a final straw for me.

Donny asked if I thought Sharon was going to do right. I told him I didn't know, we'll just have to wait and see.

Way before we were at the car dealership was when she asked Donny to make the fake bank statement. If he did that, he would be taken care of. Not only would she buy him a car, but she'd pay his way through school. I was under the impression this bank statement had something to with a car she was trying to get, but Donny said no, it wasn't.

Sharon asked him to make the bank statement to use in order to get a house in Charlotte.

Later, Sharon said she couldn't use it and what Donny did was unacceptable, which voided her agreement with him. She claimed the statement had too many mistakes on it.

Donny made the actual bank statement like she asked, but it didn't have any numbers on it. She had somebody else put the numbers in it. Sharon claimed she had somebody else at the bank do it.

Now, when Sharon first came to me about this bank statement, she said she needed something to show she had all this money coming in. "I need it to look like it was actually a statement from the bank. It's not going to go anywhere, I just need it for a flash," Sharon said.

I thought she meant that she just would briefly show it to someone, but not let them inspect it.

I went with her to Charlotte and we met with Shelley the real estate agent. While we were there, we went to the post office and Sharon sent one of her books to Fantasia Barrino in the mail. I believe it was Shelley who had Fantasia's address and that's how Sharon got it. Shelley said to Sharon that she knew she was happy to be getting such a fine home. Sharon agreed.

This house was in Fantasia's neighborhood and you had to pass it to get to the house Sharon was buying. She not only took me, but several other people to this house. She was working on convincing people it was real.

What I couldn't figure out was if she was getting such a big house like that in Charlotte, why was she always in Columbia?

She did take all of the fake documents to Charlotte to use with the real estate agent. I think the one Donny did was in there, too.

It looks like the receipt from Mary Louise for making the accountant letter Sharon wanted was before me, in October 2010 and then mine was done in August 2011. I was told to help her with this letter because it needed to be done for the attorney. She told me she had someone at the bank do this letter before, but it wasn't good enough.

Sharon said the attorney told her to sit down and write a letter, which she brought to me so I could type what she wanted on it. The attorney wanted her to have a letter ready so that when the money came in, the money could be distributed the way she wanted it to be. Sharon dictated to me what to write in modifying this accountant letter; otherwise, I wouldn't know what to put or how to spell anybody's name that she was talking about.

Right after that, I saw a letter saying Wachovia had made a settlement for $600 million dollars for discrimination for holding her money back, the original $81 million. She said it was racial; the white people at the bank act like it's not right for black people to get this kind of money.

My friend, Felicia, told me those figures were out of this world and not to believe it.

I thought it was so crazy because I thought at least someone at the bank would have known Tyler Perry, which is where she said her money came from. I can't believe it would've turned out this way. I remember asking Sharon how Tyler Perry got the rights to her book so fast, since it had just come out on the market. She said, "Bobbi Kristina, Whitney Houston's daughter, had a copy and gave it to Tyler Perry, and that's how that started."

Sharon was going to show me her top of the line BMW. She said it was in the garage. And this was right before she moved to the Woodman Farms house. I never did get to see it. She just talked about it, and it was a conversation piece on several occasions. Stereo and Byrd wanted to get fancy, but she told them to cool out because people get crazy and'll start asking her for money. She was trying to keep it modest, on the down low.

At this point, I had to choose to stop believing her. She's living in a fake world.

Speaking of asking for money, I gave her one hundred dollars in cash for a ticket to go with her to the Oprah show in Chicago in June 2011. It never happened. When I asked for the money back, she said a guy named Rob had stole all the money.

I should've been more careful, especially when I saw

she had a way to make a phone call and make it look like it's coming from another number. She would cross the lines somehow. She pulled through a phone number once, but when I called it back, it was from a fire department in San Diego, California. It may be like a call forwarding thing or an app on her phone. It looked like she called me from the fire department number but it was really just her own phone. She disguises her number to call people sometimes.

I think that I became the new Mary Louise and then Linda became the new Carol for Sharon. Linda took over the assistant role with Sharon once Carol had started asking too many questions.

When we met at Red Lobster, Tom and I and Lena Clay (who had a movie production or film company, local), Sharon wanted to talk to these people about filming for her. I was on to Sharon, but didn't know who to talk to and Sharon was blocking me out. I tried to quietly tell Lena what kind of person I was discovering Sharon was and Lena went and told Sharon.

I went through a lot with her. She made you feel like you were her friend. But, she kept people at odds, so you wouldn't talk to someone else she was dealing with and find out things weren't true. I got myself caught up in a bad situation. Of course, she changed phone numbers so I couldn't get anything resolved.

**The *Be Smarter than a Con* Takeaway: There are many resources available for those interested in publishing a book. From writers conferences to hundreds of websites with advice on formatting and links for self publishing, an aspiring writer can get his work into the marketplace. **

CHAPTER THIRTY FOUR
Player: Sammi Collins,
Real Estate Consultants

Sharon set her sights on the high end home in exclusive Woodman Farms, located in the Northeast portion of Columbia, South Carolina. This house was far away from her normal stomping ground of Garners Ferry Road. Several exits down the interstate, it was centrally located in an area known for beautiful brick estate-sized properties and horse farms.

Prices range from the high $350s to over two million dollars. In Columbia, South Carolina, the median sold price is $142,000, so this neighborhood is clearly upscale. The masterpiece golf course is a principal attraction of this lovely community. Woodman Farms sounds like a perfect place for Sharon to call home.

The existence of this neighborhood and Sharon's overwhelming desire to live there sets up another legitimate company to become embroiled in Sharon's saga. Real Estate Consultants is the real estate management firm that ultimately rented the executive home to her.

Linda originally located the house in Woodman Farms. "My attorney said I need to find another place to live because of my wealth. People will be after me and I need to be away from everybody," Sharon shared with Linda. "Plus, I need to live somewhere big enough to film the reality show."

Sharon also said the attorney was paying for the home until her funds were released. A common justification for her extravagant choices, her team of attorneys are funding travel, residences, legal fees and more.

And now for a quick economics lesson: in the real world, clients pay attorneys, not the other way around.

Now that Linda had found the house, she went out with Sharon and Calvin to look at it. Once that happened, Linda's involvement with the house acquisition ended.

At that point, Sharon has Melissa to research the house in the Multiple Listing Service to get the rental details. The company listing the property showed it as available immediately. As a real estate professional, in a normal situation, I would've signed her up as a client and shown her the property myself. Commissions are still paid on rentals, but the money is nominal when compared to a sale. However, even though she was adamant about moving into that house, I still didn't believe she was serious about it. I was already spending far too much time with her and didn't want to begin a world tour of rental properties, only to earn two hundred dollars at the end of it.

The home itself was amazing. Less than ten years old, it was an all brick, four bedroom, two and a half bath mini mansion. With twenty five hundred square feet, the home featured a two car garage, sprinkler system and so much more. The Multiple Listing Service description read, "Absolutely beautiful two story home in the gorgeous Woodman Farms community! Spacious great room with cathedral ceilings, gas fireplace and built-in bookshelves, wired for surround sound. Cozy sunroom. Gourmet kitchen with granite countertops, tile backsplash, gas cook top, built in microwave, custom cabinets with pull out shelving and storage. Master suite features tray ceilings and bathroom with dual vanity, whirlpool tub and separate shower! Backyard deck overlooks tile patio and lush landscaping."

The hardwood floors on the main floor were immaculate. The graceful white columns separating the dining area from the formal living room gave a feeling of extravagance. Painted a pale blue, the master suite was soothing and spacious.

Linda heard the attorney was handling everything. In reality, it was Ms. Sullivan who was handling the deal.

Patricia Sullivan waltzed into the Irmo offices of Real Estate Consultants, finely dressed and ready to deal. She tells the staff she represents an important person who wants to rent the house in Woodman Farms. This mystery tenant is going to be famous and needs a lot of privacy.

The property managers find this scenario suspicious. They felt something wasn't right about the situation, but could not legally prevent the rental from happening.

Everything on the application checked out as legitimate.

Ms. Sullivan gives the information requested to secure the property and rents it under the company names of Dream Development, LLC and HYPD Publications, which is Ms. Sullivan's company. Real Estate Consultants had to go ahead, so the house was leased in June 2012.

Over the course of the next several months, neighbors begin to complain about vehicles being parked in the street. Sharon claimed to be filming for her reality show, which would explain the people and the trucks. The crew and cameramen were obvious and borderline obnoxious at times, all the better to keep up the appearance of legitimacy.

Linda spends hundreds of hours with Sharon at the Woodman Farms house. Melissa visits, too. For someone who craves privacy, Sharon sure does let a lot of people know where she lives.

A pretty long run, the Woodman Farms house is set up as a year lease, but she only makes through January 2013.

The first sign of difficulty came quickly. At the beginning of her third month in the house, rent wasn't paid yet for August so a Rule to Vacate action was brought under Judge Maurer at the Dutch Fork Magistrate on September 11, 2012. Eight days later, the case was settled and Sharon had paid the back rent.

In typical Sharon fashion, another Rule to Vacate was filed again on October 15th. Yet again, she wiggles out of it and settles with the landlord on October 30th. That brings her totally up to date through October's rent.

Trouble hit through a couple more bounced checks. With rent in the vicinity of twenty six hundred dollars a month, you need a decent income to support that kind of cash outlay each month. The second bounced check turned out to be the last.

Behind on the payments, Sharon tries to catch up for the two months' rent she owes. She plays the "attorney's gonna pay my bills" game, claiming she'll have a check from the attorney's certified account to make up the outstanding balance. However, what she actually presented to the property manager was a starter check, dated January 18, 2013, in the amount of five thousand dollars. Sharon signed the check, which was drawn on TD Bank and even made the notation, "late payment." Also typical, she pays almost the amount due, which would've been five thousand, two hundred dollars plus late fees. She wants to give close to the balance, but still always short pays, just on principal.

Knowing how long she could game the system, Sharon hangs on until the first week of February at Woodman Farms. The property management firm had already filed for eviction through the local magistrate's court and turned in the insufficient funds check to the solicitor's office for prosecution and collection.

She moves out in the middle of a Thursday night, taking all her belongings and beating the coming eviction by a matter of days.

Sammi Collins, the owner of Real Estate Consultants, is furious. "I need to get that money for my property owner," she said. "It's unreal what this woman did. Who writes a bad check for five thousand dollars on purpose? I've been trying to get in touch with her or Patricia Sullivan to make this check good. They owe the money, regardless of them moving out."

The investigator from the Richland County Sheriff's Department came out to the property management office to take Sammi's statement. Both the property management firm and the rental house are both located within the boundaries of the county, so the jurisdiction is clear. Sammi already sent the insufficient funds check to the Richland County Solicitor's Office to prosecute, but the investigator pulled the check from that office to include with the overall set of charges he was working. As far as Sharon knows, the enormous bad check came and went, free of consequences and most importantly, free of taking any actual money from her grasp.

By February 21, 2013, the house was cleaned, repaired and back on the market. A better tenant was hoped for by all involved.

The *Be Smarter than a Con* Takeaway: If you receive a bad check, there are several important steps to take for the recovery process. It may take several days for your bank to let you know the check had insufficient funds. Be aware you are still liable for any monies sent from your account to others, so if this check causes your account to have a negative balance, be prepared to react. Call the bad check writer and let him know he needs to make his check good. Don't let excuses convince you to just let it go. Next, send him a Bad Check Notice via certified mail, detailing how much is due, the name of the person who wrote the check and the bank on which it's drawn and a date for payment. If the person doesn't pay, you'll have the documents required to pursue prosecution. Check with your local solicitor for procedures on filing charges.

CHAPTER THIRTY FIVE
Player: Rogie McElveen

∞∞∞∞∞∞∞∞∞∞∞∞∞∞∞∞∞∞∞∞∞∞∞∞∞∞∞∞∞∞

"She has the heart of Dr. Hannibal Lector and the skill set of Bernie Madoff."

With that assessment, Professor Rogie McElveen began his tale of involvement with Sharon Johnson. A respected member of the academic community, Professor McElveen offered to assist Sharon with the book she wanted to write. It was clear her lack of formal education would be a difficult barrier, but as an educator, he was drawn to her need and obvious desire to grow her writing skill set.

Introduced through a family connection, it's all relative, especially when dealing with Sharon. Wilamena, also known as Nekey, is a long time acquaintance of Sharon's and the niece of the first person to actually put together Sharon's manuscript for *The Fight for My Love*. Nekey skirts the edge of Sharon's orbit, hoping the tales of wealth and fame are true. She stays far enough away, though, to not be pulled into the dark hole of true believers. The same wasn't to be for her uncle, unfortunately.

The professor soon found himself embroiled in a fantastical story, surrounded by unsavory real-life characters.

***

I heard Sharon bought a bookstore recently. Kind of ironic.

I was in Orangeburg, lecturing at Vorhees College, when Sharon would ask Nekey about me. I kept telling Nekey that there's a certain lingo that even the nouveau riche don't use. When Sharon kept on asking about me after everything was over that we were doing together, I said even though she has great comedy to herself, she's a nut job. Tell her the next time she asks about me, tell her to call the Moore, Taylor and Thomas law firm and speak to my attorney.

"Hell, tell him to fuck off. I have two attorneys," Sharon said back to Nekey.

I met Sharon right before Easter in 2004. We met through Nekey and we had gone to pick up something that Sharon got for Nekey's baby. I found it odd that when you enter someone's home, unless maybe it's family, you usually turn on the light. Sharon kept us in the dark.

It was over at Byron Road Apartments. It's like 9:30pm at night and by that time it was dark. The lamp she had was really like 60 watts and really dim. She's sitting in a white night gown, mostly in the darkness, when I hear her voice.

"I understand you're a professor," Sharon said.

"Well, I'm more of a lecturer."

"I've got a book I've been writing over the years, my life story about what I've gone through with this man."

I acted interested and, at this time, I had no idea she was a drug dealer. She's been a drug dealer since Henley Homes. You know, the ones they tore down. It was rumored that her brothers owned Club Rolex and it was one of the biggest drug busts in South Carolina history. They buried drug money somewhere and Sharon told me that she still visits her brothers, even recently. I don't know if that's true, though, about her visiting them.

All Sharon ever did was sold drugs, had babies and lied. She was known for that. The lady in the dark.

But before I knew everything, I'd ask, "What's up with your friend?"

"She's just different like that," Nekey said.

Four months later, I encountered Sharon again. She showed up at my house uninvited. I lived across from Nekey at that time. I'd just gotten in from Benedict College and she must have been driving by. Sharon lived in Carriage Place Apartments by then, she'd already moved from Byron Road, but was still in the Garners Ferry Road area. She saw I was home, I think she was stalking me, basically.

She had this woman with her and I could tell she was a crack head. Now, at that time, Sharon had an entourage who did things for her that were being paid with drugs. She dealt crack, never did anything other than crack.

"I need you to come to my house," she said.

I balked.

"What you think, I'm going to kill you or something?" She can be funny, and say funny things out of the blue.

"Call me after sundown on Saturday. Maybe we can set up a time."

I heard back the following Tuesday, and I ignored her call. This woman's not serious.

I called her on Thursday and I then went over to Carriage Place with Nekey. When we arrived, I noticed that she a barrage of people in her home.

The guy that died from AIDS, Carl, was very loyal to her. He'd do anything for her and they went together. She was his drug supplier. She was with Calvin, the brainiac, at this time. She goes to get her manuscript and comes out with these two notebooks and said, "This is my book. About eighty pages and another one hundred to one hundred twenty pages, written on front and back."

"What is this?" I began to read and couldn't understand it, it wasn't even verbiage. I saw a lot of sentence fragments, more of writing in a diary but not for the masses. She wrote the way she talked.

I tried to tell her about the different writing styles, for research, for journalism, for literary purposes, for academia.

"I told you I'm not educated," Sharon said.

I spent three months with her, all the time when I wasn't at Synagogue. I would take a word at a time and have her explain to me what she meant. I'm a journalist by trade and had to talk to her like she was a third grader. But she did tell me that she had gotten her GED.

Years later, she asked Melissa to help her get the GED, which she actually didn't have yet.

I'd ask her what these little words would mean and have her explain her thoughts. I told her she'd have to change the names in this book because you're subject to libel. She didn't want to listen to me and I said I couldn't work with her. She finally relented.

Her thing was frying fish. I wanted her in her comfort zone and she would make fish and grits while we worked. She cooked for me. I was careful about not eating anything from her house because of the fiends she surrounded herself with. But, she personally was very clean.

"How big can I become?" she asked me. That's when I told her the Tyler Perry story.

"You know, NeNe, Tyler Perry? Many of his plays are based on his experience and the women in his family. I think that once you get everything in order, even if I'm not working with you, you should try to publish your book."

"You really think so?" Reading her emotions was easy, or so I thought.

"When you get your manuscript ready, it could be good." There were rumors at the time about Tyler Perry getting writers block and looking for properties to use as the basis for his movies and plays.

I gave her the Tyler Perry idea. She takes pieces from people and she regurgitates it.

So, anyway, I'm in Byrd's room where the halfway functioning computer is. By the way, I came to love Sharon as a sister, never as a friend, because I don't use that word loosely. As I spent more time with her,

I began to realize something wasn't right. Someone would call and interrupt us, she'd walk away, take the call and then go outside. She'd say, "Boo, I'll be right back." I know she was making drug deals while I was there, which was a dangerous place to be.

I started being scarce. She kept wanting to get together, though.

"Sharon," I said, "I can meet you."

She called me on my cell, I was just out of my lecture. She had an idea and she said, "I've already started writing a second manuscript."

"I can't come to your house with all those people there. What we're doing is important, I don't want all those people to know."

"Boo, I will take care of it."

I was pissed when she took the manuscript and everything we did and gave it to Ms. Sullivan, whom Sharon claimed was a renowned publisher. Sharon said that Ms. Sullivan rewrote the whole book. I told her that it wasn't her story anymore, if she changed everything we'd written.

I was probably the thorn that unraveled her when I started throwing out litigation. Something's wrong in her world.

I heard about the conference and the birthday party in 2010. I wasn't invited to anything. What has this woman accomplished that she'd have such a regal affair? I wasn't good enough to sit on the satin seats!

Ms. Sullivan made a bold statement, saying this woman had been so successful that she could fill up a ballroom three times over with her money. The rumor was that she'd sold the book to Tyler Perry. My lawyer said that if she has that much money, she was supposed to give me five percent for putting the book together for her out of its original state and from anything else we'd work together on in the future. My lawyer would go for more than that, if possible.

She went forward with everything, but I'm not mentioned anywhere in the book, not even a thank you. "Nekey," I said, "tell her I no longer have time for her lies."

"Sharon wants to come to your house in North.

"You tell that lying sack of shit, absolutely not."

"Sharon said she's having a conference and she has the line up and the A listers. Ms. Sullivan is no longer in the picture. It's Linda Wilson now."

"Where does Sharon keep finding these people? Well, I hope Ms. Wilson is smarter than Ms. Sullivan."

I was there when the heart graphic that's on the first version of her book, The Fight for My Love, was drawn by a crack head, a young white girl who came from a good family and lived off Garners Ferry, right behind the Circle K. A very good artist, she drew the heart by hand. She drew several copies in red ink and pink. The best one was with a red Bic pen, and we decided together which one and it became the drawing used. It was taken somewhere to be scanned. That's the day she became S.D. Johnson, Author. I told her she didn't want to use her full name, so we branded her as "S.D." for the cover of the book.

Cynthia, Calvin's aunt, was the one doing the typing for Sharon's manuscript when I wasn't around. I told Sharon not to work on it when I wasn't there so I could be available to make corrections. But you know Sharon, she went ahead anyway.

I started talking to people who knew "Tim," the abuser from her book and six out of the ten stories didn't match up with the stories Sharon was telling me. He did do her wrong, though. He was her daughter's boyfriend first, then Sharon started messing with him. She said in the book he tried to molest Byrd while she was asleep. Nothing means anything to Sharon, so she continues to be with him after Byrd wakes up and tells Sharon he was molesting her.

After she's changed her persona to S.D. Johnson, I remember it was a Wednesday, around five o'clock. It was rainy, too, and I got wet going to her place. When I arrived, she was in the kitchen. Everything always took place in the dining area.

"Sharon, what do you want to look at?"

"Calvin and I was talking…." I cut her off and said, "I work with you, not your family."

"Calvin said he doesn't think you should profit off my pain."

"What degree does Calvin have, a paralegal degree?"

"Calvin, tell Rogie what you were talking about."

Calvin chimes in with, "Yeah, I don't think it's fair that you get a percentage."

"Calvin, I don't know what crack house you just crawled out of, but you don't have any education and you're not going to railroad me. What right do you have to be in this business?"

"I'm her husband."

"You're not even common law. How long you been out of jail now? Don't get in my business."

I turned my back on him, then took on Sharon.

"You're familiar with the law. Remember that media law book I brought you? Don't play me, I did my research on you a while back. I know what you're doing. I teach communications, I learned to read facial expressions. And why are all these people always here? Why do you have this entourage?"

"They like being around me."

"You are attempting to use me and you would have probably gotten away with it if the brainiac hadn't opened his mouth. Calvin, I'm glad you read while you were in prison, and you know the law is the law in South Carolina."

I canceled any and all appointments with her after that. I would see her occasionally and I was cordial. I stopped dealing with her after the Calvin incident.

"Remember, I named you S.D. Johnson and people know I helped you. If you ever profit off this book, you can believe I'm coming for you." That was right at the end of our relationship.

Two years passed by and someone told me Sharon's book is out. I'm her first white collar crime victim. Tell Sharon for me, I'll go to every media outlet and talk to everybody that will let me talk about what she did. Nekey told her what I said and Sharon has kept me away from herself ever since.

Now, I don't know what turned, but a few months ago, Sharon was looking for me to ride to Atlanta to accompany her to a radio show interview. Now, she's got to keep feeding the streets all of this stuff to try and combat what she knows is coming.

That women's conference was her biggest con

because it gave her license to scam. She breeds on your sympathy.

She never paid me a dime. If I was a crack head, I would have made out! I work off percentages. But Sharon, I wanted to believe in her and knew that she had a story that the ghetto would buy. She has something to which every woman, regardless of race or social standing, could relate. I saw the potential in her story.

I told Sharon, "You are going to need financial planners, someone to create trusts for your children." I never saw the documentation of $81 million. Sharon knows I'm skeptical. Like money, I need to see the watermark. I.S. Leevy's wife and I worked together at Benedict, so I could have checked on that story of documents saying that I.S. Leevy Johnson was her attorney.

I would hear over and over that Sharon has the money coming. It's going to be Friday. Friday, Friday, Friday.

"Friday is the close of business, Sharon" I would tell her.

"What's that?"

I explained to her how banks work and then she used that information to continue to perpetrate the money fraud later.

I kept a diary from when I first started working with her, making notes throughout the process. I dealt with Sharon like I was dealing with a student. I told Sharon, "you need to polish yourself. The gold tooth has to go."

"Can you help me find somebody to do my teeth?"

Every firm has a certain amount of pro bono that

they have to do. I told her she could probably get it done for free, but I didn't find her a dentist.

You've got to remember you're dealing with a lump of sand, it's not even clay. People around her helped to mold Sharon and I'm thinking that if she has the right people, what better than to have a college professor believe in your work? In real life, it doesn't work to kick people to the curb when you're done.

Throughout this process, Calvin's drug addiction was coming to the forefront. Sharon wouldn't sell to Calvin. She would literally fight him. Calvin came to my condo because Sharon had this thing about always knowing where he was. She was trying to help him get clean and I went to several NA meetings with Calvin. I had become part of their world. Sharon wasn't benevolent in getting him clean, likely it just would save her money.

Calvin is well read and comes from a good family and he and Taci strayed after their mother died. After talking to him, I could tell that this man had more to him than what we saw on the surface. This feeling was before he started getting into our financial business.

I don't think Calvin was aware of the scams she was running at that time. When I met him, he was doing construction work.

His sister, Taci was helping them start a janitorial service so he'd have something else to do. After the book stuff I had done with Sharon, Nekey and I had a janitorial service we put together, kind of small. I was trying to invest my money from Benedict for the future. We got a bid and it was for student housing on Beltline for Midlands Tech. Sharon heard about it and went to the bid requester and told them we were basically office cleaners and didn't know anything about cleaning housing.

I confronted her. "You can't even spell janitorial. You are playing a game you don't know anything about."

She was too smooth and actually stole a bid from me on the janitorial service with the company she and Calvin had called P&P Cleaning Service.

When the $81 million story came out, Calvin was thinking she was getting advances and so forth. She told Linda that Calvin thought she was paid by Tyler Perry the eighty one million.

She is just deceptive. Sharon has an app on her phone that rings back to the Richland County sheriff's department. There's an app that you can dial any number in and it makes you think you're calling a different number.

Sharon told Nekey in May she was going to Richland County to see if there was a warrant on her. I don't believe she would do that.

She was introduced to a life that she won't turn back from at any cost. Right after the Fourth of July in 2011, it was Monday morning, Sharon came over and Nekey said Sharon wants to talk with us. Sharon told me she had something going on with Michael Vick. I'm sitting Indian style on Nekey's couch, listening to this mess.

"Boo, I will give you $50,000 and pay you the rest of your five percent."

"There's nothing about the rest, there is no rest. When can you get this money?"

"Friday."

It's always Friday. That promise was in 2011, but the big blow up with Calvin was in 2004, so this scam has been going on a long time. She is starting to unravel.

She had perfumes for this and that person, talking about doing celebrity perfume lines, and said something about Al Sharpton.

"Sharon, it all sounds good, but if my attorney has to get involved, we will go after more than five percent. Honestly, I'm happy for you."

She was going to publish stuff for Michael Vick, which was based on her buying into Linda's publishing company. She also mentioned Governor Sanford. That part was real, but for Tom and Linda. Sharon had nothing to do with it.

Again, I can't stress enough, she has the moral compass of Bernie Madoff. She's not only a narcissist, but she's a psychopath. I'm so sorry that I put her manuscript together and gave her the Tyler Perry idea. She even took the suggestion of financial advisors and having a publicist too far and has ruined so many people by using this angle.

**The *Be Smarter than a Con* Takeaway: If you suspect your neighbor (or anyone) is a drug dealer, there are signs commonly associated with this activity. Frequent traffic to the home, visitors that only stay a few minutes, visitors coming at inappropriate times, like the middle of the night – these are details worth reporting to the authorities. If you see the neighbor slap hands with a guest at the beginning and ending of a short conversation, you may have witnessed an exchange, with the money given the first time and the drugs given the second time. **

CHAPTER THIRTY SIX
Player: Tom Blackstone
And The Fuse Is Lit

Known by many, Tom Blackstone is a former football coach who became embroiled in a legal battle and lost everything. After prison, Tom returned to South Carolina, which had been his home for many years. He started fresh and began a new company to help aspiring authors. It was through the publishing world that Sharon crossed his path.

***

In May of 2011, I received a call from Milt Ronderson, a business associate I had known for many years. Milt knew I owned a publishing company and he said he had a client that was interested in speaking with me about the publishing company.

Milt went on to say that his client was worth over eighty one million due to Tyler Perry purchasing her book rights. Milt would not give me this person's name because he said he wanted to talk with her again to confirm her interest.

He wanted to know if I was interested. I told him I was.

The next day, Milt called and said the lady's name was Sharon Johnson and he was setting up a conference call for later that evening. He said Sharon's fiancé, Calvin Jones, would also be on the call.

We had the call and it lasted about thirty minutes. Sharon basically said she was interested in getting into the publishing business as a partner and would like to meet face to face.

On May 17th, 2011, I met with Sharon, Calvin, Milt and his partner Andy Roland. The meeting lasted about one and a half hours. I covered the whole spectrum of publishing. At the time, we were in very serious negotiations with both a governor and Michael Vick to publish their books. I was looking for a partner with capital to invest so we could easily fund our projects. That day, Sharon and Calvin agreed to purchase ten percent of the publishing company for three million dollars.

Milt was sure Sharon had the money and confirmed he had seen her Wachovia Bank statement showing eighty one million. Because of my past relationship with Milt and knowing his character and professionalism, I did not do any further due diligence regarding Sharon Johnson. That would later prove to be a monumental mistake.

In June of 2011, Sharon signed the agreement to purchase ownership in the publishing company. It had been renegotiated to thirty three percent for six million dollars. Sharon said that her funds were being frozen for a short while due to some minor issues with the IRS.

We began to spend a lot of time together and seemingly getting to know each other better. Sharon appeared low on funds and wanted to borrow some until her money was freed up. We loaned Sharon thousands of dollars, paid multiple personal bills for her and her children to help her stay in her apartment and keep her car.

Sharon's problem with the release of her funds lasted for several months. She said she was hiring attorney I.S. Leevy Johnson's law firm to help. She kept saying the funds were to be released by Wachovia on a particular date. Then she would go to the bank and say a new IRS lien was showing that had to be cleared up. All the while, we were fronting her bills.

After several more months, at our suggestion Sharon agreed to speak with famed attorney Willie Gary. She said she would meet with him but it just needed to be her and Calvin.

Sharon claimed to have the meeting. She had supposedly an agreement with I.S. Leevy's office that paid them six percent of additional money Wachovia had to pay her via federal court. Wachovia had supposedly worked with the IRS and was fraudulently withholding her funds. Sharon said her attorney Clarence Davis, who negotiated her $84 million settlement said he could get $80 million from Wachovia. Sharon later said Wachovia's first offer to I. S. Leevy was $600 million.

Every other day, Sharon was going to attorney

meetings and federal court meetings. First, it was with Judge Joe Anderson and then with Judge Margaret Seymour. Ultimately, when it took over a year to get her money, I wanted her to reach out to the local and national press. For some reason, she said she eventually would. But, every time she would say "let's just wait a little longer, I'm gonna get my money soon."

She was so certain she was gonna get her funds in 2011 that I used money I had left and money I borrowed to pay her bills instead of my bills. That decision caused me and my kids to voluntarily leave the apartment we had stayed in for five years and never got behind on our payments.

Sharon swore the money would be released very soon. When it wasn't, she hired Gloria Allred to take over and deal with Wells Fargo, who bought out Wachovia. Sharon made the mistake of saying Gloria and her husband came to meet with her here in Columbia. There had been many suspicious things in our dealings, but this was a major red flag because: number one, Gloria Allred wasn't married and number two, Gloria was on the Piers Morgan show the same night Sharon said she was in Columbia.

Now, prior to the Gloria Allred story, Sharon said she went to Los Angeles and hired Al Sharpton. He promised she would have her funds in two weeks.

Due to this Gloria Allred red flag, I had my son Jeremy call the Piers Morgan show and also Gloria Allred's office. Piers Morgan's office said Gloria was live on his show from another city, but wouldn't confirm what city. On television, it certainly didn't appear to be Columbia, Charlotte or anywhere close to here. Gloria's personal assistant wouldn't say where she was, but she did confirm that Gloria had not been in South Carolina in over two years. Sharon was clearly lying.

About a year earlier, Jeff Downs had went to I. S. Leevy's office, Margaret Seymour (Judge) and called Willie Gary. I. S. Leevy's office and Judge Seymour told Jeff they didn't know Sharon. Willie Gary said it's all in Sharon's mind.

We didn't believe it. We thought for privacy's sake they told Jeff that, but it wasn't true. We believed those people told Jeff that, but it couldn't possibly be true.

Now, we know it WAS true. We took this Gloria Allred issue to Sharon. She tried to lie her way out of it. She first said she never said Gloria Allred, she said she said Gloria's daughter.

I told Sharon I was close friends with I. S. Leevy Johnson and I knew Judge Seymour well; she was over a trial I knew about.

Sharon begged me not to, but I said I needed to get some answers. I was to meet with I. S. one Friday evening and Judge Seymour on Saturday morning. I was actually not meeting with either, but she thought I was.

After my meetings Sharon thought I had with Judge Seymour and I. S. the night before, I called Sharon Saturday afternoon and told her we needed to talk. She sounded really nervous and wanted to know if everything was okay. I gave her an emphatic "NO, everything is not okay. As a matter of fact, nothing is okay."

She wanted to talk on the phone but I wouldn't.

I told her I would meet her at the Richland County Library in two hours.

I knew in my heart that Sharon had been lying about everyone and everything the entire time and she had no money.

***

Tom is so overcome with frustration that he pens a letter to Sharon in mid-June, 2013 that read as follows: "Sharon,

I heard about the gathering you had at the Medallion Center. I suppose that replaced the women's conference that you advertised to be at Brookland Baptist Banquet Hall. Brookland confirmed that they had to cancel your Women's Conference for non-payment of the fee required. This is what caused you to change your whatever it was on the day of the event from Brookland to the Medallion Center. Who changes an advertised event from one location to another location on the day of the event? Of course you are lying about why you changed it.

You spent a great deal of time calling everyone you could think of asking them to come over to the Medallion Center. You obviously sold no tickets to the event. The word on the street is that it was shabby and very unprofessional. Sharon, you know this is something you could not pull off without us.

You had last year's conference at the Hilton, two days of events with entertainment and heavy hors d'oeuvres on Friday at the meet and greet, all day Saturday speakers, a full course served banquet dinner via Ruth's Chris restaurant. A multitude of first class door prizes, an A+ quality program with paid advertisers, gave out gift baskets and had sales tables outside of the doors Friday and Saturday. Even had an announcement from the Mayor of Columbia. All of this of course set up by me and others that had been sooo good to you and you were telling us every lie in the world.

This year you advertised door prizes for this event, yet there was no door prizes. You also had no programs, no name tags and no gift bags. No programs for a Women's Conference? Why not, Sharon? Could it be because you did not have me and the others who financed your event at the Hilton last year to come and take care of everything for you? You also advertised a sit down dinner. Instead you had a buffet style serving of fried chicken, cole slaw and green beans, and it appeared you purchased it from Sam's Club.

Also, we made contact with Victoria Rowell of the Young & Restless who you advertised as your featured speaker. Remember her? You are telling people that she had a family emergency and could not make it. That is a lie. She says you did not pay her fee and did not have the money to pre-pay her flight into Columbia, yet you continued to advertise that she was coming when you knew she was not. She called it AWFUL!!

By the way, I heard that you were served at the event with a civil law suit for fraud and non-payment of a loan because you borrowed $35,000 and told the people you had $81 million in Wachovia/Wells Fargo Bank. Good luck with that. I heard they'd been looking for you for over 10 months to serve you. Of course you lied

to people and told them you don't know why they
served you because you already paid it. Why would
someone serve you with a lawsuit if you had paid them,
Sharon? You have become accustomed to people
believing your lies, no matter how ridiculous they are.

Gee thought you were still living out in Woodman
Farms but you left there at midnight and left the rental
company holding over $5,000 in unpaid fees. Yes, they
have notified law enforcement. I am sure wherever you
are living is a far cry from Woodman Farms.

You gave the man at Chinese American a bad check
to secure a space for your clothing boutique and he
decided not to trust you at all. Who writes a bad check
to the people going in the door, Sharon?

Nothing good is going to happen to you or for you,
Sharon, because you continue to mock God with your
lies and all of your schemes and deceit. You have been
told that you cannot mistreat God's people and get away
with it. That is true for all of us. You have taken people
who did nothing but show you and your family love and
you have abused them in every way imaginable. To
make things worse, you have slandered the names of
those same people who have paid your bills and helped
you do any and everything needed.

There are severe consequences that you will soon
have to face for your actions. Then everyone will know
the fraud that you are. Everyone will know that
virtually everything about you is a fabrication. That you
are nothing but a lifelong con artist who cares nothing
of the harm you cause others.

The sad and unfortunate part about some of your
victims is they don't even realize they are victims. I

don't know if it's because they are caught up in greed and don't want to acknowledge all of the red flags that are everywhere; or, if they are just that blind. I won't call these people's names because they know who they are and this is about you, Sharon, and all of your lies and deceit. Below is a brief summary of some of the victims and how you have deceived them:

1. Andy Roland and his company: You reached out to these people and showed Andy a fake Wachovia bank statement with $81 million dollars on it. You told him you received these funds from Tyler Perry, you had sold him the rights to your book. Under that assumption, you had these people set up the Dream Development corporation, a conference call with Calvin, your children, Taci Jones and a trust attorney to go over how you were going to give all of them millions of dollars. You also had Andy meet with Dr. Partridge to facilitate/ oversee the funding project of initially $500k to help him build a church (which you later increased to two million dollars in order to lure Dr. Partridge in to get money out of him).

You told Andy you were looking for another book publisher because your current publisher (Ms. Sullivan) had taken advantage of you and stolen the book sales from your first book, which was tens of thousands of dollars. This is how Linda and I met you. You told us you were interested in the publishing business and wanted to invest in our company. However, every time it was time for you to actually fund these projects something would ALWAYS come up on your end where you were not able to keep your word. One of your main excuses were you were so stressed out and had to go to emergency and would have to cancel your appointment. There was always one excuse after another, until finally Andy realized you did not have any money and everything about you was based on a lie! Once Andy caught on to you, you stopped taking his calls and started scandalizing his name to people, including to me. This was done so that people would not have anything to do with Andy or believe anything he had to say about you.

2. Barbara McDaniels: You stated Barbara was money hungry and was stressing you out because she was always bothering you about money. You took Barbara out to the "View" subdivision and had her to pick out a home and even do paperwork on the home along with your daughter, Aneshia, based on you having all of these millions of dollars. Barbara even posted a picture of her and the Realtor standing outside of the house. The last I heard, Barbara still has boxes of her things packed up waiting to move! How can you look her in the face or talk to her on the phone knowing you have lied and deceived her and that you have no money, let alone millions! Who does that to their own family!

3. Patricia Sullivan: Some people say Patricia is in this conspiracy of deception and fraud with you. Personally, I go back and forth with my position on her. The reason is because of all the lies you have told on this woman. You showed me and others a check for $50k you said Patricia wrote you for copies of your book you said she sold. You said she had been stealing money from you based on the book sales. You also said she tried to deceptively have her company name on the house in Charlotte you were trying to buy. But the truth

is she put her name on the house because YOU were trying to get her to buy the house with the promise you would give her millions of dollars! The problem was Patricia could not show financial proof to afford the home. What Patricia doesn't realize, that was a blessing in disguise because she would have ended up buying YOU a home that you were NOT going to pay her back for because you don't have any money!

I (along with others) could never understand if someone had done all of the terrible things you said Patricia had done, why would you still have her around! It was later discovered you may have sold 100 copies TOTAL of your book, if that, certainly not enough to warrant her writing you a check for $50k! Patricia never stole any money from you and all of the negative things you said about her were all lies! The truth is Patricia has been giving you money and doing all kinds of things for you, including writing bad checks for thousands of dollars for you!

I have no doubt you have told Patricia all kinds of lies on other people including myself. It's your way of keeping people from ever getting close to one another and for nobody to ever trust or believe anything the other person says. This is your M.O. and if people would just open their eyes, they would see the pattern!

4. Dr. Partridge: After your initial promise of $500k to him, you came back and promised two million dollars for him and his church. This promise was done when you needed the initial deposit to give Wess Morgan as your keynote speaker in 2012. You had Linda Wilson go with you to meet with Dr. Partridge to request the funds. If Dr. Partridge would think back,

you even got up from the table when it was time to discuss the funds and said you had to go to the restroom. By the time you came back Dr. Partridge had already agreed to loan you the funds, with the promise of two million dollars once your funds were released from the bank!

I know Dr. Partridge has heard at least a hundred times from you as to the reason why the funds have not been released as of yet! I would be curious to know what reasons you are giving now, or do you even mention those particular funds anymore and have moved on to another lie! How do you continue to talk about the goodness of GOD when HIS spirit is NOWHERE within you, because if it was, there's no way you could repay good with evil, which is what you have done and continue to do!

The truth is you have no funds in the bank and no money period! Once you realize someone has finally figured that out you cut off all communications with that person and proceed to scandalize their name, like you have done to mine and several other individuals.

5. Wess Morgan: This man considered you a friend with no strings attached. He did not ask or expect nothing more than friendship from you. But you decided for your own selfish and lustful reasons to promise this man $10 million. You told him you would buy him an $800k custom tour bus and underwrite his recovery fest event. Based on your word, he goes out and orders this bus and starts the process of putting together the recovery fest.

Once everything got underway, you stopped taking his calls and would not return his calls or text messages.

This was very devastating for Wess, he had put his reputation on the line based on promises you had made to him and now he was left trying to pull everything off. He did not understand why you would do something like that, eventually he moved on and by the grace of GOD he got through the ordeal.

Then, you turn right back around and reach out to Wess again! Telling him your attorney and accountants had gotten everything worked out and you would be wiring him the funds. At that time, which was October 2012, the weekend of your birthday, Wess came to Columbia to perform at a local church. You knew he was coming to town and you wanted him to come over to your house in Woodman Farms. For whatever reason that was important to you, enough so that you made Wess another promise regarding the funds.

Wess came to your home and he told you to your face, please don't tell him you are going to do something and you know you can't do it. He does not care about the money, but he does care about friendships. You told him you were definitely going to do what you said and that he would have it by that Monday. You even asked Wess if he could stay over until that Monday, but he had another engagement and could not stay. So you promised Wess it would definitely be wired to him on Monday. It never happened! Wess confirmed with me that he has not spoken to you since that weekend. Why would you do that?

6. Talitha Long: You and your children have said on several occasions Talitha will pretty much believe anything, she's kind of slow. Well, I don't know if that's

379

true or not. However, I do know Talitha has been a really good friend to you and has helped you so much that she did not even take care of her own financial responsibilities at times.

Talitha's home went into foreclosure because you kept telling her you would be getting your funds released soon from the bank. You promised her at one time a million dollars and would buy her a hair salon. She continued to believe you, even though her home was foreclosed on and she was ultimately evicted from her home.

She is a single mom with three children to take care of, and yet you showed no mercy or compassion for her or her children. You continued to take from her (and probably are still taking) with the promise of giving her all this money, when you know there is no money and allowed her to get evicted! She is your best friend! How can you sleep at night, knowing what you are doing to people?

7. Kandi Buttons: You had started going to Kandi to do your hair and for whatever reason you started making her a promise of buying her a home in Charlotte. You and Kandi drove to Charlotte to meet with the real estate agent to look at homes. She found a home she liked and you told her you would purchase it for her. She even took her mother over there to look at the home as well. You were supposed to send the funds to the real estate agent to purchase the home, but you never did. As far as I know you have not spoken to or seen Kandi since that time! Who does things like this when nobody asked them for anything!

8. Jeff Downs: You met Jeff through me. I got him

to help pay your bills and give you money at different times for over a year. You promised Jeff when your funds were released you would look out for him for helping you. He even paid for your birthday dinner at the Capital City Club in 2011.

After a while, Jeff started to become skeptical and doubt you even had any money. Jeff brought those concerns to me and said he started doing some investigation into some of the things you had said. He spoke with Willie Gary (who was supposed to be the attorney working with Jeff Johnson of the I.S. Leevy law firm). Willie Gary informed him he did in fact speak with you, but whenever it was time for you to send over documentation to show where you had these funds in the bank, you would come up with a reason why you did not confirm. He came to the conclusion you were lying and that you did not have any funds and he moved on and never had any more contact with you. Jeff also spoke with Jeff Johnson and he told him he did not represent you and did not even know who you were. Jeff then spoke with federal Judge Margaret Seymour who was supposed to be the judge handling your case against the bank and the IRS. She had never heard of you and did not know anything about a case with the bank unlawfully holding a single female's money in their bank.

Once Jeff realized and had proof you were lying, he confronted me about it. I initially defended you, because I believed you and everything you were saying. At that point Jeff even thought I was a part of your fraud and scam. I shared Jeff's concerns with you and you tried to calm him down. Jeff advised you, if you did not repay him for all of the money he had given you or show him proof of the funds being held in the bank, he was going to the authorities and tell them you were running a scam. Telling people you have $81 million dollars in the bank, so that they would give you money and services with the promise of you looking out for them when your funds were released. When in actuality you did not have ANY money in the bank! You then decided to repay Jeff for all the money he had given you to stop him from going to the authorities on you. Why wouldn't you just show him proof of the funds if you really did have them?

9. Linda Wilson: You promised Linda and I you were going to invest in the publishing company, but you were not going to be able to do it until your funds were released. You showed Linda a Wachovia bank statement for $81 million dollars and said the IRS had a lien on the account for around $29k.

From that point on, Linda started helping you financially and any other way she could on a daily basis. She would spend up to 10 hours a day with you, every day! She, like Talitha, started giving you money and paying your bills (even paying Calvin's child support, car payment and Talitha's car payment on occasion). Ultimately, Linda fell behind in her mortgage payments because of giving you money with the promise the funds would be released numerous different times. Even when her home went into foreclosure you continued to tell her, "don't worry about, we are good, I will have my money and I'm not going to let you lose your home." This promise you were going to get your funds and take care of Linda's home went on all

the way up until the first week of January 2013. You
told her you had borrowed the funds and were going
to make a deposit into her account and give her the
confirmation number. She waited for you to call her
back with the number, but you never did. When she
tried to call you to inquire about it, your number had
been changed. She then went to your home in Wood
Creek Farms and realized you had moved! She has not
spoken to you since.

Her daughter, Misty who had befriended your
daughter Aneshia (who asked Misty to be her baby's
Godmother, which she accepted) tried to reach Aneshia.
She realized Aneshia had blocked her telephone number
from her phone. This is the same person who had spent
several hundred dollars on Aneshia's baby, who would
babysit and buy the baby different things when Aneshia
did not have the money such as Pampers, milk and a
special neck brace for the baby. Misty and Aneshia
never had any cross words or disagreements, but yet she
blocked her number and they have not spoken since.

10. Mary Louise & Gabriella Davis: You met
Mary Louise at WoodForest National Bank in 2010.
You asked her to become your personal assistant to
deal with business issues involving your company,
Dream Development. Mary Louise signed a contract
services agreement with you. You told Mary Louise and
Gabriella you had $81 million dollars that was being
held up by the bank and you needed to borrow $5,000.
You promised them a home that you said you owned
plus double their money back. They had you sign a
promissory note and of course you did not pay them
their money back and they had to file a civil lawsuit

against you. At that time you just stopped taking their calls. The home that you promised to give them you did not own and you were actually squatting in the home. Mary Louise and Gabriella have experience great hardship over the loss accredited to you.

11. Your Business Manager: I had the opportunity to meet him at your home in Woodman Farms. He seemed like a decent person and was trying to make some things happen for you in the "Reality TV" world, along with securing some celebrities for your fragrance line. He is the one who brought Fantasia to your table in hopes of creating a fragrance line for her. You signed a letter of intent with Fantasia and her people to create this fragrance. With this agreement, you promised to spend a minimum of $100k to market and promote this line.

You also promised him, to my knowledge, $30k as a donation to his church. You had Linda call him and tell him the wire transfer for those funds would be coming to him in a few days. It is my understanding that none of the above promises were ever kept. Fantasia does not have a fragrance line created by you and neither your business manager or his church ever received the $30k dollars!

12. You hired BeBe as your publicist. You and Patricia Sullivan wrote her a bad check and she terminated her business involvement with you immediately. Yet you lied and told your business manager that you had paid BeBe. BeBe confirmed she turned that check over to the Solicitor's office.

There are many other victims that I will not include in this email but they will come forth. May God show

you the same mercy that you have shown all of your
victims.

**The *Be Smarter than a Con* Takeaway: Keep
records and notes on any deals you make with people
with whom you don't have a long track record. If you
have proof you've been conned, take it to the police.
Give a statement. Pursue prosecution, and be relentless
if necessary. You're not the only victim, I assure you.**

CHAPTER THIRTY SEVEN
Player: Patricia Sullivan

The Queen Mother. The Co-Conspirator. The Power Behind the Throne. The Postmaster.

Huh? Yes, really. The postmaster at an official United States Post Office, Patricia Sullivan had a real, legitimate job. Her hobby, however, was defrauding in the name of Sharon.

For years, her involvement in Sharon's scams has been up for debate. In her absence, Sharon talks about Ms. Sullivan with contempt and disdain. Sharon says Ms. Sullivan is a vulture, taking advantage of her lack of business acumen, stealing her book profits and generally making her life difficult. The core group of victims have argued among themselves over her role. Finally, in the summer of 2014, definitive evidence was uncovered, solving the mystery.

Whenever Ms. Sullivan was mentioned, it was always said she was from Greenville, living in the Simpsonville suburb. However, a glimpse of her recent driver's license, which oddly was only valid for six months, listed a permanent address in Columbia. It turns out she's using her daughter's address for her identification. She did live there, but not anymore.

The driver's license with only six months of validity is troubling. Investigator Hinson said that the Department of Motor Vehicles doesn't normally issue licenses with such a short time period. My question was, "what if she lost her driver's license, the physical card, and needed to have a new one made, wouldn't the DMV put the new date of issue?" Say you obtained an original license in January 2004 that is valid for ten years. But, if you lost the license in September 2013 and got a new one made, then wouldn't it only be valid for four months?

No, that's not how it works. It would still retain the original issue date, according to the investigator. Her license, which was used to secure the event venue for the 2013 Empowering Women to Excel conference, was only valid for six months, expiring in November, 2013 – yet, this expiration date should be impossible.

In her official capacity, she's been lauded by the USPS as an instructor at their regional conference in Charlotte, North Carolina. She leads a double life, sitting on the board of the United Way and behind everyone's back, she brings a knife – the better to stab you with. The City of Columbia Police stopped her in May, 2013, charging her with Driving Under Suspension and Operating a Vehicle on a Highway without Registration and License Due to Delinquency. Curiously, two days later she has a driver's license document in her possession. The strange ID and the traffic charges are just the beginning. She has a twisted history of defrauding through her publishing business, and a number of schemes she's cooked up with Sharon over the years.

During the time Linda was helping Sharon with her business needs, she heard numerous times about the success of Sharon's book. "When I first looked up Ms. Sullivan's information under HYPD Publications, Sharon's book had sold around twenty copies. That's why the check I saw from Ms. Sullivan made out to Sharon for fifty thousand dollars didn't make any sense whatsoever. Sharon said it was for money she was owed for book sales. Yet none were ever really sold," Linda said.

The check was yet another piece of propaganda.

A recurring theme in the books in which Ms. Sullivan has a hand is truth. Or rather, the lack thereof. She counsels Sharon to name a version of her book, "Truth Be Found." Dr. Handsur is convinced to name his book, "Tell The Truth – Be Prepared and Pay a Price." She's infatuated with the idea of truth, but only on her terms.

Ms. Sullivan has been sued several times by people she's promised to publish. A prominent African American psychologist engaged her to publish his memoir, and had to fight her to get his original materials back. The book was published, but his lawsuit was in progress at the time of his death, leaving the fight to his heirs. She holds her shell publishing company out as a way for unknown authors to find their work in print. Person after person falls for her pitch and pays enough to keep her in business for another month.

Sharon's book has been a key feature for Ms. Sullivan's publishing endeavor, with the reviews written by her and for other authors she publishes, she writes the review and posts it under Sharon's name. They're intertwined like a strand of DNA, it's hard to see where Sharon's con ends and Ms. Sullivan's begins.

Intimately involved with one another, some of Sharon's biggest cons hinged on help from her best partner, Patricia. The fancy house in Charlotte near Fantasia, the dynamic duo's first fake contract written on the house was in Ms. Sullivan's name, not Sharon's. The rental in Woodman Farms happened through Patricia's arrangements for Sharon with the property managers. The women's conferences were jointly planned by these two for easy money. The long, drawn out evasion of Dr. Partridge when he wanted his thirty thousand back included many references to things Ms. Sullivan was supposedly doing for Sharon. The game Sharon ran on Mary Louise and Gabriella was based on her need to "get away from" Ms. Sullivan, where she had Patricia on the phone helping her convince these women of the story of the moment. Even for the swindle she ran on me, the book we were working on was first published by Ms. Sullivan and Sharon feigned unhappiness with the services she provided. She wanted me to improve the manuscript and help with her "new" publisher, Destiny Image.

Not every scheme is a joint effort, though. Ms. Sullivan has her own claims to fame. Real estate is the American dream, owning a house is the hallmark symbol of capitalism and prosperity. She owned an average home in the Simpsonville area, valued in the

high $180s. In real estate, you often see move-up
buyers who purchase larger or more expensive homes.
However, you don't usually see someone go from a
house worth one hundred eighty thousand to one
offered at almost seven hundred thousand.

Always thinking big, Ms. Sullivan engages an agent
and writes a contract of sale on a home in Greenville
listed at six hundred sixty five thousand dollars. It was a
cash sale, with the only contingency being the house
must appraise for the sales price. The sellers were a
prominent couple, with one of them appearing daily on
the local news as an anchor. Naturally, they were
excited to sell their house and wrote a contract on a
brand new home for themselves. Then, in a chain
reaction, those people wrote a contract on a new home
for themselves as well. Following this chain, you have
three families who all believe they're selling their
current homes and buying new ones. Plus, the
commission on a sale of that amount at six percent
would be forty six thousand, with half of that split
between the two real estate agents, one working for the
seller and one working for the buyer. Ms. Sullivan's
agent was due twenty three thousand dollars. The agent
purchased non-refundable tickets to Disney for herself
and her children based on her income from this sale.

Ms. Sullivan ran her line of bull all the way up to
and beyond the closing date, saying she was working
with a famous author and was due to be paid a large
sum from an investor in her publishing business. How
she thought she could worm her way into this expensive
house is puzzling, as she was never able to close the
deal.

The sellers were beyond angry and sued for performance. Ms. Sullivan stuck to her story, even in the face of a lawsuit. They won a judgment against her for ninety thousand dollars. As of today, she's paid ten thousand towards it. They were lucky to get anything, since it's been a couple of years since the judgment and nothing else has or will ever be paid. Her real estate agent went ahead to Disney with her children, even though she couldn't really afford it. Ms. Sullivan later lost her home in Simpsonville to foreclosure, and moved to Columbia to be near Sharon.

Things must be tough to lose her original home to foreclosure. Tough enough to borrow money from family, Patricia leans on her aunt when she's down and out. Inflating the heads of her relatives with a lot of hot air about Sharon's success and the money she's about to have, Ms. Sullivan gets the green. The aunt, like all the others, gets the shaft. She's forced to resort to suing her own niece for payment. Only the death of Patricia's mother, her aunt's sister, was enough to quiet the lawsuit.

A new convolution in Patricia's publishing juggernaut is the television show, The Another Level Show. This twisted effort of Sharon and Patricia claims to air on Channel 21 weekly for "conversations about your community interest – family – today's culture – age appropriate issues – youth – news – sports – people empowering people – celebrities and MORE!" If you're thinking local access cable, you're way above the production value of this show. Think Sony Handycam, no microphones except on the handheld and a setup in a hotel lobby. Patricia leads these shows by interviewing the targets they bring on to talk with them in hopes of gaining legitimacy. If you can find the Channel 21 that carries The Another Level Show, you're a genius. It's not on YouTube, online or on air. Or anywhere, for that matter, other than the minds of Sharon and Patricia. Briefly, Cousin Louis posts the videos on his YouTube channel, but they quickly disappear.

One of the guests interviewed was the fashion show director slated to bring Ceira's fete to the stage in early March 2014. Patricia peppers him with questions about fashions for young women while Sharon ogles the dresses twenty sizes too small for her bulky frame.

This show's purpose, like everything else, is to get something of value from the victims. This is America, anyone can set up a company and make herself president, chief cook, janitor, you name it. But this show isn't real and the titles they've bestowed upon themselves are ludicrous. Sharon's list includes: Producer, Host and Co-Executive producer, Entrepreneur/Dream Development LLC, SAC Gear – Designer Clothing, Barrio Bath and Beauty Products, OFS Magazine (Out in the Street), Author of The Fight for My Love and The Fight for My Love, Final Chapters and Founder of The You, Too Foundation. Patricia's list is just as impressive: Executive Producer, Host, Co-Producer, Director and Set Designer, Business/Entertainment Manager, Publisher – HYPD Publications LLC, Author of You Can Write a Book – We All Have Stories. What's Yours? And, Dirt Between My Toes.

In June 2014, a posting on a scam report website accuses Ms. Sullivan and her company of using The

Another Level Show to abscond with ten thousand dollars. "One of our managers knew the owner of this company for some years. She was supposed to publish a book and made this organization believe she was part of a new TV network and requested $10K upfront for position. She stated we would have contract that evening but need a upfront check. Cashed the check that day without giving contract and have been missing in action since. DO NOT UTILIZE this person."

A month later, the poster reports a resolution of a refund after sending several emails. From her usual MO, she likely used the money for something she needed right then and then conned someone else to have the money to pay back the first victim.

The entire premise of The Another Level Show is fraudulent. Patricia and Sharon continue their years-long partnership with this fake show for now. Who knows what they'll get into next.

**The *Be Smarter than a Con* Takeaway: Even people in positions of trust can be dirty. Just because a person has a lofty title, the title or position doesn't provide any more sense of character or right and wrong than what he or she already had. **

THE STING
All Good Things Must Come to an End

CHAPTER THIRTY EIGHT
Unraveling

∞∞∞∞∞∞∞∞∞∞∞∞∞∞∞∞∞∞∞∞∞∞∞∞∞∞∞∞∞∞∞∞∞

Jeff Downs spent months trying to convince his friends of Sharon's lies and deceit. Frustrated day and night, Jeff grew impatient with the lack of progress from Sharon's promises of big money to repay him. His personal investment in her world had grown to almost $100,000 and every day her story of when and where she'd have access to all her funds changed ever so slightly. The most damning part of her scenario – she never seemed to have any cash of her own, as she always relied on others to pay her way.

Jeff was already on the hook for a promissory note he co-signed with Sharon in early 2012 for which no payments had ever been made. Legal proceedings were brought by the lender in June 2012 against both Jeff and Sharon. Sharon successfully hid from the lender and the case eventually went on the inactive roster at the Richland County courthouse. It took almost a solid year for the lender to catch up with her and finally serve the lawsuit.

After months of cajoling Tom and Linda, they began to see the light. Towards the end of December, 2012, Tom and Linda had confronted Sharon enough with the truth that she cut them out of her life. "I just can't believe Linda," Sharon said to Melissa as they sat in the waiting room at Palmetto Baptist Hospital's Birthing Center. Aneshia had just delivered a new daughter two days before and a crowd had gathered to see her and the new baby.

"Linda is tellin' lies about me. What's worse, she's asking me for $27,000 to keep her house outta foreclosure. I ain't helpin' her no mo'," Sharon declared. I didn't know anything about Linda's situation and was quite surprised to hear Sharon talk about what I thought was her best friend in such a derogatory manner.

Family members were present at the hospital, but no one from a camera crew was anywhere in sight. When questioned about the lack of coverage from her "reality show," Sharon said they'd already been there earlier in the day and she was tired from filming. It was curious, since she mentioned the presence of the camera crew all the time, but they were never actually around whenever someone saw Sharon.

Sharon referenced an email that Linda was sending around to people who knew her, trying to convince them Sharon was a fraud. This email was actually a truthful depiction of what Tom and Linda knew at the time about Sharon's scheming.

As the new year rolled in, Jeff, Tom and Linda brainstormed to create a list of anyone they knew that was part of Sharon's circle. This list was several pages long and had basic details on how they thought each person was involved. My name was on the list.

"I think we know a mutual crook," Jeff said when I answered his call in early February, 2013.

"Oh, who would that be?" I asked.

"Sharon Johnson," he replied.

That was enough for me to request an immediate meeting to hear what Jeff had to say. I already knew him from the real estate world, so he had instant credibility with me. We met the very next day, with Jeff producing a copy of the "vicious" email Sharon mentioned at the hospital for me to read. It contained the following:

Sharon D. Jackson, Scam Artist

Over the past 8-10 years, Sharon D. Jackson has defrauded numerous victims. Sharon's primary scam is telling trusting individuals one of two stories. 1.) Her daughter Barrio died and she sued the hospital and was awarded $81 million or 2.) Tyler Perry gave her $81 million for the rights to her book. It is possible that she has told individuals more fraudulent stories regarding $81 million but these are two that we know of.

Sharon has told these individuals that her $81 million is being held up by Wachovia Bank, Wells Fargo Bank or the IRS for different reasons and when this money clears she will not only pay them back but do many things above and beyond for them. By using the lure of her receiving $81 million she gets individuals to loan her money, pay her bills and/or provide her with services. Sharon has provided several of these individuals with a fraudulent Wachovia Bank statement showing that she has $81 million on account. The fact is there is no $81 million and there never has been $81 million. It is all a scam to get money and services from any and everyone who she can scam.

Sharon's whole life is nothing more than a long string of lies, fraud and deception. Virtually everything Sharon has acquired over the past ten years has been financed through her fraudulent schemes. She has no job and she has not sold enough books or fragrances to buy anything of any real value in spite of the lies she tells people. There is an investigation going on regarding Sharon's fraud and over the next few months a Federal Grand Jury will likely convene and indict Sharon on a long list of charges.

She has recently moved from Woodman Farms where she was renting to avoid many of the people she has defrauded. It is also common practice for Sharon to rent a home or apartment and then after getting 2 – 4 months behind on the payments, just moving in the middle of the night to avoid paying the rent owed. Sharon by her own admission has moved at least 95 times over the past ten years. Also common practice for Sharon is to change her phone numbers, which she has recently done to avoid dealing with the victims who have realized finally that she has been running a scam.

Sharon is a master manipulator. She works hard to keep her victims away from each other. A common practice to achieve this means is Sharon will tell different victims that they don't like each other or they told her negative things about each other.

We have met with the authorities and have been advised to meet with anyone we are aware of that may have been a victim of Sharon's fraudulent schemes. It is critical that Sharon is not able to continue defrauding individuals while the investigation is still going on. Sharon will soon be brought to justice for her crimes but with cooperating victims, hopefully no one else will become a victim.

I was floored at the allegations. Yet, deep down I had always felt something wasn't right with Sharon's stories. Things she mentioned never came to pass and her endless promises to support the Meals on Wheels program with a donation of $250,000 rang false. Her payments on jobs we did for her became slower and further behind. You can only give someone the benefit of the doubt for so long. She knew I was a Christian and worked that angle on me, too, with all of her "I jus dnt understand, but to God be the Glory" crap she'd text when I wouldn't immediately do her bidding.

After reading the email of allegations and talking to Jeff at length, I began what turned out to be the longest research project I could've imagined: searching for the truth about Sharon Johnson.

The internet is a wonderful tool for myriad purposes, enabling research to be fast and efficient if you know where to look. A quick search of the county government's official website revealed Sharon as a defendant in dozens of cases spanning the course of several years. Minor efforts to stop her reign of terror, these cases never amounted to more than a blip on her radar. Her games have gotten progressively bigger and bolder. Now it's time for someone to stop her.

CHAPTER THIRTY NINE
Reaching Out

We immediately starting working the list of potential victims. Little did we know how many there would be. The initial list created by Jeff, Tom and Linda was an excellent beginning.

The ones who we wanted to gather that day at the sheriff's department were obvious choices for the first contacts. A key to understanding how someone targeted by Sharon would be interested in talking about it is knowing how she treats a person with whom her business is finished. Sharon hates disloyalty. Once she's gotten all she can from you, she drops you like a hot potato. Worse, if you've figured out her scheme before she's completed the con, you're labeled a traitor and summarily dismissed from her world. She's on the phone, but of course using a new phone number by then, telling everyone she can about your unbelievable act of betrayal.

Getting as many victims on the phone as possible

became priority number one. Having a strong showing at the sheriff's department was a crucial first step in turning the tide on Sharon's personal crime wave.

How many victims were out there for us to find – no one had any idea. One comment from a known victim would lead to another possible person taken in by Sharon's deceit. Getting the names and phone numbers right, along with convincing total strangers to listen to you about Sharon was challenging.

Admitting you've been foolish enough to believe a con artist is difficult, at first and always. You feel embarrassed, stupid and pathetic. Sharon counts on your reluctance to speak up. Keeping you silent, so you can wallow in your own pity party, allows her complex operations to continue without interruption.

Now we were asking people to step out in faith so she can be the one who's silenced.

"Have I ever done anything to hurt you," Sharon asked me in the summer of 2013 during a phone conversation well beyond the awakening brought to me by Jeff Downs and in the heart of the investigation.

"That's a hard question for me to answer, Sharon."

"Have I ever done anything to hurt your feelings?"

"Yes, you know you have."

"What?"

And that's where the conversation got weird. If I answered her truthfully, we would STILL be on the phone. She already knew I mentioned being unhappy about her choosing another graphic designer for her magazine project, so I went with the easy route.

After I found out Sharon wasn't what she seemed, Linda was kind enough to make contact with Smith

Publicity's president. Just for my own piece of mind, I wanted to confirm whether or not Sharon sent the money I gave her to Smith for her book promotion.

The response was, "NOOOOO, we have never heard from Sharon. If I had, I would have absolutely talked to you first before even responding to an inquiry from her. What a nightmare for you. Wow!"

CHAPTER FORTY
Summit at the Sheriff's Department

◇◇◇◇◇◇◇◇◇◇◇◇◇◇◇◇◇◇◇◇◇◇◇◇◇◇◇◇◇◇◇◇◇◇◇◇

"Are you riding in on a white horse to save us all?" Jeff asked me while I waited on hold with the Richland County Sheriff's Department.

"No, not at all. I just think we need to let the police know what's happening with Sharon and all of these people she's taking advantage of. She needs to be stopped before anyone else is hurt," I replied.

The people who felt most aggrieved found time in their schedules to meet at the Richland County Sheriff's Department on Valentine's Day, February 14, 2013. One year ago to the day, Sharon had signed a contract with Melissa for over sixteen hundred dollars' worth of design work. Oh, how things had changed.

The cold, damp day did nothing to deter the nine victims from having their issues heard by the Financial Crimes division. We gathered in the cramped lobby with the other folks who had business with the sheriff's department, all of whom looked at our unusual group with quiet interest.

After leaving messages for the police and not hearing anything back, the decision was to simply show up. No appointment, no apologies.

When you walk into the Sheriff's Department, they like to know something about you. So, they collect a photo ID and your reason for coming. I asked for the investigative supervisor, for whom I'd left a couple of messages. After a short wait, Investigator Hinson came down to the lobby to collect me. He was not the supervisor, but at least someone was beginning to pay attention.

"I'm here with a large group," I said when he pulled me into the secondary lobby, just on the other side of the metal detector.

"Let me just take you upstairs first and get an idea of what we're dealing with before I get a big group talking to me all at once."

"Ok, that's fine," I said as we entered the elevator. "But do you realize, though, who is in the lobby with us?"

"Who?"

"Tom Blackstone."

Eyes wide, he stared back, "You're kidding. Is he in on it?"

"No, he's a victim. Just like the rest of us."

"That makes this interesting," he said as we stepped off the elevator and down into his small personal office.

The supervisor popped his head into the office, "What's this about?"

With the best short summary I could manage, I explained the gist of the situation to both officers in the

412

three minutes I'd been allotted.

Hinson told the supervisor about Tom being in the lobby, which seemed to help move things along. They went down and brought up the entire group of the remaining eight victims present into yet another supervisor's office. We crammed around a too small conference table for a presentation on how they would approach the investigation.

"One at a time, we will take your statements and make the case," Hinson declared. Lots of questions followed from the victims, mainly centered around when and how soon could we start giving our statements.

Those who brought documents were told to bring everything back when giving individual statements so the evidence could be collected in a particular order.

"We're connecting the dots in this type of case," Hinson said. "Follow the money. That's how we'll get this done, by connecting the bank accounts and the money that flows in and out of her hands. Every time she swindles someone out of money, the instant she walks into a bank to cash the check obtained through the swindle, she's also just committed bank fraud. That's in the purview of the Secret Service, which is how we'll make the case."

Names and phone numbers were provided by each victim. With assurances we were being taken seriously, the group was dismissed and made our way to the parking lot.

With a much lighter mood, the feeling was positive that something, anything, would and could finally stop Sharon from defrauding and conning the innocents.

It was an amazing moment, that "ah ha!" when you realize that not only are you not alone in your shame of being a victim, but your darkest suspicions about her were exactly right all along and there are plenty of people who want to make sure justice is served.

I had set a time to give my statement and Linda was ready to give hers just as quickly. Knowing Sharon moves around frequently, we encouraged the group to keep in touch so any new information could be shared with the authorities right away.

Linda, Tom and I were standing by the parked cars when a new arrival appeared. It was Taci. She headed straight for us, her cadence of quick, short steps making her look quite intense.

"Am I too late?"

We told her no, not really. We gave her Hinson's name and encouraged her to go inside to meet him. She claimed to be just in town from Georgia, running later than she'd planned.

"Sharon's gotta be stopped. She's unbelievable," Taci declared and rushed into the Sheriff's Department. If she said anything to Hinson or not is unclear because we weren't inside with her and left before she returned to her car.

Taci looked just like another victim, wanting to share her story of victimhood.

CHAPTER FORTY ONE
Investigation

Lying is such hard work. But even with the best liars, no one is perfect.

"There will be no doubt by the time we confront her," said lead investigator Hinson. The strategy is to gather the evidence from as many victims as possible and know the details inside and out before Sharon's brought in for questioning.

The victims waited patiently on the authorities to build the case. Months went by, with fear and disappointment prevalent among those who so desperately wanted to see her off the street.

Sharon may have suspected, but didn't let the possibility of capture slow her down one bit.

Over the course of the investigative period, emails were sent to the sheriff's department with updates on Sharon's activities.

In May 2013, she planned her next series of cons. Even while she set plans in motion, the core group of victims was determined to stop her and the authorities were slowly working on bringing her to justice.

Sharon told several people she was opening a high end women's clothing store called Her Boutique. "Ok, ok, you are dragging it out of me," Sharon cooed to Melissa at a meeting set on a Saturday afternoon. "I wasn't going to tell anybody for another two weeks, but I'm gonna open a store with clothes for plus size women. We'll sell jewelry, fashion bags, shoes and have a new/used rack for celebrity clothes."

I found her story of the store opening to be completely unbelievable, but since it was Sharon telling it, you had to be cautious with the information to find if there was any truth.

Opening a retail store is a complicated matter involving leased or purchased space, inventory, business licenses, legal organization of the business entity, staffing, scheduling, advertising, promotion, basic utilities such as power and telephone lines, credit card processing services and start-up cash. The likelihood of Sharon being able to secure all of these facets of operation is slim at best.

Her story became even more fantastical when she divulged the details of the inventory. First, the rack of used celebrity clothes is supposed to come from Fantasia Barrino. Sharon would have you believe the clothes are simply given to her by Fantasia so they can be sold in this store. Second, the line of women's shoes she will carry is to be privately designed for her, called SDJ Shoes, by the famous rapper Lil' Wayne's "baby mama." "You know Lil' Wayne's baby mama?" Sharon asked. I feigned ignorance, as she somehow believed that I didn't follow pop culture, which always made conversations with her easier so she wouldn't think I knew what she was talking about most of the time.

There is no way anyone is designing a line of footwear for this woman. Definitely not Toya, Lil' Wayne's baby mama.

Naturally, the store location was Garners Ferry Road. From other sources, the exact location was learned and investigated. The initial look at the store gave us its location, but nothing more. The front door and all the windows were covered in brown paper, so looking inside was impossible. A week later, we were able to gain access to the interior of the unit and surprisingly it was partially painted in a peach color as Sharon mentioned. We questioned the property owner, who said the unit was going to be rented by someone, and the make-ready work had started. However, the check written for the rent and security deposit bounced, forcing him to cancel the agreement and change the locks. He has not collected on the check. Her year-long lease turned into a two week stretch of floating a bad check and somehow hoping to get away with it. Luckily, the owner deemed her unacceptable and saved himself a lot of heartache in the future.

Her need to feed her giant ego continued and the concurrent scam of the women's conference was in play at the same time as the so-called boutique. The Saturday meeting showed her determination to pull off another conference by any means necessary. She demanded a promotional flyer, postcards and a website to be created. As you now know, the program called for Fantasia's mother to provide musical entertainment and Victoria

417

Rowell, the actress from the soap opera The Young and the Restless, to give the keynote address.

Along this same time, the devil called early one morning to say she had moved to Charlotte in the neighborhood near Piper Glen called Ballantyne, where the television network has bought her a house.

Yeah, of course they did. They bought me one, too. They give those out like candy at Halloween.

The investigator made contact with the victims to relay a bit of progress. With the cooperation of a key player, the case would be ready for summary and presentation to the Secret Service. The decision to travel that route meant the federal system would start at the top with the most serious charges, including securities fraud, and then work their way down to the lesser charges. No state charges would be filed until the federal system completed their process.

While there hadn't been much in the way of participation from the larger group of known victims, once the Secret Service takes over, everyone will be all in. What's more, Ms. Sullivan is more culpable than we thought previously.

The more Sharon maneuvered, the more the victims themselves began to investigate things she'd said and done. It's hard to believe no one thought to check out if she had a criminal record by a simple web search before this point, but the gullible folks chosen by Sharon as marks just don't think that way. The trusting nature of humanity is Sharon's bread and butter.

By entering the particulars in the county's public index search, one will find dozens of entries under the names Sharon Johnson, Sharon D. Jackson, Sharon

Denise Johnson. First, you see an entry of an arrest
in September 2008 for Breach/Breach of Trust with
Fraudulent Intent, Value $5,000 or more. That case
was disposed of in November 2009 with a guilty plea,
resulting in a sentence of 30 days or $500 on time
served. Several other charges are listed over a ten
year time frame, with a common theme of financial
dishonesty.

Sharon also has a debt collection from Ford Motor
Credit against her and an active case from a private
lender for the promissory note she and Jeff Downs co-
signed to pay for the Empowering Women to Excel
conference in February 2012.

Another big one was almost overlooked: the
judgment from 2008 for $3,000 from a lawsuit brought
by another unlucky landlord. She won the case, but will
likely never collect the proceeds.

The lender on the promissory note from 2012 lived
frustrated and angry with his inability to have Sharon
served with his lawsuit. Searching for her was usually
a dead end. Her ability to move every few months and
stay under the radar kept her perpetually in the wind.
As the months rolled forward, Sharon's continuous con
game reeled in more and more victims. People who
had no awareness of their involvement in 2012 were
fully read into the situation in 2013. This situational
awareness started to work against Sharon in a big way.

The very public women's conference in 2012
could have been the last one in the series. But Sharon
wouldn't leave a chance to promote herself untaken, so
her ill-fated date of choice for 2013 fell on Saturday,
June first.

Even with her last minute change of venue, it was still apparent she would be in attendance, wherever it was held. Plans were made by the lender to have a process server show up with the papers and serve her at the event.

Remember what happened at the conference? The preaching, speaking in tongues and faith healing? You still haven't heard the best part of the story yet. We arrived at the conference and waited for the server to get her. Armed with a hidden video camera in an innocuous looking ink pen, a Flip video recorder and three iPhones, we were ready to capture the action. Instead, we suffered through an hour and a half of preaching and fawning over Sharon by the speakers, right from the podium. Text messages back and forth with Tom and Linda were staccato missives, "Where is he," "He's having trouble," "Guy can't come, now what?" "Look up process servers online and call somebody," "How about the sheriff's department," "It's not happening."

There were three of us there, so one by one we left to excuse ourselves to the restroom. Once out of the ballroom at the Medallion Center, we headed to Panera Bread for dinner. No way were we going to eat with Sharon's crowd.

We had no plans to go back, instead focusing on eating a good meal and talking about the failed operation. Shockingly, Linda called and said they'd solved the problem and the lender and the process server were on the way, right now. We had to go back.

Linda had the lender call my cell, as he was unfamiliar with the Garners Ferry Road area since he lived on the other side of town at the lake.

"I know you don't know me, but we were at the conference and I can give you directions to the Medallion Center," I said.

"You're right, I don't know you. Why would you help me?" the lender asked.

"Because Sharon is dangerous and needs to be stopped."

"This better not be a ruse. I left my daughter's graduation party to come do this."

"I assure you, sir, it is not a ruse. She's there. We are on our way back now. Text me when you get there."

He agreed and off we went down Garners Ferry to return to the conference. We sneak in the ballroom's back door and sit at an empty table in the back. There were several to choose from, so blending back in was an easy matter. Hidden camera in hand, we film the faith healing in progress, trying to get a shot of Sharon at the same time.

The room breaks for the promised banquet-style meal and the text exchange with the lender begins.

"Back at the Medallion Center. Sharon's at the third table on the back row in a white dress."

"She's walking out of the room."

"They're serving dinner so everyone is up and about."

With the crowd in disorder, worry sets in that Sharon might disappear. Clearly unfounded, Sharon's in her element as the adored one, so she's not going anywhere.

The lender makes it to the Medallion Center, staking out a vantage point in the upper parking lot. His message, "waiting on police. Saw WIS TV walk in w/

camera."

Sure enough, the NBC affiliate started interviewing the celebrity speakers and then moved on to Sharon. Our clandestine video pen in hand, we walk out in the hallway and get close enough to record the interview on our own cameras. As soon as the on-camera interview began, the message was, "Now, now, they're going to interview her for WIS."

The process server still wasn't on site, so the interview came and went without Sharon being served. Holding back from telling the reporter she was covering the wrong story was difficult.

Another set of back and forth texts for the next twenty minutes, "she's at her table again, sitting with Calvin," "she's outside," "she's back," and finally the result was at hand. The process server appeared, wearing khaki shorts and a striped polo. He looked around for a minute or so and as soon as Sharon saw him, she made a bee line straight for him. He confirmed her identity and walked her out the front door, where they were met by a single Richland County deputy. The service was quick, with Sharon back in less than five minutes. A quick pit stop in the ladies room to get a wad of tissue, then she rushed back into the conference and collected three ladies (including Ms. Sullivan), who turned right around and went outside, clearly visible through the plate glass doors.

Sharon pitched a first class fit. Screaming, thrashing about. It was a sight. Truly brilliant.

We had what we came for, so it was time to slink out the door unnoticed.

Beyond the conference, keeping up with her is

important. She moves every few months, so you have to be quick on her trail.

Her tenure at Duck Point Apartments was fairly short, ending in early July 2013. For about nine days, none of us knew where she was. She definitely had moved. The truck was no longer in the parking lot at Duck Point, like it had been since February.

Taci worked on a tactical misdirection, calling Linda and Tom with news of Sharon's move to lower Richland to a small house owned by an elderly lady. Tom and Linda rode over that way, but didn't turn up anything.

Starting to get nervous that we'd lost her, I began to stalk her daughter's Facebook page. Sharon unfriended me, so I could no longer see her posts. Her daughter also unfriended me, but failed to change her privacy settings. Everything she posted was still visible. Thank you, Facebook, for making it complicated to change your settings.

On July 10th, Ceira posted two photos of a burned out apartment with a fire truck in front, captioned, "Block is hott, literally." Oh, boy, now we've got something! And yes, she spelled hot just like that, "hott."

The perspective on the photo looked like it was taken across the street from the burned apartment. The first thing to do, search for Ladder Nine to see what areas this fire company serves. Shockingly, they cover from Shandon over to the Garners Ferry Road area. Now we're on the right track.

Harnessing the power of Google, I searched for "Apartment Fires, Columbia SC." There had been three reported fires within the past ten days. I read each story and looked at the accompanying video or photos. The third story fit the bill. The photos of the apartments matched the apartment in Ceira's pictures! The apartment complex wasn't named in the story, but it did say they were in the Byron Road area. So, back to Google street view for Byron Road. I drove down the road on the computer screen until I found the apartments in question. Turning around one hundred and eighty degrees, I saw the apartment complex name.

A quick call to Linda with the information led her to promise she and Tom would check it out in the morning. I could barely sleep, waiting to see if I had, in fact, found Sharon.

Tom's text came early, around 7:30am. "WE FOUND HER." He sent a picture of Sharon's truck, sitting in the apartment complex parking lot. Now we can keep up with her location for the authorities. When they're ready to arrest her, we can lead them straight to her.

Knowing part, but not all, of Sharon's story was exasperating. Piecing together her life of con games was a complicated process. Naming the players and victims one at a time, our investigative work started to show real results. The discovery of her 1995 marriage to John Stearman was a good clue and the many discussions with him through traditional mail and email proved enlightening. After finding his name in Barrio's obituary, we sent a title researcher to the county to see if the marriage license was legit. After the document was in hand, it was a simple matter to find the federal inmate information and mailing address. John's commentary was simple and clear – he doesn't hold a grudge against Sharon, but hasn't had anything to do with her in almost two decades. The continued validity of their marriage will be quite a surprise upon his release. Sharon makes no mention of him; if she ever had any feelings for her husband, they're long gone.

The love interest in Sharon's psychotic manifesto, The Fight for My Love: Final Chapters, is a character named Tim. She said his actual name was Alex and in May, 2013 he was killed in a motorcycle accident in Eutawville. "I'm in Atlanta at a casting call for my movie and got a text that Alex was dead," she said on a Sunday night phone call in late May, right near the time of the women's conference.

"That's terrible. I'm so sorry to hear about it," I said.

"Yeah, it's bad I guess. He was 44 years old."

"That's so young." It really is young, but when this man's obituary was checked, he was really only 37 years old. Again, the lie served no purpose.

"How do you feel about it?"

"I don't feel no kind of way. Just blank."

After chasing this man for years, tolerating abuse both personally and of her daughters, Sharon has no feelings at all when informed of his death. Hatred would be expected, and even relief that he couldn't hurt anyone else – these would be natural emotions. Sadness could be there, if not a personal sadness, but for the children he left behind. Not Sharon, though. She's got nothing. Devoid of emotion on things that no longer fulfill a purpose for her, the death of Alex is just another part of the day's news, ready to be consumed and forgotten by tomorrow.

The summer of 2013 dragged on, with little communication from the sheriff's department and not much word on Sharon or her activities. For all anyone knew, she'd gone dark. But remember, when Sharon's talking, you better listen closely.

Back in April, 2013, she tells several people about buying a book store. Big dreams happen in small ways with Sharon, so she convinces the owners of City Knowledge Book Store in Columbia Place Mall to turn over their "almost out of business" store to her in mid-May. This store is located in a dying mall, replete with a significant vacancy rate and a surrounding neighborhood no longer wealthy enough to support a large retail center. The anchor tenants remain, for now, powered by the national brands they represent, such as Macy's, Burlington Coat Factory and Sears.

Since her first attempt at opening a store didn't pan out, she tries her hand at becoming a book seller.

Word on the street about City Knowledge wasn't good. Bankruptcy loomed, so the ownership made a deal with Sharon to take over the operation and store lease. The Facebook posts announce new ownership first on May 17th and again on June 27th. The pitch used to entice customers read, "We are now under new ownership. We have a clearance sale going on. Lots of &5.00 books also 20% to 50% off books, Come on in to see what we have. We will be doing special orders so stop in so we can order your next book for you. Our new number is 893-655-8725." Typed exactly as it was presented on the Urban Knowledge page, this post has several technical errors a business owner, especially someone who supposedly loves books and would have grammar skills, wouldn't make. The devil's in the details, and here, the devil is Sharon.

The store's identity was up for debate, with Sharon choosing to drop the established name and go for Books and Other Things. She ordered a new phone number and listed her name, along with Books and Other Things, in the Citysearch directory for the Dentsville area.

A surprise phone call from a friend tipped off the store information, so a quick recon run out to Columbia Place Mall was in order on the last day of August, 2013. Sure enough, the City Knowledge storefront was no more. But contrary to the public posts, no signage was present for Books and Other Things either.

In the space formerly occupied by City Knowledge was a closed retail store, labeled as Good As New in block letters over the entrance and security gate. Just to be sure, every store in the mall was checked to make sure she hadn't moved the book store to another unit within the mall.

The friend with the information claimed Sharon had opened a resale store and traded services in order to get the signage done for free. So, the Good As New name made sense, but it was still a closed store.

The perfume kiosk worker across from the store entrance was a wealth of knowledge, though. When asked if he had ever seen the store open, he gave a resounding yes. "Oh, yeah, they were open with the new name there for about a month and a half," he said. "I saw a few people in there. They had mainly books and t-shirts."

Amazed that she pulled off an actual store, but not at

all surprised it was already a failure, the kiosk operator was queried on the finer details of the operation. "They've been gone now about three or four weeks. They are closed, like closed for good. Nobody's been back."

Still, there wasn't any concrete confirmation this operation was Sharon's. A photo of Sharon from the women's conference was shown to the kiosk guy, who easily confirmed her identity. "That's her, that's Miss Cindy. Um hmm, she was one of the owners."

Miss Cindy. That's a new alias for Sharon, to be added to her growing list: Sharon, SD, Cheryl and now Cindy. Calling her one of the owners is curious, too. The logical possibility for her partner is Patricia Sullivan, who had a cache of t-shirts from years past that could've been the clothing portion of the store's inventory. Ms. Sullivan's involvement with the book world also makes her the natural choice.

To further establish the truth of the store story, a deputy from the Richland County Sheriff's Department happened to be on duty during the reconnaissance visit and answered questions about the Good As New. This deputy was familiar with the store, including its inventory of books and t-shirts. "I never shopped in there, but that's what they had, books and a lot of t-shirts. They've been gone now for three weeks."

The layout of the mall is a stacked two-story, with escalators traversing the two stories every so often. Sharon's store is right near the bottom level termination of one of the escalators. Her boldness knows no bounds, as she opened up this store mere feet away from the Richland County Sheriff's Department Substation in that very mall. Running her game, literally right under the noses of the Sheriff's Department, fear of being caught never entered her mind.

For a full month and a half of operation, Books and Other Things or Good As New (whatever name was being used) sold merchandise to customers. Unknown numbers of people have given cash or credit cards to Sharon for their purchases. If you've shopped there, check your bank statement immediately and cancel your credit card. Leaving your viable account information in her hands is dangerous.

The store's short run is not surprising. Rent is due on the first of the month, every month. The second month's rent of her operation was likely funded with a bad check; the three week time frame is just about right for the management to have the check returned and give her a deadline to make it good. True to form, she runs out with bills still due, creating another victim of fraud in the process.

By digging a little deeper, the name Miss Cindy wasn't an alias for Sharon at all. The original manager of the bookstore was an older lady named Cindy. She was the one who ran the store for years and the name given by the perfume kiosk attendant was hers. But, he very clearly recognized the picture of Sharon as one of the owners of the revised bookstore called the Good As New.

Mall management is handled by a company called CBL & Associates Properties, based in Myrtle Beach, South Carolina. By virtue of the lost revenue from City Knowledge's intact lease, they've unknowingly added their names to the victims list.

Until she's arrested, there will always be one more con from Sharon. Up next: baby clothes. October, 2013 rolls around and word on the street is she's opening a consignment shop on Two Notch Road for baby clothes and accessories. Her fictitious line of children's clothing, Sac Geer, may be a player in this new front. Her luck also seems to be running out on Garners Ferry Road, causing her to branch out to local competitor for King of the Hood, Two Notch Road. With a reputation for street walkers, gangs and drugs, parts of Two Notch are downright scary. Not to say plenty of legitimate, successful businesses aren't located along Two Notch Road – there are hundreds of them – but the overall connotation of this area is negative.

Ms. Sullivan has a family member who works for a name brand baby food and clothing manufacturer. She's previously provided a good bit of clothing rejected as seconds for Sharon's endeavors, so this person could be a start-up source of material for the consignment shop.

CHAPTER FORTY TWO
Justice for All?

◊◊

Sharon's not the smartest person in the room, although she always thinks she is. The surprise of justice would be a bitter pill for her, especially after more than a decade of successfully eluding the authorities and any real consequences from her illegal and immoral actions.

Cooperating agencies – the Secret Service, the FBI and the Richland County Sheriff's Department – could've come together to stop Sharon's reign of financial terror. But even with a lot of prompting from the non-badge wearing public, she remained at large.

A con is a rush. For Sharon, it's an addiction. The only way for her to stop is to hit rock bottom; for Sharon's sociopathic tendencies, though, the only way to find rock bottom is to have it shoved in her face by the authorities.

She may have gotten away with decades worth of fraud, but the very real emotional and financial pain she left in her wake still hurts today for those she conned. The civil suit against her and co-defendant Jeff Downs was decided by Judge Cooper in Richland County in August, 2013, ruining Jeff's credit with the judgment of almost forty thousand dollars. Sharon will never be able to pay it, leaving Jeff a lifetime to do so on her behalf and to the detriment of his family.

The monster she's become rages on, while a proper reckoning waits. A string of unreturned phone calls and emails to the Sheriff's Department became the victims' very own trail of tears. Communicating everything we knew to the proper authorities, trying to do the right thing, became an exercise in total frustration. The investigator would throw a bone every few months by actually returning a phone call or even agreeing to a meeting. The refrain heard time and again was, "this will be a marathon, not a sprint." In no way did the group of victims ever imagine the marathon would be a year long, fruitless process.

The promise of Secret Service involvement, the tying together of the numerous bank accounts, the legitimately filed complaints taken from a few of the victims early on – there is a reasonable expectation of performance from the investigative team. Bad checks for thousands of dollars go unprosecuted in this case, along with the other serious charges that could be brought at any time. Inaction is the mode of operation with Richland County law enforcement. Perhaps it's a symptom of a larger problem, not only with Richland County but with law enforcement as a whole.

Robbed? Assaulted? Violated in some way? We're sorry, that's a shame. Let us take a report, give you a case number and don't call us...we'll call you.

The police force has been relegated to a battalion of note takers and case filers. Investigative action is apparently no longer a function of the job. Departments are focused on reducing officer overtime to meet their budgets. A violent crime will still warrant an active response to the call and if they're lucky enough to arrive during its commission, the perpetrator will be arrested. Anything else must not be important.

Tactics taken to address crime and even gang activities border on the absurd. For example, the South Carolina State Fair and several high schools in Richland District One have banned students from wearing camouflage. Camo has become a gang color, so by not allowing anyone to wear it, they believe they're combatting the gang problem. The gangs will find another way to communicate their allegiance; the removal of this clothing option is a minor hindrance. The overarching issues of societal disarray, irresponsible parents, a decaying educational system and lack of consequences for criminal behavior mean the criminal justice system will have an uphill battle for control of lawlessness.

Sharon's case falls under the purview of the Fifth Circuit Solicitor in Richland County. This circuit has a long history of reducing or dropping charges altogether for even the most violent criminals. The hope of the victims was Sharon's case was different. The hope remains strong for justice, but the slow reality of a paralyzed police force and prosecutor is painful for those she terrorized.

Richland County's growing reputation for gang

activity is a contradiction to the accolades of its top lawman, Sheriff Leon Lott. Sheriff Lott has been recognized both nationally and internationally for his expertise in community policing and the development of a skilled officer force. He travels the globe, teaching police in countries such as Germany and Israel. Yet somehow, his own back yard is falling apart.

A large part of Richland County includes the City of Columbia, which has its own police force. A high percentage of Richland County's crime occurs within the city limits.

From 1998 through 2007, the number of gang related crimes in South Carolina had skyrocketed to 5,245 reported incidents during that time frame. Offenses range from simple assault, intimidation, weapons law violations, aggravated assault, kidnapping, murder and even more. Even in this dated crime report, Richland County led the way in with the highest number of gang incidents.

Today, that's still the case. The visibility of gang crime in 2013 is very high in this area. Public attention gets totally focused on the out of control shootings when an eighteen year old college student is shot while waiting for a cab in Five Points, a popular college hang out and entertainment district.

With all of the crime in this county, perhaps a con artist like Sharon Johnson is not worth the trouble of arresting; and as one of the Captains asked us once, "she hasn't killed anyone, right?" As victims, it's worth it to us. She's a rampant force of destruction.

If the Richland County Sheriff's Department had acted in a timely fashion when Sharon's case was first presented in February, 2013, a whole host of cons could have been prevented. The Sheriff's Department is indirectly responsible for allowing the following known injustices:

1. Taking advantage of a disabled minister through her scheme of paying with out of date starter checks from a closed bank.

2. Everything related to the fourth annual Empowering Women to Excel conference: everyone conned into appearing, all guests, both The Medallion Center and Brookland Baptist Church, the actress Victoria Rowell, and every single service provider who wasn't paid or paid in full. Not to mention the charities for whom Sharon promised donations.

3. The Chinese American property owner who intended to rent retail space to Sharon for a women's store but was paid with a bad check.

4. Columbia Place Mall and the Urban Knowledge Bookstore, who both sustained losses after allowing Sharon to "take over" the store. In typical Sharon style, she moved out in the middle of the night, bills all unpaid.

5. Duck Pointe Apartments, who lost rentable space by allowing Sharon and her family to stay, working the system long enough to avoid eviction until July, 2013.

6. Real Estate Consultants, who still has been unable to prosecute the bad check Sharon wrote to them for five thousand dollars because the Investigator pulled it from the Solicitor's process to include with the case that's never been made.

7. The publicist with the same story – an unprosecuted check for one thousand dollars.

These seven cons are just a few small highlights of her criminal career during the bulk of 2013, that's just one single year. What's more, there are surely others that have yet to be uncovered. Had Sharon been arrested and the story covered by the local media, additional victims would likely appear in droves.

One last ditch effort was made to contact the authorities after Sharon's indignant voice mail in November 2013. The investigator, his superior and even the assistant to the sheriff were tried. To his credit, the Captain called back within twenty four hours as per agency protocol.

"Capt. Hughes, Richland County Sheriff's Department calling."

"Yes, sir. I'm trying to reach you about Sharon Johnson."

"Is that the woman you and the other woman came to talk to me about a few weeks ago?"

"Yes, sir it is, but it was over three months ago now, not just a few weeks. Is anything ever going to be done to take this person off the street?"

"I'll have to look into it."

"She called me this week with a fairly threatening phone call and even confirmed something I said in my statement to your department last February. She's out there running cons on people, can't you pick her up for something? How about the bad check she wrote in January for five thousand dollars? Can't you at least get a warrant for that?"

The Captain was gruff, virtually dismissing the call. "I'll speak to the investigator and see where he stands. Have a nice day. Good bye."

Two days later, the investigator called, surely cajoled by his superior to wrap up this never-ending case. The plan is to go forward with the state charges and use everything he has right now to go before the judge on the Tuesday before Thanksgiving to get the warrant. If he can actually put Sharon behind bars before the holiday, a whole host of her victims will truly have something for which they can give thanks.

Involvement with Sharon hasn't been all bad. The blessings from her evil presence continue to evolve. First of all, a friendship with Linda Wilson would've never happened. She is a truly good person and has been invaluable throughout the process of this investigation. Secondly, increased awareness of criminals and the malevolent deeds they commit has been extremely helpful. Here's an example of how the lessons learned from dealing with Sharon have positively impacted my life.

This extreme example came in the form of a robbery. On October 9th, 2013, our office was robbed. The unknown subject entered the building in the early afternoon, went behind the front desk, rifled through the drawers and took the petty cash, a set of car keys, money from our employee Avery's bag and Avery's wallet. The subject went out into the parking lot, hit the unlock button on the key to see what prize was won, and drove off in Avery's 2012 Toyota Rav4 (Avery's wallet was still in the car). The theft wasn't discovered until the end of the business day, around 5:00 p.m.

The Lexington County Sheriff's Department responded by sending a female deputy approximately one hour after the initial call for help. The deputy took the report, called in the missing vehicle's VIN and tag number and handed over a case number. Nowadays, you don't even get a copy of the report without downloading it from the county website or going in person to the sheriff's department office.

While the deputy was taking Avery's statement, I went across the parking lot to MedCare Urgent Care. The MedCare office faces our parking lot and their security cameras should have a clear picture of the perpetrator. The manager wasn't available, so the best they could do was arrange a meeting with their IT guy for nine the next morning.

I returned to the office and told the deputy I might have something. "We're going to be getting the video from the MedCare cameras," I said.

As she looks at her watch, she drawls, "Well, I'm fixin' to get off, so ya'll can call the Sheriff's Department pretty much any time to come and get that, if you ever get it."

Getting actual evidence is an inconvenience when your shift is almost over.

The robbery was disturbing on many levels. First, the obvious violation of our safety was a problem, especially since the perp had a master key to the building from Avery's key ring. That meant we had to stay until almost 9:30 p.m. to get the building rekeyed. Second, Avery was left without a car. At the age of twenty, she's unable to rent a car, so she's left with nothing. Her family lives over one hundred miles away, so they're not able to help her immediately, either.

After thinking about it all night, I went in early and addressed the class of students who were there for post license training in real estate. Surely someone saw something helpful.

I implored them to tell me anything at all seen out of the ordinary. A female student recalled seeing a young woman in a red hooded sweatshirt and blue jeans sitting in the grass beside the MedCare building.

As soon as she mentioned the girl, three male students chimed in that they, too, had seen this woman, but not at MedCare. She was at our building, pacing the sidewalk. "She had the red sweatshirt and blue jeans, she was white, in her thirties or forties, had black hair pulled up into a pony tail," the men all said just about together.

Ok, now we're getting somewhere. Maybe this woman had someone over at MedCare and was just bored and waited outside. Maybe not.

Class started at 8:30 a.m., so I let the instructor proceed while I visited the Assemblies of God Ministry Resource Center, whose building is adjacent to ours and directly behind. Our offices are connected by an enclosed breezeway.

With the same routine, I asked if anyone saw anything unusual yesterday. "No, not really, except for the woman who came in asking for money," offered Michelle.

"Asking for money? What did she look like?"

"Tall woman, black hair, wearing a red top and blue jeans. She walked right past me, I was in the kitchen making a late lunch and had to ask her twice if I could help her."

The woman told Michelle twice she needed money. "This is a church, right? You give money to people."

"We're the district office. Let me get some phone numbers of people who can help you."

"No, that won't work. I'm getting thrown out of a motel right now and need help now."

The woman didn't wait on the phone numbers and marched right out the door. That's the last Michelle saw of her.

Instead of going to my nine o'clock appointment at MedCare to view the video, I grabbed my keys and Becca (Sharon's favorite person) for a field trip.

We jumped in my car and took off down the frontage road. The Executive Inn is within walking distance of our office, so I thought it was a logical choice to investigate. We drove around the parking lot twice looking for Avery's car. It wasn't there.

We cautiously circled back around and parked near the front entrance. I pulled my concealable .32 caliber pistol out of the dash and slid it onto my belt, covering its presence with my sweater. "Let's go inside," I said as Becca hesitated to get out of the car.

There are several hotels in close proximity to our office. We often refer students to virtually every other one but this one. It's not a place the average person finds acceptable. You expect an episode of COPS to be filming there any minute.

We made our way into the small office, where the female proprietor greeted us. "May I help you?"

I told her who we were and what happened. "By chance, did you happen to evict a tenant yesterday matching this description: white female, thirties, red sweatshirt, blue jeans, black hair?"

"Yes. Yes I did," she said without a moment's

hesitation.

"Oh my gosh, can you tell the police about her? If I call them right now, will you talk to an officer if we can get one over here?"

"No, I can just tell you. She goes by Susie. Let me get a copy of her driver's license for you, we get one on all of our guests."

Holy cow, we have her driver's license. Not only that, we also got the boyfriend's driver's license, credit card and cell phone number.

"When's the last time you saw her?"

"Yesterday around three o'clock when she was checking out. She was driving a silver SUV."

Holy cow again, she's got Avery's car! We rushed out the door, paperwork in hand. As we jumped in the Porsche, the adrenaline was pumping.

"Becca, I swear if we find this car, I'm dropping one of our businesses to start a detective agency!"

"Yeah, that would be awesome!" Becca said.

"Let's try some of these other no-tell motels right around here. Maybe she went to another one just like this one." Going left out of the parking lot, we spied a series of possibilities across the interstate.

The first hotel, an almost new Holiday Inn, wouldn't fit the bill, but the two adjacent properties were definitely feasible. Looping around the parking lot of America's Value Inn proved fruitless. To its left, the lesser West Columbia Extended Stay rents rooms by the week and by the month. The two-story, low rent mecca beckoned.

We hit pay dirt on the far side. A silver Rav4 was backed into the last parking space.

"Oooh, is that the car?"

"Looks like it," Becca said. "Need to check it."

"Yep, I'm on it." Parking the Boxster in the middle of the parking lot, I jumped out and left the car running and the door open. A quick look at the back of the vehicle confirmed it wasn't Avery's. But in the twenty seconds it took to check, we'd drawn a crowd.

Residents from all the rooms on our side came out to see what we were doing. Double decker rows of faces stared our way. One of the male residents called down to us, "Hey, honey, what you lookin' for?"

"Susie. Where's Susie?" What possessed me to say that, I'll never know.

"You lookin for Susie?"

"Yeah, have you seen her?"

"She was here last night."

"Baby, was she driving a car like this silver one?"

"Sure was. She brought her boyfriend a steak dinner and baked potato."

"Oh my God, she's got my girlfriend's car. She stole it from Avery, that car is all she has in the world! We gotta get it back, where is she now?"

That exchange was enough to bring the two homeless guys from the balcony down to the parking lot for a little face to face. Anyone staying at this motel is a long term guest without anywhere else to go, so they are essenTially homeless.

Becca whispered out of the window, "Hey, he's got a knife."

Homeless guy number one sees me eyeing the knife in his front pocket. Knife is really an understatement. It was more of a machete-sized knife, on the order of the

444

Crocodile Dundee reference, "Now, that's a knife!"

"Honey, don't you be worrying about this here knife."

"I'm not. I've got my pistol on me."

"Oh, well I'm a felon, so I can't carry a weapon." Apparently, this giant knife doesn't count as a real weapon. Ok, then.

"I've got a Concealed Weapons Permit, so we're good."

Satisfied, homeless guy number one starts to speculate about Susie's whereabouts. He even makes a few phone calls. Homeless guy number two offers us a souvenir keychain with the University of South Carolina logo. This fella is also very interested in my car.

"Do you want to take some pictures of the Boxster? Let me shut the door so it looks right." A crowd of about fifteen encircles the car. Homeless guy number two asks a lot of questions about it, which I was more than happy to answer.

Becca gets out of the car to join me in the impromptu car show.

Homeless guy number one determines Susie is probably over at Tree Man's trailer. "I know where she's at. I can show you where his trailer's at."

"Can you give me the address? I have a GPS that's pretty good at finding things."

"No, I don't know no address, but I can show you where to go. I got a car here but they done took my DL from me, would you drive my car and I can show you how to go?"

"No, baby, I've got this girl here with me and I

don't think we'll all fit in your car. How about we find somebody else here with a driver's license who would drive your car so we can follow you over there?"

We canvassed the crowd and found a woman with a current license who was also friends with Susie. Reluctant to take us, we assured her we didn't want any trouble, and only wanted to get the car back for Avery. She sidled up next to me, speaking in a barely audible voice, "You need to call the cops when you get there. Susie needs to go to jail. But, keep this on the down low, ok?"

I nodded "yes" for her and off we went. The homeless crew piled into the white Pontiac with Georgia plates while Becca and I turned the Porsche around and fell in behind them. Becca texts her boyfriend that if we disappear, someone should look for a guy called Tree Man who lives in a mobile home near Wal-Mart on Highway 1.

Sure enough, we turn down a side street off Highway 1 and I knew even from a distance that we'd be turning by the stolen green shopping carts from Bi-Lo. The gravel road led to a small trailer park. The Pontiac went about halfway down the road and then started backing up towards us. Throwing the car in reverse, we scooted backwards and over to the right to get out of the way.

"The car's here, the car's here! Call the cops, call the cops!" Everyone from the homeless car was screaming like crazy. I dialed the non-emergency number for the West Columbia police department and asked for the dispatcher.

"Dispatch."

"Yes, we need an officer on the scene immediately.

We have located a stolen vehicle."

"What's your location on this supposed stolen vehicle?"

"I assure you it's stolen, I have the case number from the Lexington County Sheriff's Department from yesterday. Please call them to verify if you need to. It's a silver 2012 Toyota Rav4." I realized then that I didn't know where we were, as the GPS just shows a big arrow in the middle of nothing, since we'd turned down a gravel road.

"Hey, guys, what street are we on?"

They didn't know either, so the two main homeless guys jumped out and looked around to find a street sign. Homeless guy number two has a genius idea. He walks up to the front door on the closest trailer and knocks. "Yo. Man, what's your address?"

He got the information and I relayed it to the dispatcher. "An officer is on the way."

"Look for the white Porsche, it's the only one."

The lady driver of the Pontiac wanted to go down to the trailer and talk to Susie. She promised to not tip her off, so we let her go ahead. In the meantime, I repositioned the Boxster as a road block. There was no way I'd let Susie escape with Avery's car.

"Becca, can you drive this car?"

"NO. Why? Don't make me, why are you getting out of the car?"

"Put your foot on the brake, the ignition's on the left, turn it to start the car."

Amazingly efficient, the West Columbia officer was on the scene in three minutes' time. Homeless guys one and two were all over the cop, trying to tell him the situation. I was out of the car and walking toward him when he pointed at me. "You. Tell me what's going on here." I summarized the situation and ran back to the car to move it out of the way enough for the officer to get past.

"Let's follow on foot. I don't want to take my car back there if I don't have to."

Becca and I started walking down the gravel road, taking pictures with our iPhones as the scene unfolded. Always helpful, homeless guy number two offered to stand guard over the car. "I won't let anybody mess with it." And you know what? I believed him.

By the time we got to Tree Man's trailer, the officer was bringing Susie out by the arm onto the wooden deck that served as a front porch. "Ma'am what's the story here on this vehicle?" he asked her as we approached.

There's Avery's car! The Rav4 was beyond the ratty rust-stained trailer, under a tree and almost behind the corner of the house. It looked to be in good condition, no visible body damage or anything wrong on the outside.

"Yes, I stole it. Yes, I took their money." She admitted it right away.

"Ok, have a seat here on the porch. Let me have the keys," the officer demanded and her compliance was immediate. She produced the car keys from her purse, which were now missing Avery's keychain.

Homeless guy number one was fluttering around us, saying he sure was glad we found the car.

"Becca, here's my phone. Facetime Avery. Show her the car."

While the officer continued to interrogate Susie, Avery came on the screen. She hadn't even been able to get out of bed because she was so upset. "Look, look! We found your car!" Becca pointed the phone towards the car so Avery could see it.

"What? Where? How did you do that?" She couldn't believe it. Becca sent her the location from the iPhone's map so she could find us.

Over the course of the next three hours, the Lexington County Sheriff's Department investigators arrived on the scene, talked with the West Columbia officer and the suspect and processed the vehicle.

My husband also arrived with sandwiches from Chick-fil-A for our crime scene tailgate.

The very same deputy that took the report the day before was called to transport the suspect to the Lexington County Detention Center. In one of my weaker moments, emotion overwhelmed me as Susie was handcuffed.

"Take that, bitch! Your ass is going to jail!" The fist pump in the air was probably a little much, but I was really excited that we caught her and recovered Avery's car.

The criminal was charged with Grand Larceny Over $10,000 First Degree and Burglary Third Degree, Second Offense. Bond was set at twenty thousand dollars. We kept a watch on the jailhouse inmate list over the next several weeks, just to make sure she hadn't been released. Two weeks after her arrest, a new charge was added: Distribution and Manufacture of Methamphetamine. The bond was increased by another five thousand dollars.

Her trial was set for April, 2014 in General Sessions Court. She skipped out on her bond, which was posted by a professional bail bondsman and currently remains at large. If the police were to ask, we could always offer to locate her for them; clearly, they're not looking.

People are conned every day, in all walks of life. Use the lessons found in this story to protect yourself and your loved ones. At the end of this book is a section called End Notes and Resources, full of basic information on dealing with similar situations.

You don't have to live your life as a victim. You can turn things around. Reach out to another person, even if it's not the authorities. Seek help and tell people how you really feel about a situation. If you see someone doing something wrong and you can help the intended victim, you should warn him. The more information a person has when deciding to become involved in a con man's scheme, the better chance he has to escape before it's too late. Now that you know what to watch for and the lessons to apply, you can be better prepared. If you're the target of a con artist, and you realize it, stop it from happening and tell everyone you know so the deceiver is exposed. Don't be embarrassed – be empowered. Take a stand for what's right, you'll be glad you did. Be smarter than the con!

Not every story has a happy ending, including this one. In the last few days of 2013, the authorities had yet to act against Sharon Johnson and her crew. The only consolation is her eviction from the apartments on Byron Road, right before the holidays. At least she was inconvenienced for a little while. But with Sharon's decades-long history of gaming the system, one more eviction on her record barely registers as bothersome. In fact, it's blessing in disguise, making it just a little bit harder for the authorities to find her if they ever actually try. For Sharon, it's just another day in the life of a world class con artist.

END NOTES AND REFERENCES

SOCIOPATHS

If you've only ever thought of a sociopath as a serial killer or as a character in a scary movie, you'll be shocked to know sociopaths are a part of the general population at large. These people are dangerous and unencumbered by conscience. Sharon Johnson is just one example.

To give you well known references as a counter-point, two famous examples of sociopathic behavior are Jim Jones and Charles Manson. First, Jim Jones was a master of delusion, convincing over nine hundred followers in his private jungle compound to drink grape flavored water laced with cyanide and Valium. Next, Charles Manson delivered a 1970s murder spree and has been denied parole for the five killings on twelve occasions over the past forty years. His intense stare and repeated statements about not killing anyone because all he has to do is think it and it happens are classic delusion.

Several helpful guidelines are available for specific definitions and warning signs about sociopaths. First, a definition of sociopath would be helpful: A person with a personality disorder manifesting itself in extreme antisocial attitudes and behavior and a lack of conscience.

Psychology Today contributor M.E. Thomas provided a list on their website, found at *http://www.psychologytoday.com/articles/201305/how-spot-sociopath,* in May 2013 with the hallmarks of this behavior:

How to Spot a Sociopath:
•Superficial charm and good intelligence
•Absence of delusions and other signs of irrational thinking
•Absence of nervousness or neurotic manifestations
•Unreliability
•Untruthfulness and insincerity
•Lack of remorse and shame
•Inadequately motivated antisocial behavior
•Poor judgment and failure to learn by experience
•Pathologic egocentricity and incapacity for love
•General poverty in major affective reactions
•Specific loss of insight
•Unresponsiveness in general interpersonal relations
•Fantastic and uninviting behavior with alcohol and sometimes without
•Suicide threats rarely carried out
•Sex life impersonal, trivial and poorly integrated
•Failure to follow any life plan

The Sociopath Next Door by Martha Stout is a terrific book with insight into typical behaviors someone you might encounter in your life uses to manipulate and intimidate you into following his or her plan.

She postulates that four percent of the population are sociopaths.

Based on the details from *The Sociopath Next Door* and Natural News, keep this top ten list of sociopath red flags handy:

1. Sociopaths are charming.
2. Sociopaths are more spontaneous and intense.
3. Sociopaths are incapable of feeling guilt, remorse or shame.
4. Sociopaths invent outrageous lies about their experiences.
5. Sociopaths seek to dominate others and win at all costs.
6. Sociopaths tend to be intelligent.
7. Sociopaths are incapable of real love.
8. Sociopaths are excellent storytellers.
9. Sociopaths never apologize.
10. Sociopaths literally believe what they say becomes truth.

BACKGROUND CHECKS

Learn how to do a basic background check. Check your local county's website and enter the person's name into the Public Court Records Search. Anything filed should appear and these searches are almost always free. For a detailed, state-specific criminal background check, many states offer this service through one of their law enforcement divisions. For South Carolina, it's SLED (SC Law Enforcement Division, www.sled.sc.gov). North Carolina has Department of Justice, State Bureau of Investigation. California has the Department of Justice. Your state will have something similar, uncovered easily by an internet search.

For a criminal background check, you'll need personal information such as the person's legal name, alias or maiden name, date of birth, social security number and possibly additional information. Expect to pay a fee for this search.

If you plan to run a background check on a person as a part of your job or for rental purposes, a credit check must use a Consumer Reporting Agency as required in the Fair Credit Reporting Act.

You can also use a paid service online, of which there are dozens. Some of the more prominent ones include US Search, Intelius, Been Verified, People Finders, KnowX, PeopleSmart, Background Report, Instant Checkmate, People Wise, and the obvious Backgroundchecks.com.

Once you have your report, be on the lookout for felonies, sex offenses and misdemeanors. The offense date and description are important, but the disposition is the most important of all.

We are still innocent until proven guilty, so if a charge is listed but not processed or the defendant is found not guilty, take that information into consideration when evaluating the results.

SPOTTING A LIAR

Becoming a student of body language can help you out a liar. There's a neat website called blifaloo.com that offers these signs of deception:

Body Language of Lies:

• Physical expression will be limited and stiff, with few arm and hand movements. Hand, arm and leg movement are toward their own body the liar takes up less space.

• A person who is lying to you will avoid making eye contact.

• Hands touching their face, throat & mouth. Touching or scratching the nose or behind their ear. Not likely to touch his chest/heart with an open hand.

Emotional Gestures & Contradiction:

• Timing and duration of emotional gestures and emotions are off a normal pace. The display of emotion is delayed, stays longer it would naturally, then stops suddenly.

• Timing is off between emotions gestures/expressions and words. Example: Someone says "I love it!" when receiving a gift, and then smile after making that statement, rather then at the same time the statement is made.

• Gestures/expressions don't match the verbal statement, such as frowning when saying "I love you."

• Expressions are limited to mouth movements when someone is faking emotions (like happy, surprised, sad, awe,)instead of the whole face. For example; when someone smiles naturally their whole face is involved: jaw/cheek movement, eyes and forehead push down.

Interactions and Reactions:
• A guilty person gets defensive. An innocent person will often go on the offensive.
• A liar is uncomfortable facing his questioner/accuser and may turn his head or body away.
• A liar might unconsciously place objects (book, coffee cup, etc.) between themselves and you.

Verbal Context and Content:
• A liar will use your words to make answer a question. When asked, "Did you eat the last cookie?" The liar answers, "No, I did not eat the last cookie."
•A statement with a contraction is more likely to be truthful: " I didn't do it" instead of "I did not do it."
• Liars sometimes avoid "lying" by not making direct statements. They imply answers instead of denying something directly.
• The guilty person may speak more than natural, adding unnecessary details to convince you... they are not comfortable with silence or pauses in the conversation.
• A liar may leave out pronouns and speak in a monotonous tone. When a truthful statement is made the pronoun is emphasized as much or more than the rest of the words in a statement.
• Words may be garbled and spoken softly, and syntax and grammar may be off. In other words, his sentences will likely be muddled rather than emphasized

Other Signs of a Lie:
• If you believe someone is lying, then change subject of a conversation quickly, a liar follows along willingly

and becomes more relaxed. The guilty wants the subject changed; an innocent person may be confused by the sudden change in topics and will want to go back to the previous subject.

• Using humor or sarcasm to avoid a subject.

HOW TO FILE A CASE IN MAGISTRATE'S COURT

Magistrate's Court is a court of law where you may file a case against someone if you believe you or your property has been injured in some way. The limit for damages in this type of court is $7500 or less. There are several different types of forms and cases you can file at the Magistrate's Court level.

The first step is to figure out the county in which the person or business is located. You will need to file your case in that county. Look under County Government in the yp.com directory.

You'll fill out a statement, called a Complaint, with a statement of what happened and a list of the parties involved. The other component to the Complaint is the Summons, which is the document that informs the other party about the case. As the person filing it, you are called the Plaintiff. The person or company you're filing against is the Defendant. The Defendant will have thirty days to respond in writing and then your case will be placed on the court calendar for a hearing.

Be sure to bring any supporting documents you have to the hearing for the judge to see and use when making his or her ruling.

A really important part of this process is the serving of the Summons and Complaint on the Defendant. Try your best to find out a solid address before submitting your initial paperwork to the court. If the person can't be found to serve the documents, your case is dead in the water.

I'VE BEEN CONNED. NOW WHAT?

If you've been caught in the net of the scammer, you can escape. Don't be afraid to push your questions on the criminal and offer to have your attorney, accountant or other professional get involved. Tell the criminal you no longer have whatever it is he or she wants from you. If you're part of a financial crime, check out the person or company on fraud.org, which is part of the National Consumers League. Your local police department in larger towns and jurisdictions should also have a financial crimes division who would be interested in any type of financial fraud.

Common types of fraud include: Advance Fee Loans, fake credit card offers, charity scams, credit repair, fake checks, supposed free government grants, investments, jobs where you're asked to pay an upfront fee, magazine sales (often door to door), internet phishing and multi-level marketing scams. Expose the wrong doers, and you may save more than yourself from the pain and loss perpetrated by these scammers.

CRIME STATISTICS

To find out crime statistics for your area, a good tool to use is **www.raidsonline.com**. Simply enter your address or for a more general search just enter your city's name. You can see layers and layers of crime data, based on offender type and law enforcement agency information.

FINALLY...

The clues and body language cues listed above don't automatically make a person a liar. Look to make judgments based on a person's base line of normal behavior, but don't discount the feeling you have telling you, "something just isn't right." Your intuition is probably correct.

The next book in the Liar Series from Real Life Publishing Company is *My Husband is a Liar* by Melissa Sprouse Browne. Available June, 2015.

From *My Husband is a Liar*:

And I quote. . .
    "The scent of Mark's body overpowers me as I fall asleep in his arms. Sometime later, after dark I am roused from my sleep by a tickling feeling in my ear. I reach up, my hand feels something and I'm momentarily confused. I awaken fully and find the engorged head of Mark's cock rubbing up against the side of my face. He is straddling my head, his balls hanging over my ear. It tickles as he slowly moves them over the surface of my ear.
    I turn my head to look straight up. The musty smell of his sweat overcomes me as I lean up and draw his balls into my mouth with a light suction. I can taste the cum left there from last night. From my vantage point, I can see straight up the shaft, a full six inches. It throbs each time I pull on his balls. Mark moans softly, his ecstasy such a welcome surprise. I continue to suck his balls and while I do so, I see a glistening drop of cum forming on the very tip of his beautiful cock.
    I slowly come to realize what I've been dreaming about since I was eleven is here with me now, in my bed, with a rock hard cock and a beautiful face. I reach around him and grab his gorgeous tight ass with both hands and pull him towards me. I look up into his face, up into the biggest smile I've ever seen. I know he desires me and it makes me feel giddy."

Wow, that was terrible. I've seen a lot of terrible things, but the letter from which those lines originated is one of the worst for me. What would make this passage so terrible, other than possibly the graphic language? You see, this letter was written by my husband. Yes, my husband. As a woman, you don't expect your supposed soul mate to write explicitly about his homosexual dreams and exploits.

The perfect marriage, an idea little girls dream about. Turns out, it's the funniest thing I've ever heard. Walking down the aisle more than once, you learn the fairy tale is far from a sure thing. Husbands lie about a lot of things. In the case of my marriage to Beau, not only did he lie to me, he lied to himself since childhood. Clearly, my marriage was doomed from the start, based on a lie so destructive no union could survive.

I'm but one disillusioned spouse in a world where husbands lie for many reasons. Is he lying about being gay? Does he lie to your face, claiming to love you one minute and taking out his anger on you in the next, torturing you through abuse? Is he hiding a gambling addiction? Or worse? In this study of the myriad untruths wives and girlfriends face, we examine the stories of real women who share how they uncovered the deceptions and what it took to survive and overcome their personal tragedies.

***

Other titles by this author:

Unit History: The 755th Field Artillery Battalion – This compilation is a history of the 755th Field Artillery

Battalion from December 1944 through May 1945. It includes an account of their vital participation in the Battle of the Bulge, which gained its members the Presidential Unit Citation. Available on amazon.com.

The Caregiver's Training Program: What You Need to Know to Take Care of Your Parent in their Golden Years – The Caregiver's Training Program gives you practical, immediately useful tactics for caring for your aging parent. This book provides the step by step instruction you need to understand what to do, who to call and how to find help when you need it. Use The Caregiver's Training Program to guide your day to day activities while planning for the future of your parent's care. Available on amazon.com.

Visit **www.reallifepublishingcompany.com** for a complete list of titles available from our great authors. Be sure to like us on Facebook and Goodreads.com.

www.ingramcontent.com/pod-product-compliance
Lightning Source LLC
Chambersburg PA
CBHW021037090426
42738CB00006B/124